Kulturstiftung Sibirien

Oral History Meets Linguistics

Edited by
Erich Kasten, Katja Roller, Joshua Wilbur

Verlag der Kulturstiftung Sibirien
SEC Publications

This publication has been made possible with the generous support of DFG GRK (Graduiertenkolleg) 1624 "Frequenzeffekte in der Sprache", Albert-Ludwigs-Universität Freiburg.

frequenz effekte
graduiertenkolleg 1624

Bibliografische Informationen der Deutschen Nationalbibliothek:
Die Deutsche Nationalbibliothek verzeichnet diese Publikation in der Deutschen Nationalbibliografie: detaillierte bibliografische Daten sind im Internet über <http://dnb.d-nb.de> abrufbar.

Cover photo by Michael Rießler, showing an interview situation with Komi speaker Andrey Hozyaynov in Kel'chiyur, Izhemskiy Rayon, Komi Republic.

Gestaltung:
Kulturstiftung Sibirien gGmbH, Fürstenberg/Havel

Herstellung:
Books on Demand GmbH, Norderstedt

Electronic edition: www.siberian-studies.org/publications/orhili.html

ISBN: 978-3-942883-30-6

Printed in Germany

CONTENTS

Introduction 7
Erich Kasten, Katja Roller, Joshua Wilbur

1 Documenting Oral Histories in the Russian Far East: Text Corpora for Multiple Aims and Uses 13
Erich Kasten

2 Documenting Endangered Oral Histories of the Arctic: A Proposed Symbiosis for Documentary Linguistics and Oral History Research, Illustrated by Saami and Komi Examples 31
Michael Rießler and Joshua Wilbur

3 "Our Ice, Snow and Winds": From Knowledge Integration to Co-production in the Russian SIKU Project, 2007–2013 65
Igor Krupnik and Lyudmila S. Bogoslovskaya

4 Fading Memories and Linguistic Fossils in Jewish Malayalam 83
Ophira Gamliel

5 Owls, Sasquatch and Tsun' Dye: Uncovering Indigenous Englishes through Oral Storytelling 107
Sonya Kinsey

6 "La Geste d'Asdiwal": A Structural Study of Myth in the Light of Oral History and Linguistics 121
Michael Dürr

7 On Pits, Progressives and Probabilities of Use: Memories from Wales and Their Implications for Corpus-linguistic (and Historical) Research 147
Katja Roller

8 A Difficult Term in Context: The Case of French STO 159
Annette Gerstenberg

9 Hidden Dialogues: Towards an Interactional Understanding of Oral History Interviews 185
Cord Pagenstecher and Stefan Pfänder

Notes on the Contributors 209

INTRODUCTION

Erich Kasten, Katja Roller, and Joshua Wilbur

This collection is intended to provide an overview of studies, methods and databases at the interface between linguistics and oral history research, and with a particular focus on minority languages and contact varieties. The inspiration for this interdisciplinary project originated in the workshop *Oral History Meets Linguistics* which was arranged by Bernd Kortmann, Stefan Pfänder and Katja Roller and took place in December 2015 at the Freiburg Institute for Advanced Studies (FRIAS). At the workshop, a number of questions were addressed, including:

- What can linguistic approaches to oral history data look like?
- What challenges and opportunities do such archived data present for linguistics research?
- In which way can historians profit from close collaboration with linguists?
- Are there archived oral history materials currently unknown to linguists that could be useful for future research? Or, concomitantly, what about linguistic data that could be useful to oral historians?

A number of linguists, historians and anthropologists participated in the workshop, and benefited from the lively discussions and interdisciplinary exchange of ideas, resources and know-how.

In this, one thing became quite clear: linguists and historians stand to profit in multiple ways from close collaboration. However, no significant discourse between linguistics and oral history studies has really come to life in the literature. This collection attempts to close this gap by providing contributions from linguists concerning various target languages, as well as from historians and anthropologists, and in doing so, presenting a multifaceted interdisciplinary examination of approaches to orally remembered historical events.

In the first chapter, *Documenting Oral Histories in the Russian Far East*, Erich Kasten discusses text corpora for multiple aims and uses with examples of Itelmen, Koryak and Even texts that have been recorded by him and his team since the mid-1990s in Kamchatka. The focus is on a quest for new ways to transmit endangered languages and traditional knowledge to younger generations. The use of electronic media and archives on the internet facilitates open access and sustainability of the data. In addition to that, conventional print media and DVDs still serve, for the time being, important functions, especially in more remote places. In this, younger community members are encouraged to practice endangered vernacular and cultural knowledge in recorded life histories in order to allow these to survive. Through such hybrid publication strategies, the language data can simultaneously be made available for different uses, such as the preservation of linguistic diversity within the community and for scientific research and comparative analyses by linguists, historians and cultural and social anthropologists.

The following chapter by Michael Rießler and Joshua Wilbur on *Documenting Endangered Oral Histories of the Arctic: A Proposed Symbiosis for Documentary Linguistics and Oral History Research, Illustrated by Saami and Komi Examples* argues that documentary linguistics can provide valuable resources for social science research, particularly for studies in anthropology and oral history. In this, the authors focus on an approach to collecting linguistic data on endangered languages using digital technologies that can make this useful data available outside of linguistics. With their thorough annotations and "thick" metadata the recordings from various Saami and Komi groups can be easily used not only for linguistic, but even for comparative historical research. This discussion can even be seen as a set of best-practice guidelines for digital archiving and publication of such data. Examples of oral histories in linguistic data are provided showing how similar political socioeconomic transitions which these specific communities went through over the past decades are documented. They conclude that both linguistics and oral history stand to benefit significantly from cooperative research.

Igor Krupnik's and Lyudmila S. Bogoslovskaya's chapter *Our Ice, Snow and Winds* shifts the focus to the Russian "Sea Ice Knowledge and Use" (SIKU) project. SIKU was the first scientific program in the Arctic that systematically collected indigenous nomenclatures for ice, snow, and weather phenomena in local languages and dialects. This documentation contains elders' and hunters' narratives on the use of sea ice, safety in ice hunting and traveling, and practices of ice- and weather forecasting. Similar to the approach in Kasten's chapter, this addresses the practical aim of ensuring continued use of traditional knowledge under pressing problems such as the current challenges of climate change. While the bilingual lexicon (dictionary) of local ice terms illustrated in this chapter did not have a place in indigenous culture, it appeals to today's hunters, elders, youth, teachers, ice scholars, linguists, and heritage specialists. This work relates directly to the recent book by Alexandra Lavrillier und Semen Gabyshev "An Arctic Indigenous Knowledge System of Landscape, Climate, and Human Interactions", published in 2017 by the Kulturstiftung Sibirien, that discusses Evenki reindeer herders' and hunters' knowledge on the basis of their own vernacular.

Ophira Gamliel's case study on *Fading Memories and Linguistic Fossils in Jewish Malayalam* relates to preceding chapters as it underpins the urgency to record endangered language data before it potentially falls into oblivion within in the near future. Similar to Kasten's chapter, Gamliel shows through personal accounts how her awareness of this important issue increased and how she eventually became fully involved in this project. By relying on concrete linguistic findings, the paper challenges accepted and, arguably, biased notions regarding the oral history of Kerala Jews as reconstructed in foreign languages (Portuguese, English and Hebrew) from the late 17th century to the present. The chapter argues that the linguistic description of a castolect on the verge of extinction is crucial to the study of the sociocultural history of minority communities.

In her chapter on *Uncovering Indigenous Englishes through Oral Storytelling* with the example of the Witsuwit'en people from north central British Columbia, Sonya Kinsey clearly shows how a community tries to cope with the dramatic loss of their particular vernacular. Although language revitalization efforts are underway, they have not shown the expected results so far. During her fieldwork, Kinsey noticed that a break in dialectal language transmission often coincided with a break in cultural transmission—as is also demonstrated in Kasten's, as well as Krupnik and Bogoslovskaya's chapters. She emphasizes how traditional storytelling practices are at the heart of many indigenous communities, and are important modes of transmitting history and culture from one generation to the next.

This finding relates to the following chapter of this volume: Michael Dürr discusses the *Structural Study of Myth in the Light of Oral History and Linguistics* using the example of "La Geste d'Asdiwal" by Claude Lévi-Strauss. Referring to an iconic text collected in the heydays of early linguistic data collection on indigenous languages at the beginning of the 20th century, Dürr directs our attention to a closer linguistic analysis of the original text, an analysis that obviously has been neglected so far. He questions that characteristics or traits were selected as relevant for previous analyses which were based on Franz Boas' English translation. In contrast, these previous analyses are compared here with the information structure of the original Sm'algya̱x text. Furthermore, through in-depth text analysis, the author reveals some implications in particular genres of stories, such as *adawx*, and discusses how the use of Sm'algya̱x directional particles can lead to the core of structuralism.

Katja Roller's chapter on *Memories from Wales and their Implications for Corpus Linguistic (and Historical) Research* outlines how oral history interviews from Wales can be used for corpus linguistic analyses of Welsh English grammar. The study presented explores how consciously people from Wales and from London perceive different grammatical features of Welsh English (determined through questionnaires) and whether the features perceived more consciously are more frequent in spoken Welsh English. A positive correlation between the features' conscious perception and their usage frequency in Welsh English could be found, providing evidence for usage-based theories of language.

Apart from these linguistic implications, Roller argues that analyses of constructions such as the non-standard habitual progressive can also yield fruitful insights for oral historians, for example, in that they illustrate daily practices and routines at different times in (remembered) history. Roller also observes that in oral history collections speakers from a specific region do not necessarily speak the local dialect, which can complicate the situation for the researcher. Kasten noticed the same in his material, when, after enforced relocations in later Soviet times, local groups "took their particular dialects with them" to new environments where the same language was spoken differently by others. Therefore, for precise language documentation, it is important to document the individual background of each speaker in the metadata, including information on e.g. where the speaker's family is from or may have migrated from in the past.

Annette Gerstenberg combines sources from linguistics and oral history research for the analysis in her chapter *A Difficult Term in Context: The Case of French* STO. The author makes use of two databases compiled in the 2000s with elderly French speakers: the linguistic corpus *LangAge* and the oral history collection *Zwangsarbeit / Forced Labor 1939–1945*. Based on these sources and data from newspaper archives she explores how the historical term STO (*Service du Travail Obligatoire*) is used and what meaning can be attributed to it in different contexts. Among other things, the author finds that STO referring to "a person doing Forced Labor" (as opposed to the common meaning "the institution of Forced Labor") is mainly used by speakers with first-hand experience of working in STO. This suggests that specific shades of meaning of the term STO are constructed based on individual personal experiences.

In the concluding chapter on an *Interactional Understanding of Oral History Interviews*, Cord Pagenstecher and Stefan Pfänder bring together oral history, conversation analysis and interactional linguistics. This chapter studies dialog patterns in video-taped testimonies of Holocaust survivors. The biographical interviews are understood as the results of a recorded interaction: the narration and its layers of meaning are co-constructed in a working alliance between interviewer and narrator, with both participants using specific verbal and non-verbal resources. By analyzing examples of repetitions and of re-tellings within testimonies, the authors explore the potential of interdisciplinary cooperation between historians and linguists in understanding the dialogical character of oral history interviews.

The detailed analysis of linguistic and contextual implications of certain interview situations given in this last chapter relates to the broader issue of appropriate recording techniques that has been discussed thoroughly in some of the earlier chapters. Kinsey noticed that storytelling provides opportunities to record longer, uninterrupted samples of speech. Such stories are also more likely to contain authentic local constructions, providing a more comfortable natural type of response from indigenous speakers, as opposed to the standard question/answer format of many linguistic interviews. Kasten emphasizes how certain recording techniques can bias the outcome of documented oral histories, especially if they are geared towards aesthetic or commercial uses, in contrast to scientific and community needs that are clearly prioritized in the endeavors of the authors of this volume. However, as the discussion by Rießler and Wilbur has shown, even film projects can produce valuable data for such purposes, depending on the experience and interest in a reliable and trusting cooperative relationship between the producer, the community and anthropologists. This is not always a given, as stressed by Anna Gossman-Stammler during her presentation at the Franco German Seminar "Gateway to the Arctic" at the Alfred Wegener Institute in Potsdam in November 2016. She had had similar rather negative experiences with a BBC film crew in Yakutia, as addressed in Kasten's chapter. However, there are other more promising examples such as those demonstrated in the films by Christian Vagt and Stephan Dudeck, and by Anastasia Lapsui and Markku Lehmuskallio, which were shown and discussed at the Berlinale film festival in 2017. These films often contain full soundtracks in the given Nenets languages and express indigenous views more clearly.

Rießler and Wilbur indicate that language documentation projects often include legacy data, and thus cover a greater time-span, which then allows for diachronic comparisons. The advantage of incorporating earlier text recordings for current analyses and—after modernizing their orthography—for community use is addressed in Kasten's chapter with regard to the Kamchadal texts, recorded by Jochelson about 100 years ago. Around the same time, Henry Tate provided the "Story of Asdiwal" to Boas's text collections of the First Nations of the Canadian Pacific Northwest that is discussed by Dürr. These forms of re-use direct our attention to the particular value of legacy data for revisited oral history and linguistic analysis with more advanced technical and methodological means, as well as for the repatriation of cultural knowledge in order to sustain endangered languages and cultural memories of the given people. It should also make us optimistic with regard to the future use of current data collections.

Finally, as Roller points out, a combination of linguistic and oral history approaches can give the people who made and experienced history, through their own words, a central place in developing a richer understanding of the past, and in keeping it alive. This aspect has been the main concern in many contributions of this volume and may serve as common ground for further discussions on oral history and linguistics in the future.

1 DOCUMENTING ORAL HISTORIES IN THE RUSSIAN FAR EAST: TEXT CORPORA FOR MULTIPLE AIMS AND USES

Erich Kasten

Introduction

With the emergence of American cultural anthropology at the end of the 19th century, new concepts gave more weight to studying people's own interpretations of their traditions. For Franz Boas, it "seemed supremely important to document the anthropological material through uncensored accounts of natives in their own words and in their own language, to preserve the original meaning" (Boas 2001: 19). But such "salvage anthropology" was by no means aimed at sustaining the endangered languages and cultures. Thus Michael Krauss is "struck, even shocked, that as revolutionaries, discoverers of cultural relativism, they [Boas, Jochelson, and Bogoras] wrote so little in their JNPE [Jesup North Pacific Expedition] contributions to protest or even express regret about the then very active colonial suppression of the languages and cultures" (2003: 215). But nevertheless, the enormous amount of texts that were collected by Franz Boas and his collaborators in the indigenous languages of the peoples of the North Pacific rim (see Dürr, *this volume*) today—more than 100 years later—provides many First Nations of the Canadian Pacific Northwest essential and highly appreciated foundations for their efforts to revitalize their languages and cultures. Thus, unintentionally, important additional or multiple uses of the data once recorded came to light later.

In similar ways, more recent text corpora originated for indigenous peoples in the Russian Far East. At the outset of my own fieldwork in Kamchatka in 1993, when an initial project was explained to the locals at a community gathering in Kovran, the strong wish expressed by the Itelmens was to preserve their language, which was at that time in a critical state of endangerment. Keeping this request in mind, the information to be collected from local people for the purpose of that project[1] was recorded, whenever possible, in the given indigenous language. This way, as a later spin-off from this scientific project, a primer on Itelmen language and culture (Khaloimova et al. 2012 [1997]) was produced as early as 1997, as the first volume in a series of eagerly awaited community learning tools (Kasten 2009b).[2] The same strategy was applied in following projects, even though these projects had to prioritize other programs and

1 "Ethnicity processes", funded by the German Research Foundation.

2 http://www.kulturstiftung-sibirien.de/mat_31_E.html [24.01.2017]

different aims.[3] For all these projects most of the information was knowingly recorded in the given indigenous languages. As a result, much of it already has been and will later be returned to the communities who support sustaining endangered languages and indigenous knowledge, in the form of learning tools. During the last decades, this philosophy and implicit agreement on sharing and returning recorded data has become the basis for most collaborative field projects with indigenous peoples, especially on the North Pacific rim (see Krupnik 2000, also *this volume*).

For most institutions and funding organizations (see note 3) it has been the policy or recommendation to encourage sharing data at a later point with the wider public, beyond their paramount project aims. In one instance, however, Ulrike Ottinger, the producer of the film project "Chamissos Schatten", refused to allow such supplementary use of the recordings as non-profit learning tools for the given indigenous communities. Her decision was justified with reference to the funding guidelines for that project. However, it turns out that the main sponsor of that project, the *Kulturstiftung des Bundes* (The German Federal Cultural Foundation) does not actually provide such guidelines. In fact, as a public institution, it is not only obliged, but usually committed to supporting the aim of maintaining the cultural heritage of indigenous peoples and, thereby, cultural diversity in general. But despite the producer's decision, the audio of the recorded texts on Chukchi language and culture will still be used for publishing community learning tools, as these are the intellectual property of the people who provided the information in the first place (Lewinski 2004) and secondly of the consultant who conducted the interviews, chosen because of his connection to the local culture and language competence. Nevertheless, it is regrettable that these learning tools will not be released, as with most other volumes in this series, together with the DVD, which contains the recorded texts, because the producer was not prepared to provide the footage of these interviews.

In total, about 170 hours of Itelmen, Even, Koryak, and Chukchi language data are stored at the Foundation for Siberian Cultures as part of a more comprehensive ethnographic digital video pool. They originated over the past 20 years more as spin-off results from ethnographic fieldwork projects that where, firstly, directed towards other aims. But the full value of the collected data has become apparent only later with the data now even being employed—after their scientific or commercial usage for exhibition and film projects—for important community-oriented purposes. Fortunately, this opportunity has been seized upon and an extensive text corpus for the peoples of Kamchatka has been compiled in time, as much of this knowledge has been rapidly vanishing since then (see below). This is important since special programs

3 Among these were scientific projects on property relations (Max Planck Society), ethnographica in context (German Research Foundation), traditional ecological knowledge (UNESCO), math in cultural context (US National Science Foundation) and international exhibition projects on peoples and cultures in Siberia at the Museum of Natural History (Münster), the Central and Regional Library (Berlin) and the Linden-Museum (Stuttgart).

for preserving the cultural heritage of these peoples have been unlikely to receive the needed full-scale funding as they are usually seen as not responding to specific scientific research questions.

In the following, it will be discussed how a given text corpus can be made available for multiple follow-up uses. But first, various recording methods will be scrutinized with regards to possible limitations or biases of the given data. These data refer to oral history that is defined as "a field of study and a method of gathering, preserving and interpreting the voices and memories of people, communities, and participants in past events."[4] Even though its most prominent genre are life histories, this definition should also include tales or stories, since they often contain historical information not only about events in the distant past, but also about worldviews and behaviors that have been transmitted over generations. (For particular story genres that may carry elements of political discourse, see Dürr 2017: 126ff., *this volume.*)

Methodological Considerations

Should oral history be recorded in the indigenous language or in a lingua franca?

In the case of Itelmen, most speakers—even those belonging to the elder generation—were already more fluent in Russian than in their indigenous language in the 1990s. Yet even then we were still able to record life histories from the last remaining fluent speakers—that is from those to whom the language was transmitted in the natural way as their mother tongue. Most of them are no longer alive today. However, for neighboring Even and Koryak, one can still find, especially in remote locations, a sufficient number of speakers who are still in full command in their own language. But even there, most of them are now only able to communicate fragmentarily in their language or with constrained grammar and lexicon. This leads to restrictions for a researcher expecting data only in the indigenous language if he or she is mostly interested in the ethnographic or historical content of the recorded text. In this particular case, the information may be less complete if the speaker is encouraged to speak in his or her indigenous language for linguistic documentation purposes.

Furthermore, recording a text in the respective indigenous language may entail a considerable time lag until the text can be analysed with regards to its content, as it has first to be transcribed and translated into a language understood by the researcher. Most researchers who decide to cover a larger geographical area for comparative reasons or for getting a broader and more balanced view, are not—or hardly can be—in command of all the various languages spoken in the given area, with all their often diverse dialects and local variants. Therefore, in order to capture the subtle nuances of

4 http://www.oralhistory.org/about/do-oral-history [24.01.2017]

the documented language material the researcher often works in teams with various indigenous experts who are familiar with the given local vernacular. Working up the recorded texts later can turn into an extremely time-consuming process that has, in our case, sometimes stretched over several years. Clearly, this often exceeds the deadline for submitting the expected results or for providing reports on a funded project in time. Therefore, researchers in projects who have to focus on the immediate analysis of a specific research question regarding ethnographic or historical content might be inclined or well-advised to record the data in Russian or whatever relevant lingua franca right away.

On the other hand, whenever we had the opportunity to record oral histories from some of the last fluent mother-tongue speakers in their own language, we noticed that the information often was more precise and more complete. Speakers would even place more emphasis on certain issues that they would usually share among their group members but not necessarily with the foreigner. That means that the same life history can be told differently in the indigenous and in the Russian language—as in the latter case the speaker might also be more inclined to live up to the expectations of the foreign interlocutor, in addition to having to conform to the linguistic and communicative structures of the foreign tongue and culture.

Therefore, even with regards to content, it is preferable to conduct the recording in the indigenous language, if the speakers are proficient enough in it. This can also create a more familiar situation for the speaker, especially if he or she feels more comfortable using their own language. But in other situations, as mentioned above, it can be counterproductive to urge the speaker to use his or her indigenous language. Therefore, the researcher has to assess and to decide flexibly about these options case by case.

How can certain recording techniques influence or bias the information?

Until the end of the 19th century, there were no technical means to record sound data. But with the breakthrough of modern devices, new wax cylinder recording techniques were applied, first in the Russian Far East during the Jesup North Pacific Expedition in the years between 1900 and 1902. However, because of the limited capacity of these wax cylinders, Vladimir Jochelson and Vladimir Bogoras confined their use mostly to recording shamanic songs or incantations. Therefore, only few texts of the extensive corpora that they compiled for the Koryak, Chukchi, Yukaghir, and Itelmen languages have audio samples as well. But nevertheless, according to Boas' instructions (see above), the researchers were eager to record the information from the local people as authentically as possible, with obvious limitations that soon became apparent. Most of the texts—collected in the indigenous languages as well as in Russian—were still written or taken down in shorthand, which meant continuous stops and interruptions of the important on-going flow of the story. Jochelson explicitly stated that the tales were dictated to him, and that he had felt obliged to stop frequently for questions regarding the proper script and translation through his interpreter. Obviously, the speakers became irritated about that and frequently lost their enthusiasm (Jochelson 2016: 448).

Most notably when recording tales, it is essential not to interrupt the text flow of the story as otherwise its meaning and the plot can get lost. But even today this basic requirement may be put aside, as in the film project "Chamissos Schatten" when the recording of a tale by Maya Lomovtseva in Esso was interrupted by the producer to adjust the lighting. Understandably enough, the speaker found this annoying but carried on with telling the story. Consequently, a decisive fragment of the story was later missing and the entire recording had become useless with regard to its meaning. But, in that case, it was not seen as a problem as the intention was simply to record a segment of indigenous language. Here, just a fragment of the indigenous language was considered sufficient for insinuating exotic authenticity for the later audience of such a film. When she was asked in a newspaper interview whether she was irritated by not understanding Russian or any of the indigenous languages while filming, the producer professed quite frankly that she learnt from gesture and facial expressions alone what the given story was about.[5] Such imaginary ethnography (*imaginäre Ethnographie*, cf. Kramer 1977) was certainly a fascinating genre in the 19th century. The question is whether this approach can live up to current standards that aim at understanding indigenous concepts and look for a "respectful coexistence of various types of knowledge" (see Krupnik and Bogoslovskaya 2017: 78, *this volume*)—if local oral history and indigenous nomenclature is explicitly ignored.

But even in serious text recordings, researchers are sometimes inclined to interrupt the story in order to request more information, especially on linguistic topics. It is clear that such questions are better discussed later so as to not interrupt the narrative, after having finished the interview and when going through the audio file again with its transcript and translation. Beyond this, it has proven useful to set up recording situations in a way that the researcher disappears as much as possible into the background in order to encourage a natural conversation among local participants on a certain topic that is given beforehand (see Pagenstecher and Pfänder 2017: 193ff., *this volume*). A good example for this is a spontaneous recording during a tea-break in the tundra with Maya Lomovtseva, the same Even protagonist mentioned above, in 2000 (see Fig. 1.2). While enthusiastically telling the fox story to her Koryak and Even friends she almost forgot about the filming fieldworker, tripping over him during the story.[6]

When Bogoras and Jochelson occasionally employed, for the first time in that area, the revolutionary new sound recording technology of wax cylinders, this must have already felt like an intrusion. Descriptions of relevant field situations by Jochelson and reactions by the people indicate obvious biases of the recorded material. When

5 "Gekochter Seehund ist delikat". *Der Tagesspiegel*, 8. Mai 2016.
6 http://www.kulturstiftung-sibirien.de/mat_321_2_E.html [24.01.2017]

speakers were sitting curiously or even afraid in front of the funnel they must have perceived the situation as unfamiliar (Jochelson 2016: 448, 609). Advanced recording technologies can certainly provide better opportunities to minimize such kinds of intrusion or interference and the observer's paradox, especially if they use less obtrusive recording devices, for example low-key camcorders in contrast to more conspicuous complex professional film equipment.

Fig. 1.1 A film crew is recording a ritual in Chukotka, 1999 (photo: V. Vaté).

Fig. 1.2 Maya Lomovtseva (right) tells a story to her friends during a tea-break in the tundra, 2000 (video still, E. Kasten).

How the outcome can be biased by certain recording methods can be seen with regard to other examples from the above mentioned film project "Chamissos Schatten". In Yanrakynnot (Chukotka) first the furniture of a household had to be rearranged for the imagined visual aesthetics of the setting, which caused detrimental irritation and stress on the part of the interviewees. Another recording in Kamchatka with the Even elder Nadezhda G. Barkavtova was made in a traditional yurt that is set up for tourist shows in Esso. Immediately, the set was understood by the interviewee as a commercial project that she already had become used to in similar previous occasions—with consistent code-switching out of regard for the expectations of the particular audience, the film crew. The same topics of her life history that she addressed then had been recorded with her more than 10 years earlier, at various occasions in the natural setting of her summer fishing camp and winter hunting cabin at Kabana, several days' travel by horseback away from Esso in the tundra (see Fig. 1.3–4).[7] When contrasting these recordings with each other, it is most revealing to analyse specific features and variations resulting from the different contexts in which the recordings were taken.

Fig. 1.3
Recording life histories with Nadezhda Barkavtova (left) at her fishing camp, 2000 (photo: E. Kasten).

Fig. 1.4
Nadezhda Barkavtova, 2000 (video still, E. Kasten).

7 Her tales from these recordings have been published in Kasten / Avak 2014: 55–77, see a sample clip: http://www.kulturstiftung-sibirien.de/mat_321_1_E.html [24.01.2017], while more editions on her life history, ecological knowledge, and sewing techniques are still in progress.

How can linguistics influence or bias the recorded data?

Sometimes researchers with linguistic competence may overrate their abilities and risk distorting or biasing the recorded material. An early example is given in some notes by Bogoras (1917: 1, 4) when he makes judgments about rules of pronunciation in the Koryak language that are based on his earlier experiences with the Chukchi language, which he was more familiar with. Today many researchers prefer to work in shifting teams with local language experts who are familiar with the numerous different varieties or dialects of the given indigenous language in order to capture the particular subtleties that most often only a local person can fully understand (see above).

If the researcher focuses too much on text recordings, there is the risk that one relies foremost on what is told while paying less attention to the actual practices and activities. For example, in one case Jochelson's confined oral information caused his incorrect assessment of the way the *matev*, the traditional skin boat of the Koryak, is paddled (Kasten and Dürr 2016: 25–26). There are many other cases where it has become apparent how important it is to match recorded texts with visual and emotional information from real situations und practices by means of participant observation, which is the classical method of the ethnographer. Therefore, it is most advantageous if researchers with particular linguistic interests or expertise collaborate with cultural or social anthropologists, for properly contextualising the recorded data.

Another bias can occur when sound recordings of oral histories are transformed into written text or academic script. It is well known that through this procedure they lose some of their specific qualities. Often they appear as "frozen" or they suffer from changes or standardizations, especially if the given speakers transcribe the recorded texts themselves. Commonly, written texts do not capture the on-going variation that is characteristic for oral traditions. A story is rarely told exactly the same way twice, but it is continuously varied, further elaborated or provided with supplements. Today, we have adequate technological means to record and to preserve oral history in unbiased form in original and annotated audio-video files. Being thoughtfully applied in learning situations, they can simulate customary story-telling situations that are closer to natural ways of transmitting this knowledge orally and visually than through print media or textbooks. This may downplay the significance of written texts insofar as scientific transcriptions have anyway often been of limited use for the purpose of language preservation.

For example, the Itelmen (or Kamchadal) texts, recorded by Jochelson and edited later in 1961 by Worth in linguistic script could never be read by Itelmen themselves, until these were published in 2014 in contemporary practical Itelmen script (Khaloimova et al. 2014). Even today, linguistic documentation programs put first emphasis on scientific script, from which later community-oriented learning tools might be produced, if at all. Even when relevant data are hosted on the Internet for open access, the given interface is often not designed in user-friendly ways for indigenous communities. This reflects again the subordinate aim of making the texts available for practical uses and for the important purpose of endangered language preservation. Although these reasons are often given as part of the justification for funding such projects, they are seldom hardly more than attempts at maintaining political correctness.

In conclusion, the data is usually looked at with a specific preset focus according to the aims and approaches of the given scientific disciplines or film genres. Consequently, recorded life histories and related activities often reflect only confined or even biased segments of the actual stories. A too narrow linguistic view can at times miss or ignore the need to put the data into cultural perspective. The same occurs in film projects, which have to look for the most spectacular images to address a particular public. An example of this is a scene from a staged ritual after the killing of a seal that was set up for the film crew of "Chamissos Schatten" in Chukotka. Not only was the natural community involvement left out, in particular the important role that the hunter's wife takes in this ritual. During the recording the imagination of the producer Ulrike Ottinger was captured by the powerful moment (from the Western viewpoint) of seeing the film crew's cook (a Siberian Yup'ik) drinking the fresh seal's blood. Thus she did not want to pay attention to the most significant step in the entire ritual from the indigenous point of view, although the consultant was insistently pointing to it, when the hunter cut a small piece of the seal's liver and returned it to the sea—as a gift to and a reconciliation with nature. By missing this scene, the fundamental idea and worldview of Chukchi and Koryak seal hunters with regards to nature (Kasten 2009a, 2017) could not be captured in the film. In consequence, the footage is of limited value for other multiple uses, such as high-toned documentary for potential further scientific analysis.

Experiences from a Recent Edition Project on Itelmen Oral history

In addition to providing ethnological or historical information, the documentation of oral history can serve additional needs when it is used for linguistic research and/or as learning tools for preserving or sustaining endangered languages. With these potential multiple uses in mind—even to be taken up at later times or by other disciplines—we decided to record oral history whenever possible and even despite the mentioned restrictions in the given indigenous languages. Over the years we tested different formats for practical use in Kamchatka for which we developed print as well as electronic editions of the recorded texts. They can be used simultaneously for various aims and can supplement each other in favourable ways.

Here I will give an example of a first set of learning tools from documented Itelmen oral history. In contrast to our much more extensive materials on Koryak and Even oral traditions, the recorded Itelmen data is relatively confined. One reason is the already limited number of Itelmen speakers in the 1990s. In addition to this, because of other research priorities then, the later focus on documenting endangered languages was unfortunately not yet fully developed at that point.

The resulting edited volume on Itelmen language and culture (Kasten and Dürr 2015) contains life histories and tales that show particular characteristics according to the speech competence and the individual background of each speaker. There is one short story on memories of early village life by one of the last fully fluent speakers,

Fig. 1.5 "Gosha" Zaporotski, 1993 (photo: E. Kasten).

Fig. 1.6 Chatting about Itelmen texts over a bearded seal stew with Klavdiya Khaloimova, Galina Zaporotskaya, and Tat'yana Zaeva (from left) near Kovran, 2001 (photo: E. Kasten).

"Gosha" (Georgi) Zaporotski (Kasten and Dürr 2015: 46–49), who had no academic background, but who was in command of probably the most profound Itelmen traditional knowledge. When I approached him, I was surprised that he proposed to first give some thought to my request. As he obviously wanted to speak "correct" Itelmen he wrote the story down over night, and the next morning he read it from his notes, which of course was not what I was looking for. He presumably wanted to satisfy my perceived linguistic expectations to the best of his ability.

A similar problem occurred in another publication project in our series when the speaker herself helped with transcribing the recorded data and insisted on changing and correcting the grammar. In that case the editors could not publish the sound files together with the book, as these eventually differed too much from the transcript given in the volume after the speaker herself had edited it.

Similar experiences were gained when re-editing Jochelson's Kamchadal texts (Khaloimova et al. 2014) in contemporary practical Itelmen orthography (see above). At the beginning, the local co-editor and Itelmen language expert in this project Klavdiya Khaloimova tried to translate the numerous Russian terms in the original texts into Itelmen—although these had already at that time, the beginning of the 20th century, become part of the Itelmen lexicon. Understandably enough, from the perspective of a textbook author (see below) she was obviously concerned about standardizations according to this specific genre. Although, as a matter of course, the team eventually decided to leave the Russian terms as they were, as they document and reflect internal dynamics within the Itelmen language that already had occurred at the given time, and which provide important clues for further analysis of such processes. Beyond that, the occasional Russian terms do not affect the practical use of the texts, as this even reflects and anticipates more recent developments and states of the Itelmen language.

There are other chapters in the edited volume "Itelmen texts" in which the realization of the Itelmen language is obviously biased by the academic background of the speakers. Klavdiya Khaloimova (Kasten and Dürr 2015: 50–53) has published textbooks together with Aleksandr Volodin from the 1980s onwards in which they have employed standardized Itelmen, which is strictly rejected by genuine speakers who pay particular attention to preserving their local variants.

Other local Itelmen speakers, Galina Zaporotskaya (ibid.: 36–45) and Valentina Uspenskaya (ibid: 16–35),[8] were able to preserve their local and clearly differentiating vernacular, although they had an academic background as teachers of Itelmen at the Institute for Advanced Teachers' Training in Palana and in the regional city of Petropavlovsk-Kamchatski. Another text, a *Kutkh* (Raven) tale (ibid.: 84–97), is from the schoolteacher Vera Khan who—although one of the last genuine mother-tongue speakers—read it from a manuscript that she had prepared for her classes.

8 Sample clip: http://www.kulturstiftung-sibirien.de/vir_237_3_E.html [24.01.2017]

It is obvious that in the Itelmen case one had to draw mostly on the local *intelligentsia.* Most of the last few speakers of this language belonged to this group who had been able to preserve the language because of their professional engagement with it.

Another text, a *Kutkh* and *Miti* tale (ibid.: 54–65), concludes in a way that is otherwise not characteristic for this genre. The speaker Lyudmila Pravdoshina, who teaches cultural programs and Itelmen classes for younger children, adds to the tale's end the admonition that "they had forgotten their parents. But do you know your Mama and Papa"—whereas in traditional ways of storytelling such moral concepts remain implicit, they are not overtly spoken out. This tale was recorded, the same as another one on the culture hero *Tylval* by Agrafena Ivashova (ibid: 66–83), unscheduled and in a relaxed mood after a picnic near their potato field.

Fig. 1.7 Picnic with Agrefena Ivashova (left) and Lyudmila Pravdoshina (right) and her family, Tigil', 1997 (photo: E. Kasten).

There are also a number of texts that were told spontaneously and which were of prior value for our documentation. One of them was quite notable and informative; I was able to create a situation in which two speakers shared their memories about earlier village life while more or less forgetting about my presence. In this way, they did not feel pressured to speak "proper" Itelmen, but employed customary continuous code-switching between Itelmen and Russian, which reflected the natural state of Itelmen speech among elders in 1997.

Also, another recording with Tat'yana Gutorova (ibid.: 98–115) was not intended at the outset for the later given text collection. It unexpectedly came about during her granddaughter Elena Zueva's rehearsal and preparation for a concert tour in Germany,[9] and therefore was recorded in Russian.

9 http://www.kulturstiftung-sibirien.de/ver_422_E.html [24.01.2017]

In sum, what makes these texts particularly interesting is that they reflect ongoing changes not only in the language itself, but also even in the content of the stories, according to new social environments and the varying personal backgrounds of the given speakers. Therefore, collaborative projects between linguists and cultural anthropologists can produce favourable effects, as the latter can contribute by viewing linguistic data within its proper cultural context.

Generally, the transcription process proceeded relatively straightforwardly once decisions had been made about consistencies in the Itelmen script. But deciding on an adequate or proper Russian (or English) translation turned out to be more of a challenge. The question was how far the translation could diviate from the original text, or from the word-to-word translation in the scientific annotation, in order to make the text understandable or even attractive for a general readership. In the past, less attention was paid to this, and not much effort was put into editing the data for non-scientific audiences. Therefore, the Jochelson Itelmen texts have been hardly used by others apart from researchers (including linguists) until recently. The same situation occurred with the enormous corpora of informative Itelmen, Koryak, and Chukchi texts collected by Bogoras, which also deserve more attention beyond specialized academic circles.

Additional Electronic Formats of the Itelmen Oral History Text Edition

From the outset, our motivation to record oral history in the indigenous languages was in response to community concerns for language preservation. This motivated our earlier focus on print editions according to the technical means in the mid-1990s. Even later on, with the emergence of new electronic formats, these aims were still applied primarily for this purpose and not yet for linguistic documentation such as under the DoBeS programme.[10] More recently, within the framework of developing multiple uses of the data stored at the Foundation for Siberian Cultures, these aims and relevant digital technologies have been gaining more weight, especially with regard to long-term storage of the data.

New technological formats were already explored in the late 1990s during our research on the use and acceptance of learning tools. We then noticed a few important points that could strengthen or create indispensable motivation among those who are concerned about the Itelmen language in Kamchatka (Kasten 2013). Viewing and listening to elder relatives in familiar local settings by means of video recordings—even if some of them might have already passed away, but are still well-remembered—endorses identification with one's own local history and promotes cultural self-esteem. With this in mind, we supplemented the print editions of the oral histories mentioned

10 http://dobes.mpi.nl [24.01.2017]

with DVDs that contain a complete set of the recordings with subtitles in Russian and English. These audio-visual formats go back to earlier experiences when we first published relevant sound files of Itelmen speech and wordlists on CD.

Since 2000, we have been recording consistently on digital video in order to illustrate the context and to also show the body language of the speaker. Thus the DVD materials that have been produced since then are even more attractive for educational uses as learning tools.[11] However, these DVDs must be seen only as a provisional "bridge technology". In the long run, all related audio-visual materials will be available on the Internet for more convenience and free download. But for the time being, some of the most prominent target user groups—private households or pedagogical institutions and cultural centres in indigenous communities in Kamchatka and in other parts of the Russian North—do not always have adequate and reasonably priced access to the Internet and therefore still have to rely on the DVD editions. Currently, comprehensive Internet language archives are in progress that will ensure easier open access to the text corpora, with links to relevant other text corpora of the Russian North (see Wilbur and Rießler 2017, *this volume*).

The edited volume "Itelmen texts" is also available on the Internet, the same as all other publications in the series "Languages and Cultures in the Russian Far East".[12] In addition, most of the texts are accessible there in modern linguistic transcription and with interlinear glossing as separate electronic editions.[13]

The package of Itelmen learning tools also includes a primer that addresses natural learning situations at home for children at a pre-school age. It has been widely used since 1997 in Kamchatka, and its second edition came out in 2012 (Khaloimova et al. (2012). The illustrated schoolbook was followed by the multimedia CD-ROM "Itelmen Language and Culture" (Dürr and Kasten 2001). As a new feature, the user can listen to sound samples while choosing from up to eight different variants of the Itelmen language, in addition to slideshows and videoclips that illustrate the particular cultural contexts. Since its first publication in 2001, this multimedia CD has technically become out of date. Based on the same data, we produced a thematic dictionary in html-format for the Internet with sound samples of various local speech variants. This online "Itelmen Talking Dictionary" includes about 550 entries that are useful for both educational and research purposes.[14]

In addition to the above-mentioned publications that were jointly produced by the project team, Klavdiya Khaloimova published the book "Methodical recommendations for teachers of the Itelmen language" (Khaloimova 2015). This book is directed mainly towards future Itelmen teachers and is considered a particularly useful teach-

11 See sample clip http://www.kulturstiftung-sibirien.de/vir_231_1_E.html (6:25–8:17) [24.01.2017]

12 http://www.siberian-studies.org/publications/lc_E.html [24.01.2017]

13 see for example: http://www.siberian-studies.org/publications/PDF/lcitelmentexts_LiAn_Khan.pdf [24.01.2017]

14 http://www.kulturstiftung-sibirien.de/itd_E.html [24.01.2017]

ing tool at the Institute for Advanced Teachers' Training in Palana.[15] The book is a guide for teachers on how to systematically explain the rather intricate Itelmen grammar to schoolchildren of different levels with the help of short examples.

Finally, the DVD on the fall festival of the Itelmen, "Alkhalalalai" (Kasten 2015) completes the package of Itelmen language and culture learning tools. It depicts situations in which Itelmen language is used today in cultural revitalization events, although less for the purpose of communication, and more so to express Itelmen ethnic identity (Kasten 2005).[16]

Multiple Uses of the Recorded Material

In sum, the example of the Itelmen texts edition shows the potential multiple uses of recorded oral histories. The experiences gained from this project also apply to our forthcoming materials on Koryak and Even oral histories editions, as well as to publications by other authors in this series:

- The edited volume of these texts contains the full Itelmen transcripts of the recorded texts and their translations into Russian and English, with Russian and English subtitles on DVD.
- The Russian translation is meant for community members who are not yet in full command of their indigenous language, or who are no longer familiar with it.
- The English translation encourages desired cultural exchanges about these themes, especially among indigenous peoples of the North, such as in Scandinavia and North America.
- Furthermore, the English translation addresses the international academic community of linguists, who do not always know Russian.
- The linguistic annotation of the texts that is provided in addition to the electronic version of the edited volume on the Internet is even more specifically intended for further research purposes.

Conclusions

There are obvious mutual benefits in approaches to the documentation of oral history that aim to produce complex and well-integrated outcomes, and which bring together or combine potential multiple uses. The historical information can be more precise and complete if oral history is recorded in the given indigenous language. In

15 *Kafedra rodnykh yazykov, kul'tury i byta korennykh malochistlennykh narodov Severa Kamchatskogo instituta razvitiia obrazovaniia.*

16 http://www.kulturstiftung-sibirien.de/vir_237_7_E.html [24.01.2017]

the form of printed and electronic learning tools that are supplemented with DVDs, the recorded oral histories can stimulate interest in the preservation of endangered languages and indigenous knowledge, especially among younger generations. And we have seen how linguistic research can benefit if the recorded data are made available and presented in the ways as mentioned above.

Finally, this contribution has identified a number of fields in which shared interests and approaches between cultural anthropologists and linguists should be brought together in order to create valuable synergies from which both sides certainly will benefit. So far, because of its primary orientation towards language and traditional knowledge preservation through community use, we have put particular emphasis on (physical) print and DVD editions of the data. The next steps will be to focus even more on digital solutions, for example by using ELAN[17] as an archiving format, and by securing long-term storage and promoting the usage of these data via integrated language archives. These will merge various extensive text corpora that cover indigenous or minority languages of the North—from Scandinavia in the west to as far as Sakhalin and Chukotka in the east (see Rießler and Wilbur 2017, *this volume*).[18] The principle aim would be to provide easy and free access to these materials for indigenous communities, as well as for anthropological and linguistic research.

References

Boas, Franz 2001. The Results of the Jesup Expedition. In *Gateways. Exploring the Legacy of the Jesup North Pacific Expedition, 1897–1902*. I. Krupnik and W. Fitzhugh (eds.), 17–24. [English translation of: Die Resultate der Jesup Expedition. *Verhandlungen des XVI. internationalen Amerikanisten-Kongresses*, 1908. Erste Hälfte, S. 3–18, Wien und Leipzig: Hartleben.]

Bogoras, Waldemar 1917. *Koryak Texts*. Publications of the American Ethnological Society, 5. Leiden: Brill.

Dürr, Michael 2017. "La Geste d'Asdiwal": A Structural Study of Myth in the Light of Oral History and Linguistics. In *Oral History meets Linguistics*, E. Kasten, K. Roller, J. Wilbur (eds.), 121–146. Fürstenberg/Havel: Kulturstiftung Sibirien.

Dürr, Michael, Erich Kasten, and Klavdiya N. Khaloimova 2001. *Itelmen Language and Culture*. CD-ROM. Münster: Waxmann.

Jochelson, Waldemar 2016. *The Koryak*. E. Kasten and M. Dürr (eds.). Fürstenberg/Havel: Kulturstiftung Sibirien.

Kasten, Erich 2005. The Dynamics of Identity Management. In *Rebuilding Identities. Pathways to Reform in Post-Soviet Siberia*. E. Kasten (ed.), 237–260. Berlin: Reimer.

17 ELAN is an annotation tool allowing for transcribing and annotating video and audio materials. Cf. https://tla.mpi.nl/tools/tla-tools/elan/ [24.01.2017]

18 See the already existing volumes from such data bases for the Russian Far East: http://www.siberian-studies.org/publications/lc_E.html [24.01.2017]

— 2009a. Das O-lo-lo-Fest der Nymylanen (Küstenkorjaken). In *Schamanen Sibiriens. Magier, Mittler, Heiler*, E. Kasten (ed.): 32–35. Berlin: Reimer.

— 2009b. *Itelmen Language and Culture*. UNESCO Register of Good Practices in Language Preservation.

— 2015. *Alkhalalalai. The Fall Festival of the Itelmens in Kamchatka*. DVD. Fürstenberg/Havel: Kulturstiftung Sibirien.

— 2013. Learning Tools for Preserving Languages and Traditional Knowledge in Kamchatka. In *Sustaining Indigenous Knowledge: Learning Tools and Community Initiatives for Preserving Endangered Languages and Local Cultural Heritage*, E. Kasten and T. de Graaf (eds.), 65–88. Fürstenberg/Havel: Kulturstiftung Sibirien.

Kasten, Erich (ed.) 2017. *Dukhovnaya kul'tura koryakov-nymylanov, s. Lesnaya, Kamchatka. Mirovozzreniya i ritual'nye prazdniki / Worldviews and Ritual Practice of Nymylans (Coastal Koryaks), Lesnaya, Kamchatka*. Fürstenberg/Havel: Kulturstiftung Sibirien. (in print)

Kasten, Erich, and Raisa Avak (eds.) 2014. *Dukhovnaya kul'tura evenov Bystrinskogo rayona / Even Tales, Songs and Worldviews, Bystrinski district*. Fürstenberg/Havel: Kulturstiftung Sibirien.

— 2015. *Itel'menskie teksty / Itelmen texts*. Fürstenberg/Havel: Kulturstiftung Sibirien.

— 2016. Jochelson and the Jesup North Pacific Expedition. A New Approach in the Ethnography of the Russian Far East. In *Waldemar Jochelson: The Koryak*, E. Kasten and M. Dürr (eds.), 9–34. Fürstenberg/Havel: Kulturstiftung Sibirien.

Khaloimova, Klavdiya N. 2015. *Metodicheskie rekommendatsii (materialy) uchitelyu itel'menskogo yazyka*. [Methodical recommendations (materials) for the teacher of Itelmen language]. Fürstenberg/Havel: Kulturstiftung Sibirien.

Khaloimova, Klavdiya N., Michael Dürr, Erich Kasten, and Sergei Longinov 2012. *Istoriko-etnograficheskoe uchebnoe posobie po itel'menskomu yazyku* [Historical-ethnographical teaching materials for the Itelmen language]. 2nd ed., first published 1997. Fürstenberg/Havel: Kulturstiftung Sibirien.

Khaloimova, Klavdiya N., Michael Dürr, and Erich Kasten 2014. *Itel'menskie skazki, sobrannye V.I. Iokhelsonom v 1910–1911 gg.* [Itel'men tales, collected by V.I. Jochelson, 1910–1911]. Fürstenberg/Havel: Kulturstiftung Sibirien.

Krauss, Michael E. 2003. The Languages of the North Pacific Rim 1896–1997, and the Jesup Expedition. In *Constructing Cultures Then and Now. Celebrating Franz Boas and the Jesup North Pacific Expedition*, L. Kendall and I. Krupnik (eds.), 211–221. Washington DC: National Museum of Natural History and Smithsonian Institution.

Kramer, Fritz 1977. *Verkehrte Welten. Zur imaginären Ethnographie des 19. Jahrhunderts*. Frankfurt am Main: Syndikat.

Krupnik, Igor 2000 (ed.). *Pust' govoryat nashi stariki*. Chukotkam yupigita un,ipatsiugit. Rasskazy azyatskikh eskimosov-yupik. Zapisi 1975–1987 gg. [Let's our elders speak. Asiatic eskimo-yupik narratives]. Moskva: Institut Naslediya.

Krupnik, Igor, and Lyudmila S. Bogoslovskaya 2017. "Our Ice, Snow and Winds": From Knowledge Integration to Co-Production in the Russian SIKU Project, 2007–2013. In *Oral History meets Linguistics*, E. Kasten, K. Roller, and J. Wilbur (eds.), 65–82. Fürstenberg/Havel: Kulturstiftung Sibirien.

Lewinski, Silke von 2004. Protecting Cultural Expressions. The Perspctive of Law. In *Properties of Culture – Culture as Property. Pathways in Post-Soviet Siberia*. E. Kasten (ed.), 111–127. Berlin: Reimer.

Pagenstecher, Cord, and Stefan Pfänder 2017. Hidden Dialogues. Towards an Interactional Understanding of Oral History Interviews. In *Oral History meets Linguistics*, E. Kasten, K. Roller, and J. Wilbur (eds.), 185–207. Fürstenberg/Havel: Kulturstiftung Sibirien.

Rießler, Michael, and Joshua Wilbur 2017. Documenting Endangered Oral Histories of the Arctic: A Proposed Symbiosis for Documentary Linguistics and Oral History Research, Illustrated by Saami and Komi Examples. In *Oral History meets Linguistics*, E. Kasten, K. Roller, and J. Wilbur (eds.), 31–64. Fürstenberg/Havel: Kulturstiftung Sibirien.

2 DOCUMENTING ENDANGERED ORAL HISTORIES OF THE ARCTIC: A PROPOSED SYMBIOSIS FOR DOCUMENTARY LINGUISTICS AND ORAL HISTORY RESEARCH, ILLUSTRATED BY SAAMI AND KOMI EXAMPLES

Michael Rießler and Joshua Wilbur[1]

Introduction

In this chapter, we argue that documentary linguistics, particularly as we practice it in our own projects, can provide valuable resources for social science research. Especially in our experience as documenters and researchers of endangered Uralic languages spoken in the Arctic, our projects and the data we collect can be considered an additional source for future oral history studies.

We first briefly discuss the history of the relationship between oral history studies and linguistics (specifically documentary linguistics), or more appropriately the lack of any significant relationship. We then go on to explore current social science projects in the Arctic and how these have the potential to relate to language documentation as a background to the further discussion. The next section deals with documentary linguistics in general, as a field within digital humanities, and how it strives to collect multifunctional, quality data for long-term preservation of linguistic and cultural knowledge. In this, it has significant potential to inform the field of oral history and other social sciences. Specifically, even if the sizes of our text collections pale in comparison with corpora for major European languages, our heavily annotated ("thick", see § *Oral History, Language Technology and "Thick" Metadata Descriptions* below) metadata[2] make our texts qualitatively rich, and more accessible, even to oral historians, anthropologists and other non-linguists, in part because they include translations into the respective majority languages as well as English. Indeed, our extensive metadata provide relevant background information on speakers, the recording session

1 The order of the authors' names is alphabetical. We would like to express our gratefulness to Rogier Blokland, Stephan Dudeck, Erich Kasten, Sonya Kinsey, Niko Partanen and Katja Roller for their insightful comments on our paper.

2 As is common in documentary linguistics, we use the term "metadata" to refer to data *about* the content of recordings or other primary data, for instance dates, names, or descriptions of recording events. This can be compared to "annotations", which typically mean textualizations of primary recordings, such as transcriptions and translations. In the strict sense, however, annotations are of course a special subtype of metadata *about* primary data (the text itself).

itself, as well as project details; this then allows non-linguists not only to contextualize recordings, but also to filter them for potentially relevant categories such as location, recording date, and, most importantly, topical keywords. We follow this up with several examples from our own documentation projects that illustrate how transcribed recordings from such projects often include narratives that are of potential interest for oral historians. Specifically, we provide excerpts from narratives by speakers of the Uralic languages Izhva Komi, Kildin Saami, Skolt Saami and Pite Saami.

Finally, we present our vision for creating extensively linked documentations of oral histories for future research in both linguistics and the social sciences. In order to ensure the creation of multifunctional and sustainable databases for multiple fields of research, we highlight some best practices for digital data archiving and publication. Furthermore, we indicate how tagging the metadata and annotations for relational linking and keywords on relevant subjects in individual recordings allows searches both within a single archive, as well as in connection with external archives and/or search engines, for both linguistics and other disciplines, thus increasing discoverability.

Oral History and Linguistics – a Missing Link?

To begin with, we want to point out that when we use the term "oral history" we are primarily referring to an oral speech genre that consists of an individual's narrative about a historical event that he/she personally observed or participated in (this is a countable noun, as in "a collection of oral histories"). These are the oral accounts that (re)present vernacular historical knowledge or perspectives of the individuals that tell them. The same phrase is also used by the entire social science discipline that utilizes such texts to come to conclusions about such events (this is uncountable, as in "oral history as a discipline has become established relatively recently"). Note, however, that we do not use the term to refer exclusively to any abstracted analyses that are based on the study of such narratives.

A seeming lack of a relationship between social scientists and documentary linguists concerning the collection and analysis of oral histories appears to have been around for as long as both disciplines have co-existed. For instance, in discussions on oral history, linguists or the like are clearly missing, even in recent works such as in Freund et al.'s extensive list of oral history practitioners. This includes "archivists, historians, geographers, ethnographers, ethnomusicologists, folklorists, educators, museum curators, journalists, broadcasters, and authors" (Freund et al. 2015: 7), but does not mention anyone from language sciences.[3] This seems to be the case despite

3 This is perhaps even more surprising considering the obvious use of oral history materials for descriptive linguistics, as evidenced by Katja Roller in chapter 7 in this volume.

a goal which is clearly common to both disciplines: again, Freund et al. mention that oral historians "attempt to stimulate the narration of stories … rather than simply recording short responses as in a questionnaire or survey" (Freund et al. 2015: 7). While the goals of the research done on the resulting material differ significantly, the raw materials themselves are strikingly similar, although the breadth of topics that documentary linguists collect is typically broader than that of oral historians whose focus is on historical events. Indeed, at the very least concerning the observer's paradox, documentary linguistics can certainly stand to learn from oral historians, who, again according to Freund et al., "found that in their relationship with interviewees they could not claim to be detached and objective" as far back as the 1950s (Freund et al. 2015: 7). Furthermore, the ethical obligations of researchers (typically outsiders from the majority group, although not exclusively so) towards the members of minority groups they work with have obvious parallels (cf. Freund et al. 2015: 8). Finally, a number of shared practical challenges concerning the preservation and presentation are shared by both disciplines, again emphasizing how a mutual dialog could benefit everyone involved (cf. e.g. the chapters in part 3 "Preservation and Presentation" in Llewellyn et al. 2015).

In linguistics, this missing link is not quite as obvious, at least in the discourse around documentary linguistics.[4] It is most obvious in Himmelmann's seminal paper "Language Documentation: What is it and what is it good for?", in which the author lists three fields of research as examples for disciplines with a potential interest in language documentations: "linguistics, anthropology, oral history, etc." (Himmelmann 2006: 2). The author further mentions that interdisciplinary projects working on language documentation aiming for truly comprehensive results would include "anthropology, ethnomusicology, oral history and literature" (Himmelmann 2006: 15). Himmelmann even concludes that "[d]ocumentary work that aims at a truly comprehensive record of a language also has to engage with ethnobotany, musicology, human geography, oral history, and so on" (Himmelmann 2006: 28). Aside from Himmelmann, oral history studies are occasionally mentioned in name, although never in much detail (cf. e.g. Bowern 2011: 464, 480; Woodbury 2011: 162). In fact, Woodbury even mentions that one of his first language documentation projects arose out of a local oral history project (Woodbury 2003: 9). Otherwise, oral history can only be inferred in formulations concerning the potential audience of language documentation projects such as creating a "multi-purpose record" (Himmelmann 2006: 1).

4 See § *Oral Histories in Endangered Language Documentation* (below) for a more detailed description of what exactly this sub-discipline entails.

Oral Histories in the Arctic – Examples of Ongoing Projects in the Social Sciences

The title of this section is inspired by the project "Oral History of Empires by Elders in the Arctic (ORHELIA)",[5] which was carried out by a team of anthropologists led by Florian Stammler at the University of Lapland between 2011 and 2015. This project can be taken as an example for recent anthropological approaches to oral history research in the Arctic during the last century. The arctic cultures investigated by ORHELIA include different Saami and Komi groups and therefore overlap considerably with our own work. Last but not least, it was the collaboration with Florian Stammler and the ORHELIA group which initially attracted our own special interest in oral history research.

Our observation that ORHELIA recorded oral histories almost exclusively in the respective majority languages (Russian and Finnish, cf. the community DVD published by the project Dudeck et al. 2015),[6] is particularly relevant for the discussion in the present paper. This is despite the fact that the project descriptions stress "indigeneity" as well as the common language roots of the different Saami, Nenets and Komi groups (which all speak Uralic languages) investigated by ORHELIA and linked to this "indigeneity". A similar approach using non-native languages predominantly (or exclusively) seems characteristic in other projects as well,[7] although there are obvious exceptions such as those thoroughly discussed by Erich Kasten in chapter 1, or the studies presented in the book series *Languages and Cultures of the Russian Far East* (by the same publisher as the current volume).[8]

Two further examples of projects working in the same region and on similar topics are the recent works by Lukas Allemann[9] (2010, translated into English in 2013) and Anna Afanasyeva (2013). Whereas the forced relocations of Kola Saami during the Soviet Union was the specific topic of Afanasyeva's study, relocations were only one of several topics in Allemann's study on the history of Saami people during the Soviet Union. The data analyzed in both studies consists mostly of oral history recordings done with ethnic Kola Saami informants. Note that all informants mentioned by Afanasyeva and Allemann are fully bilingual in Saami and Russian (they are mentioned by name in Allemann 2010: 127–128, and personally known to us; Afanasyeva anonymizes her informants, but their proficiency in Saami can be inferred with near certainty from the given birth years between 1930 and 1940).

5 http://www.arcticcentre.org/EN/research/anthropology/ORHELIA [20.02.2017]
6 The only exception being the sub-project on Tundra Nenets (Florian Stammler, pc, 20.02.2017).
7 Cf. e.g. the seeming lack of discussion on the role that information provided in native languages as opposed to lingua franca in the contributions in Ziker and Stammler (2011), with the exceptions of chapter 5 and chapter 8, which are notably also the only contributions by linguists.
8 http://www.siberian-studies.org/publications/lc_E.html [20.02.2017]
9 Lukas Allemann joined the ORHELIA team after the project.

Like ORHELIA, Afanasyeva's and Allemann's studies cover topics related to Saami ethnic identity under Russian assimilation pressure. Generally speaking these and similar projects are typically influenced by contemporary frameworks in so-called indigenous studies and often include the specific aim to record local (or "indigenous") memories and knowledge and preserve these for later generations. The ORHELIA project description states this specifically:

> [...] the project also contributed to preserve [sic] incorporeal cultural heritage among Uralic speaking northern minorities of Europe and study [sic] the transmission of historical heritage between different generations.[10]

As linguists we are particularly interested in the different *languages* spoken by Arctic people and how *communication through language(s)* functions in Arctic societies, and we were therefore surprised to observe that the majority of oral history recordings by ORHELIA (and similar projects) were done in the corresponding majority languages. This was especially unexpected for us because methodological discussions of the oral history approach (e.g. by Dudeck and Allemann 2016) specifically mention the importance of interpreting the *context* in which the life stories are told by the informants and stress the *polyphone character* of oral histories as subjective accounts of one's personal life history:

> Ein solch polyphones Verständnis von Oral History setzt jedoch auch voraus, dass sich die Forscher und Forscherinnen mit dem Kontext beschäftigen, in dem die Geschichten erzählt werden und in den sie sozial und kulturell eingebettet sind. Das Zelt oder die Wohnung, in der wir eine Geschichte zu hören bekommen, steht nicht in einem Vakuum. Die Art der Kommunikation wird von Konventionen beeinflusst, wie sie beispielsweise in einer von Rentierzucht geprägten Gemeinschaft generell vorherrschen. (Dudeck and Allemann 2016: 85)[11]

There is of course an obvious practical reason for the predominant use of majority languages for oral history interviews, namely when a researcher team does not have any members sufficiently fluent in the relevant native language or languages. In many other cases the informants themselves may also choose the majority language, perhaps because they simply prefer to do so, because they are not fluent speakers of the native language either, or for other reasons.

10 http://www.arcticcentre.org/EN/research/anthropology/ORHELIA [20.02.2017]

11 "Nonetheless, such a polyphonic understanding of oral history also requires researchers to deal with the context in which the stories are told and in which they are embedded socially and culturally. The tent or the apartment in which we get to hear a story is not located in a vacuum. The type of communication is influenced by conventions such as for instance those that generally prevail in a community shaped by reindeer husbandry." (our translation)

What is striking to us, however, is that the multilingual context in which all Arctic indigenous societies exist today has scarcely been considered relevant by oral history researchers in social sciences. We are not aware of any ongoing methodological discussion about the potential role of language choice by the interviewer and the interviewee in oral history research. We believe, however, that the following questions are methodologically valid and should to be taken up in future research:

1. Does the choice of language influence the results of the transmission of historical heritage and knowledge between different generations, or between informant and researcher?
2. If the answer is yes, what should be best practice in oral history research, i.e. in what language(s) should data be collected, especially when informant and researcher are not native speakers of the same language?

One aim of the present chapter is to try to stimulate such a discussion in the future.

Oral Histories in Endangered Language Documentation

Language documentation (also referred to as documentary linguistics) is an emerging sub-field of applied linguistics. Research in language documentation aims at the provision of long lasting, comprehensive, multi-faceted and multi-purpose records of linguistic practices characteristic of a given speech community, often in conditions where these languages are under threat of disappearing (cf. Himmelmann 2006; Woodbury 2011; Austin 2014). Although it evolved out of traditional fieldwork methodology used primarily by descriptive linguists and language anthropologists, language documentation is no longer merely a method, as it has its own primary aims and methodologies. One of the most important purposes of language documentation is ensuring that data are available for further research on and for endangered languages, for both further theoretical and applied research, as well as for direct use by the respective language communities.

Ideally, the data pool provided by the language documenter includes a comprehensive, deeply annotated and easily accessible corpus[12] of primary language recordings, representing a wide variety of texts in terms of chronology (e.g. age of recorded speakers), geography (e.g. dialects), and other sociolinguistic variables (e.g. gender and educational background of speakers, speech registers, text genres, etc.). In addition to annotations, cataloging metadata are crucial in ensuring the intellectual accessibility of the documented data and concern both the *content* of the recorded speech sample (typically represented as orthographic or phonological transcriptions, morphosyntactic tagging, and free translations into other languages) as well as the *context*

12 The term "corpus" is typically used in linguistics to mean a database which is systematically annotated for specific data features in order to investigate a research question using a data-driven and quantitative approach.

(such as actors, places, and speech events, but even meta-documentation about the project itself, cf. Austin 2013).

Along with methodologies and best practices related to fieldwork and archiving (including questions of research ethics, protection of copyrights, resource discoverability, data standards and long term data preservation), the usefulness of the actual product of language documentation for linguistic research hinges on the quality and quantity of digitally accessible *annotations* as the basis for further analyses and data derivations. With the awareness of such collections and the increase in the quality and quantity of a number of such collections, the use of language documentations for scientifically significant corpus-based investigations on endangered and lesser-known languages as well as the role of computational methods in this have frequently been a driving topic in recent years. (For a specific discussion of these questions on our own projects, cf. Gerstenberger et al. 2016.)

While the data typically gathered in endangered language documentation projects correspond to a wide variety of genres, a common type of recording can clearly be considered oral history. Our main motivation as linguists collecting such recordings is to secure non-elicited, unplanned examples of the target language in a spoken modality on topics that speakers can relate to in a comfortable, relaxed and natural way. Precisely this approach aligns well with expectations of oral history. It is just such recordings that can prove to be valuable multi-functional sources for other disciplines as well, particularly historically oriented social sciences.

The following section provides a few concrete examples from our language documentation projects on Pite Saami, Kildin Saami, Skolt Saami and Izhva Komi for recorded and annotated texts in these native languages which could potentially serve as useful sources for oral history or other social science research looking at Arctic peoples.

Case Studies

The languages which our own documentation projects are concerned with are all spoken in the Barents Sea region and belong to the Saamic and Permic branches of the Uralic language family. The data, which we discuss below, stem from our own projects: the Pite Saami Documentation Project, which has been carried out by Joshua Wilbur since 2008 and which works with the Pite Saami language spoken in northern Sweden around Arjeplog (cf. Wilbur 2008–2017); the Kola Saami Documentation Project, which has been carried out by Michael Rießler (and collaborators) since 2005 and which works with all four Saami languages spoken (or formerly spoken) on the Kola Peninsula in Russia (cf. Rießler 2005–2017); and the Izhva Komi Documentation Project by Michael Rießler together with Rogier Blokland, Marina Fedina, and Niko Partanen (and other collaborators) which works with speakers of the Izhva

Komi dialect diaspora both within and outside the Komi Republic (cf. Blokland et al. 2009–2017).

All texts collected by our projects in the field are available at least in audio, and many also include video. In addition to our own field work data, we include available legacy data in our archives whenever possible. By "legacy data" we mean for instance fieldwork data collected by other projects (annotated or not) and stored in various language archives, as well as spoken texts which were transcribed, translated and published in books and are available with or without original audio/video recordings.

Further processing of legacy data basically follows the same processing as with our own fieldwork data, and thus includes segmentation into utterances in the ELAN program,[13] followed by orthographic transcription and translation into at least one (inter)national language. The majority of our data are transcribed and translated into either English or Russian.

As indicated above, oral histories have been collected by researchers in diverse fields, although no special framework of oral history research seems to exist in which methodology or theory would overlap between these different fields. On the one hand, in our own projects, oral history is but one of many categories found in our collected texts (more detail on this below in § *Oral History, Language Technology and "Thick" Metadata Descriptions*) since we as linguists do not have a particular focus on oral history. On the other hand, anthropologists and historians use oral history as a framework, but without any specific intention to "document" when the collected oral histories are simply a tool used to provide an empirical foundation for further theoretical study. Still other projects collecting data on the cultures and languages mentioned here neither "document" nor carry out "oral history" research, but nonetheless collect oral history without mentioning this specifically, for instance the work by the Norwegian political scientists Overland and Mikkel-Berg (2012), which is also partly based on fieldwork interviews. Nonetheless, one of the most typical goals of documentary linguistics is the recording of "natural" language, and precisely this goal provides significant common ground with oral history and fieldwork-based research in social sciences in general.

With this in mind, the following sections present some examples from our text collections that show how oral history stands to benefit from language documentation, even if such texts were not initially collected with oral history in mind. Topics covered include for instance reindeer husbandry, life in Soviet times, or the introduction of modern technologies. These examples are also presented here to illustrate the following discussion about how not only the texts alone, but our extensive "thick" (see below § *Oral History, Language Technology and "Thick" Metadata Descriptions*) metadata can and should be utilized by non-linguistics researchers not only as an

13 ELAN (EUDICO Linguistic Annotator) is free software for annotating and presenting multimodal language data, and developed by the Technical Group of the Max Planck Institute for Psycholinguistics; https://tla.mpi.nl/tools/tla-tools/elan/ [20.02.2017]

access point, but as a source of contextualization. After presenting some best practices for both archiving and publishing such texts, we share our vision for a unified digital infrastructure allowing access to a large number of documentations from various archives and with various target users in mind.

Pite Saami

Pite Saami is an indigenous language spoken in and around Arjeplog municipality in Swedish Lapland, and historically in adjacent territory in Norway. While there may be more than a thousand ethnic Pite Saami individuals (as stated, for instance, by Krauss 1997: 24), the language has suffered significantly under dominant Swedish/Norwegian social, cultural and political pressure over the course of the last half century, such that practically an entire generation of parents ceased to pass the language on to their children, resulting in a likely irreparable break in the transmission of the language (Wilbur 2014: 6–7; Valijärvi and Wilbur 2011). Currently, Pite Saami has around forty speakers.

The Swedish anthropologist Ernst Manker compiled a significant amount of research on various Saami groups, a small part of which concerns Pite Saami, particularly reindeer herders (cf. eg. Manker 1947). Otherwise, the only studies in the social sciences specifically concerning Pite Saami are very recent and can be found in Evjen and Myrvoll (2015). However, linguists have been studying Pite Saami for more than a century, and a number of texts are available which are potentially very interesting for oral history researchers. The earliest texts are short narratives with Hungarian translations in Halász 1893 and with German translations in Lagercrantz 1957 (but originally transcribed in 1921). The Swedish state agency *Institutet för språk och folkminnen* (ISOF)[14] has an archive which includes a significant collection of Pite Saami legacy materials. While many of these texts are, strictly speaking, written (even if presenting a spoken modality of language), the archive also includes several hundred untranscribed Pite Saami recordings by Israel Ruong, Olavi Korhonen and others, recorded throughout the second half of the 20th century. While we have not yet had the opportunity to examine these written and audio texts in any detail, particularly concerning their potential usefulness for oral history, a trip to the archive in Uppsala is planned for summer 2017, with the intention of eventually ingesting as many of these heritage texts as possible into our data collection.

The Pite Saami recordings we are most familiar with stem from the Pite Saami Documentation Project, which has been carried out by Joshua Wilbur since 2008, and it is these recordings we will focus on here. All recordings are transcribed and translated into either English or Swedish or both. A number of these recordings seem to be exemplary for how language documentation can provide a valuable source for

14 Swedish Institute for Language and Folklore: http://www.sprakochfolkminnen.se [01.03.2017]

oral history as these present insights into Saami culture as primary sources portraying Pite Saami life in previous decades, including the changes it has undergone in Sweden, by individuals who experienced these firsthand. One reason these recordings are particularly valuable is because they contain a number of interviews with settled Saami, i.e. those who survived mainly on fishing and small-scale agriculture, in addition to reindeer herding Saami, who tend to receive a disproportionately large amount of focus in studies on Saami culture and history (relative to the actual proportion of the Saami population in the whole of northern Europe).

In example (1), from a recording done in 2015, a reindeer herder (born in 1977) thumbs through his journal and recalls specific details about the highly unusual weather during the winter of 2014–2015:

> *(1) Men dä lij gu buhtin jåvlå vuässte, dä älgij nievrut huj spajjta, ... dä lij muohta båhtam, ja dä huj garra bivval budij. ...* årrå *jage biejven dä lij gákktse plus grader.*
> "But then as we got closer to Christmas, it started to get bad really fast, ... the snow came and then really warm weather came along, ... on New Year's Day it was six degrees above freezing." (sje20150329b.056-061)[15]

While this only documents the weather during one specific winter, it nonetheless bears witness to the effects of climate change on reindeer herding. It will potentially be a useful source for future oral history research on the effects of climate change, especially if adequate metadata on its content are available (as is the case for any archived recording; see § *Oral History, Language Technology and "Thick" Metadata Descriptions*, below).[16]

In another recording, an elderly speaker (born in 1927) presents some memories from her childhood, at which point her family still migrated seasonally with their reindeer. In this particular example (2), which was recorded in 2009, she recollects what her family did while in the village of Arjeplog on special occasions such as church holidays or market days, including their relationship with tourists.

> *(2) Da gåde ma dále lä, da lä sjaddam maŋŋel, ja* dánne inijme del omassev duogajme, dä slöjdojd ja gajka, dujijd ja málestijme guasmagav ja duogajme aj dajda turistajda ma buhtin.
> "Those huts which are here now, they were put up later, and we had all kinds of things here, we sold handicrafts and such, and we prepared coffee and also sold those things to tourists who came here." (pit090915.254-256)

15 Here and below, references in parenthesis after examples from our data indicate the session name (here: sje20150329b) and sentence/utterance numbers (here: 56 through 61) in the relevant data collections so that the source data can be located in the archives.

16 A good example for how primary oral history research can be used in scientific studies on climate change and reindeer herding in the larger Arctic can be found in Forbes et al. (2016).

With a similar focus on past lifestyles, in the following example (3), recorded in 2013, another speaker (born in 1949) provides insight not only into life on a subsistence farm by providing a simple inventory of the family's animals:

> *(3) Jå, dubben hiejman gålmå gusajd inijme, ja* gålbmå gajtsa, ja hiestav.
> "Yes, at home there we had three cows, and three goats, and a horse." (sje20131025.072-075)

But she also discusses some of the personal frustrations and limitations she experienced while living there in (4):

> *(4) Men dä sujjtijiv fiksav, dajd gajk judosijd, ja biebmov mån lägiv ja bähkkujiv ja men itjiv dä dárbahe bassat, dä muv äddne dav dágaj. Ja dä nagin dä turista buhtin diht dä almatj inij nagan biednegijd. Itjiv mån ietjá biednegijd ane, men ij lam del nåv nävvre danne årrot, men almatj sidaj ulgus vuällget, ja kan lij nagin suohtas radnav gávdnam nagin sájen, men idtjiv. Mån iv diede jus muv äddne itjij sida att mån galgav naginav adnet uddne.*
> "So I took care of the barn, all the animals, and I prepared food and baked, but I didn't have to wash up, my mother did that. And when some tourists showed up, then we had some money. I didn't have any other money, but it still wasn't so bad living there, and yet one wanted to get out into the world more, and maybe to have met some fun friend some place, but I didn't. I don't know if my mother didn't want me to have anyone today." (sje20131025.023-033)

The following example (5), recorded in 2009, illustrates some of the inherent risks involved in depending on reindeer herding as a way of life. Here, after relating the story of how a large portion of her husband's family's reindeer herd was lost because all but the strongest reindeer drowned while swimming across a large lake, the speaker (born in 1927) indicates the significant effects this event had on her husband's family.

> *(5) ja* dä virrtijin häjjtet dä gu dä iello såggoj. Dä idtjin disste dárbahe jåhtet …
> *ja* dä dale dä genugin dä dasa dán Áhkaj
> "and so they had to stop [herding] after the herd drowned. They didn't have to migrate any more … and then they settled here at Áhka." (pit090609b.029-033)

In continuing the themes from the recording in the previous example, in the following example (6), also from 2009, the same speaker's husband (born in 1927) talks about some of the activities his family were dependent on for survival after losing their reindeer herd (as described in example 5).

(6) *Dä inijmä gusajd, gålmå nällje gossa, ja* så dä gájtsajd ja dä dajna vanj viesojme ja ja dä fiskodijme ja inijme del nan buhtsuv. Men nåhkåm lidjin vanj, da uvdutj ájge lidjin urrum nåv gårrdok, att nuhkin buhtsu, så idtjin del mådde bátse, så dä sladjime danne ja pirunijd sadjijme ja årojme ja viesojme gulij ja mielkijn ja dä slaktijme nan gusav.
"Well we had cows, three or four cows, and goats, and we lived with them, and we fished and had some reindeer. But then they [the reindeer] were gone, it was tough in the old days, that the reindeer were gone, there weren't many left over, so we harvested hay here, and planted potatoes, and stayed and lived on the fish and the milk, and sometimes we slaughtered a cow." (pit090609a.009-018)

In this final example (7), again from 2009, this speaker (born in 1954) indicates how modern technology has been both a blessing and a curse to life in remote villages such as the one she grew up in before moving to town.

(7) *Mij lip aj adnám telefonav dán dåben, ja dun stuordåben aj. Men dä, jáhkav lä guäkt-jage urrum, dä Telia väldij bårtå dav telefonav, ja mån iv dav åbbå tuhtje. Da åddå telefona, da mobiltelefona, da lij, eller nåv buoraga, halva ij gullu danne, ja gu ij lä akktak eliktrisitehta dánne, dä ij almatj máhte dajd läddit dánne, så dä lä tjiervas Mån sidav dav gambal telefonav ruopto.*
"We also had a telephone in this house, and in the big house, too. But then, I believe it has been two years since Telia took away the telephone—I didn't like that very much. These new telephones, these mobile phones, they are quite good, but they almost don't belong here, and since there isn't any electricity here, you can't charge them here, so that is difficult. I want that old telephone back." (pit090823.151-161)

Kola Saami

Kola Saami is the common denomination for the four Saami languages of northwestern Russia (sometimes including and sometimes excluding the Skolt Saami now living in Norway and Finland). Today, Russian is the dominating language in practically all domains of life for the Kola Saami groups of Russia. Contacts with Russians are centuries old and go back to the establishment of the first orthodox monasteries in the area in the 16th century and subsequent Russian colonization. Russian cultural and linguistic influence culminated after the creation of the Soviet Union in the 20th century when a significant number of Russian speaking people moved to the area as a result of the industrialization and militarization on the Kola Peninsula (cf. Siegl and Rießler 2015).

Like the other languages described in this chapter, the Kola Saami languages have been studied for more than a century and a variety of texts have been collected which are potentially very interesting for oral history researchers. Unlike Pite Saami, there are published legacy recordings relevant for oral history because portions of these text collections could be described as primary oral history sources. In addition, there are many more unprocessed recordings stored in archives, for instance in Helsinki, Petrozavodsk, and Tallinn.

The four Kola Saami languages are Ter Saami, Kildin Saami, Akkala Saami, and Skolt Saami. Kildin Saami is spoken by a total number of around 500 native speakers,[17] most of whom live in the municipality of Lovozero, where the majority of them were forced to resettle to during the 1950s and 1960s.[18] Originally, Kildin Saami was spoken all over the central inland parts and the north-central coastal parts of the Kola Peninsula, and the language had several significant dialectal variants.

The neighboring Kola Saami dialects in the northwest belong to the Skolt Saami language, which is hardly spoken in Russia any longer. After their families were forced to leave Russia when the Winter War broke out in 1939, most speakers of Skolt Saami moved to Sevettijärvi, Nellim and other places in the Finnish municipality of Inari, where they still live today. The total number of Skolt Saami speakers is roughly similar to Kildin Saami (cf. Siegl and Rießler 2015), but basically all Skolt Saami speakers live in Finland today.

Ter Saami dialects were formerly spoken in the eastern parts of the peninsula, but there are practically no Ter Saami speakers left in these areas today. The last Ter Saami speakers live in various other places such as Lovozero, Murmansk or elsewhere (Scheller 2011a). The fourth Kola Saami language, Akkala Saami, was originally spoken to the southwest of the Kildin Saami dialect area, but is also moribund or perhaps even already extinct (Rantala et al. 2009; Scheller 2011a).

The examples we provide here are from Kildin and Skolt Saami, which are the most vital of the Kola Saami languages. The following short extracts provide not only instances of oral history in our own data, but describe also the approach taken in our projects to include legacy data into our corpora.

Kildin Saami

The first example from Kildin Saami is from an original speech recording stored at the spoken language archive at the Institute for the Languages of Finland in Helsinki.[19] Metadata in the archive's catalogue are sparse, but we found out that the recording was done in Petrozavodsk (Karelian Republic, Russia) by the Finnish linguist Terho Itkonen on 8th June 1965 on analogue tape, and only recently digitized in Helsinki.

17 Cf. Rießler 2013 and the estimates by Scheller (2011), who differentiates between "active" and "passive" speakers.

18 Cf. also the studies by Allemann (2010) and Afanasyeva (2013) mentioned above.

19 http://www.kotus.fi [20.02.2017]

The recorded speaker is Pavel Polikarpovich Yuryev (1936–1983) from the town of Lovozero. Additional pieces of metadata were recorded in Finnish at the beginning of the tape and include the exact location (the recording was done at the Karelian branch of the Institute of Language and Literature of the Academy of Sciences of the USSR), the profession of the speaker (geography teacher) and the reason for his stay in Petrozavodsk (he was participating in a course). The recording is 32 minutes long and includes four different topics about the life and work of the Saami: descriptions of fishing in former and contemporary times, the seasonal weather changes, making skis, as well as the oral history described below. The speaker talks almost exclusively in monologues, with only very little interference by the interviewer. All questions asked by the interviewer are in Russian, while the speaker consistently answers in Kildin Saami, although he uses many loanwords and other Russian-language influences are plentiful.

Surprisingly, we found the same recording completely transcribed phonetically and translated into English in an unpublished M.A. thesis from Indiana University (Bjarnson 1976a). We have digitized these annotations, re-aligned them with the digital audio data, and added additional annotations, such as an orthographic transcription in standard written Kildin Saami, a Russian translation, and a few additions and corrections to the original annotations. According to our conventions concerning legacy data, the original annotations are kept unchanged and all new annotations are added as additional layers.

We think that one part of the recording is especially interesting from the perspective of oral history. In this 8 minute extract, the speaker remembers a school outing to the Tundra which he organized for his students from the boarding school in Lovozero in the winter of 1963. The story starts like this:

> *(8) Кудтлоагкь куалмант ыгесьт январрь ма̄нэсьт мунн учениками авцант кла̄ссэсьт выйӣлэмь чӣррэ, пӯдзэгуэйм. Тэнн райя мыйй со̄а̄гэмь соанэтҍ запра̄ватҍ кӯһт харянҍ. Колхосс энҍтэ мӣйенҍ выйем пӯдзэтҍ, мыйй ва̄льтэмь пе̄рк мӣлльтэ, ма̄льцетҍ, пиматҍ, туберкэтҍ, савехетҍ, ро̄а̄лхэтҍ, са̄ллвас, ко̄мпас, тетра̄дӭтҍ, фатапара̄т оаккшэ э выйӣлэмь чӣррэ. Ыштэмь соан э̄л кутӭ-колмэ о̄ллмэ.*
>
> "In the year of 1963, in January, me and my ninth grade students went to the tundra by reindeer. For this purpose we got reindeer sleighs, with equipment and two wooden reindeer driving sticks. The kolkhoz[20] gave us draught reindeer, we took along food, fur parkas, fur stockings, fur boots, skis, poles, tarpaulins, compasses, textbooks, cameras, an ax and we left for the tundra. We sat on sleighs in twos and threes." (sjd19650608kotus5493-1az.200-279)

20 A kolkhoz was a form of collective farm in the Soviet Union (and other communist countries).

At the time it was recorded, this story was still quite recent for the speaker, and it includes interesting personal accounts on life and work in Lovozero in the 1960s. Note that Pavel Yurev is a local celebrity[21] in Lovozero and his biography is well-known to most local people (who did not know, however, about the existence of this old recording of him and were excited about it when we played it to them). He is especially famous for the after school club for "Young Reindeer Herders", which he established and for which he also led excursions like in the one described here. Yurev was also a local historian and the founder of a small museum at the boarding school, which later developed into the Museum for the History and Culture of the Kola Saami People.[22]

The 1965 interview described here is an oral history account of Pavel Yurev's life and work. It also provides some details about the zeitgeist in the local Soviet society of Lovozero, where for instance schooling, spare time activities, and work at the kolkhoz were intertwined. For instance, Yurev describes how the kolkhoz, as the most important entrepreneur and potential future employer of the school pupils, supported the outing with material and personnel.

Finally, this oral history also provides us with a typical example of discourse *about* the Soviet Union.

> (9) *Тэсьт ... уһчтэль ... геогра̄фья, мунн раз- моайнсэ парнатҍ пугк ча̄р баяс ... ко̄ххт адтҍ изменился ча̄рр, тэйя ыгка ... Ко̄ххт ёлешкуэдтэ̄шь пэря ... И так далее.*
> "Here, (I as) the teacher of geography, I told the kids all about the tundra, how the tundra has changed now, up to now ... How we've started living better ... And so on." (sjd19650608kotus5493-1az.255-259)

The changes in the tundra and the lives of the local people mentioned here refer of course to the alleged improvements in the economy and society in the Soviet Union. Such standard propaganda phrases were obligatory in official speeches. As a teacher and communist representing the town of Lovozero in a recorded interview (even given to a foreigner), the speaker presumably felt obliged to build such clichés into his speech.

Another example of an oral history recorded in Kildin Saami in the 1960s and included as legacy data into our corpora is about the personal experiences of Lazar Dmitrievich Yakovlev (1916–1993) from the village of Kildin. He tells about his own experiences as a primary school pupil in his village, his later studies at the pedagogical college in Murmansk, and the boarding school in Lovozero (the same as in the oral history above), where he was working as a teacher when the interview was recorded by the Russian linguist Georgi Kert in Lovozero in 1960.

21 Note also the entry about him in the online encyclopedia *Kolskij Sever,* http://lexicon.dobrohot.org/index.php/ЮРЬЕВ_Павел_Поликарпович [20.02.2017]

22 Cf. https://ru.wikipedia.org/wiki/Музей_истории_кольских_саамов [20.02.2017]

(10) *Мӣн сыйтэсьт, Кӣллт сыйтэсьт ля̄йй шко̄ла уже маӈӈа тӯййшэнч. Тэнн шко̄ласьт о̄һпнуввэнҍ са̄мь парна, кӯһт(эмп)лоагкь и выдт(эмп) лоагкь па̄ррьшэнче. Сӣнегуэйм мунн тэсьт-шэ о̄һпнувве.*
"In our village, in the Kildin village, the school only was built later. Saami children learned in this school, twelve (girls) and fifteen boys. I learned with them, too." (sjd19600000ldjkert1961a-1.04-06)

In this text, the interviewee also mentions a historically significant event: the arrival of the first native Saami teacher Ivan Andreevich Osipov after his studies at the Institute of the People of the North at Herzen Institute in Leningrad. Ivan Osipov started working in Lazar Yakovlev's village school in the 1930s.

(11) *Маӈӈа пуэдтэль мӣн сыййта Осипов Эвван Вуэннҍтре алльк, тэдта пе̄рвэ са̄мь вуэппьсэй.*
"Later, Ivan Andreevich Osipov, the first Saami teacher, came to us."
(sjd19600000ldjkert1961a-1.21)

Last but not least, typical communist propaganda phrases are also included in this interview.

(12) *Адтҍ са̄мь парна, ыжэм парна я рӯшш, ко̄гк тэсьт Луя̄вьрэсьт ле̄в, аллькэв ро̄бхушшэ е̄ммьне альн, аллькэ куаййвэ е̄ммьне, ко̄ххт се̄мятҍ се̄йе и о̄һпнуввэ, ко̄ххт пэрямп пынне пӯдзэтҍ, штобэ ванҍса коадхэ, штобэ пӯдтӭ пӯдзэ лӣһченҍ пэрямп, штобэ вя̄л колхосс о̄ллма пэрямп е̄лешкудтӭв. Тэдта пайнэмушшэ ве̄кяһт советскэ правительствэ и коммунистическэ па̄ртья. Сыйй лыһкэв пай пэрямп, штобэ са̄мь о̄ллма я̄лченҍ пэрямп.*
"Now, the Saami, the Izhva Komi, and even the Russian children in Lovozero have started working on the fields, cultivating the soil, sowing, and learning how to herd reindeer better, in order to have fewer losses and have the reindeer grow better, in order for the people to live better in the kolkhoz. These improvements are due to the assistance from the Soviet government and the communist party. They do everything in order to let the Saami people live a better life." (sjd19600000ldjkert1961a-1.41-43)

The interview with Lazar Yakovlev was printed as a phonemic transcript with a Russian translation in the text collection by Kert (1961). The original transcript was later converted into orthography by our project and included in our corpus.[23] The original audio is probably even available for this recording in digitized form in the Phonogram

23 This specific text was also included in a small Kildin Saami book called "Lazar Dmitrievich's stories" published by the Kola Saami Documentation Project (Afanaseva and Rießler 2008).

archive of the Karelian Branch of The Russian Academy of Sciences in Petrozavodsk[24] and could be re-aligned to the written annotations. Unfortunately, the archive has not made its Saami language recordings available to the public.

These two examples of oral histories collected unintentionally, i.e. collected not for oral history research but as linguistic data, also illustrate both the potentials and the limitations of the approach of reconstructing oral history data from already existing collections. This approach seems to differ considerably from the fieldwork-based participation approach (described for instance by Dudeck and Allemann 2016), which pays careful attention of the (spacial, personal, etc.) specific context of the interview situation itself and the personal interaction between the interviewer and the interviewee. The approach we describe here comes much closer to "source criticism", i.e. a critical analysis of (written) historical sources, which is a traditional method in historical sciences. However, as we will argue below, the inclusion of the *complete context* in the interpretation of oral history during fieldwork-based participation is also only an ideal and depends on the unplanned outcome of the interview, spontaneous reflexions by the researcher and his/her questions for the interviewee during the recording, as well as on the later interpretations.

Furthermore, using different layers of "thicker" (see below § *Oral History, Language Technology and "Thick" Metadata Descriptions*) and retroactively better contextualized metadata can help enable the reconstruction of context. Note also that the two examples of texts described above are not only linked to each other on different levels (for instance using "Lovozero", "schooling", "Saami teachers", etc.) but are also linked to other collected histories with shared topics. Last but not least, they are linked to various other kinds of historical data found for instance in photographs, written primary or secondary sources, and they provide information on the Kola Saami people or local northern Russian history in general. For instance, the two teachers Pavel Yurev and Lazar Dmitrievich were colleagues at the same boarding school in Lovozero and both oral histories mention events frequently taken up in current social scientific research on Kola Saami or northern Russian societies. Note also that the book mentioned above with transcribed and translated interviews (among them several oral histories about WW II, work in the kolkhoz, schooling, etc.) by Kert (1961) as well as several of the non-printed interviews listed in the catalogues in the archives in Petrozavodsk or Helsinki have obviously never been thought of as historical sources by the numerous social scientists who have been carrying out research on the topics mentioned here.

24 According to the webpage, the Kola Saami audio collection has been digitized and this text is included in the catalogue available there, cf. http://phonogr.krc.karelia.ru/section.php?id=27 [20.02.2017]

Skolt Saami

Skolt Saami is culturally and linguistically closely related to Kildin Saami, although both languages are not completely mutually intelligible and their writing systems are also standardized differently. The oral history we describe here was recorded with Zoya Mikhailovna Nosova (born in 1937 in the village of Muotka), one of the very few Skolt Saami speakers on the Russian side today. She is also considered by other community members to be the last remaining truly fluent speaker of Skolt Saami in Russia.

We want to describe this recording in detail for methodological reasons. The data originate from an ongoing project in visual arts carried out as a collaboration between a documentary filmmaker,[25] a language documenter (i.e. one of the present authors) and a native Skolt Saami speaker with the aim of collecting texts about the personal history of this speaker and her family during Soviet times. The topics touched in the interviews with Zoya Nosova are typical for oral history studies and include for instance: the protagonist's childhood in a kolkhoz where the family was forced to resettle after their village was closed down by the government, how this original collective farm was forcibly subsumed into a larger state-owned farm (which again resulted in forced resettlement to a new place), her life as a Saami teenager and young adult in the small town of Verkhnetulomsk, and the private and societal changes during perestroika. Similar topics have been central in anthropological and historical research on Northern Russian society during recent years. As a result, the interviews collected for this documentary film include valuable information for social science researchers.

Although "indigeneity" (and even exotic ideas about it) are often a driving force behind the interest in the topics of such projects to begin with, all documentaries we are familiar with concerning the Saami of Russia are done completely in a lingua franca (while perhaps including a few symbolic sentences in the native languages). The project described here is unique in having the protagonist speak exclusively in her native Skolt Saami language. This approach does not only seem sensible from the point of view of native representativeness, but it also results in many hours of recorded video useful for language documentation. In fact, the linguist (Michael Rießler) only agreed to participate in the project on the condition that the film is (predominantly) recorded in Skolt Saami and that the resulting materials are properly archived and made available for future research. Zoya Nosova, who would have been ready to be interviewed in Russian, agreed also readily under the condition that the final translations (as subtitles) are rechecked with her before launching the film.[26]

---

25 Solvej Dufour Andersen, http://www.solvejdufourandersen.com [20.02.2017]

26 Having an agreement is hardly a given; indeed, as evidenced by Erich Kasten's experience with one filmmaker, portrayed in chapter 1 of this volume, neither is keeping such an agreement.

In addition to requiring significantly more working hours for interviews, transcriptions, and translations (compared to making films in a dominant majority language), there are several crucial differences between a filmmaker's approach and that of anthropological and/or linguistic fieldwork. Although the filmmaker has a "documentation" in mind and is also carrying out ongoing research on the biographic-historical topic of the planned film (i.e. by going to archives, doing preliminary interviews before the actual filming starts, and even when reflecting on events and posing questions while filming), the research aim is typically not primarily scientific but artistic. In interviews and filming, the director has to find a compromise between the biographic-historical topic developing through the continuing insight from interviews and the plot he or she has prepared in order to present the narrative of the film to a general public in a visually, artistically appealing way. This also includes the fact that technical questions of audio and video quality and the composition of recorded sound and pictures are more important than in normal scientific fieldwork. Even in documentary filmmaking, scenes are sometimes repeated until the director is satisfied. However, care must be taken when prioritizing filmmaking aspects, as this can cause the value of the data to be diminished significantly from a research point of view, as illustrated by several anecdotes in chapter 1.

Because the informant is aware of these priorities, she dramatizes the situation somewhat on occasion. And it is likely that this specific situation of filming affects her own attitude or willingness to speak about certain sensitive questions or how she answers them. However, we believe that the recorded materials are nevertheless very valuable and usable in scientific research, for instance oral history and language documentation, because there is no clear boundary between recordings done by social scientists or linguists and those done by documentary filmmakers. Indeed, these exist on a continuum between "spontaneous" and "dramatized".[27] Indeed, as highlighted by the observer's paradox, the very fact that filming is taking place creates a special situation, and researchers also stage their interviews, even if to a more limited extent (for instance by selecting certain backgrounds or activities, or choosing the location with the best lighting, etc.). In addition, researchers typically also have a bias towards topics that are currently trending. On the other hand, a good filmmaker is very well prepared, after spending months or years becoming familiar with the topic of the film, often more than a typical linguist who focuses on linguistic aspects and has only a fleeting familiarity with the non-linguistic topics involved. With this in mind, a filmmaker's approach, if it includes constant reflection and further questioning as in the described project, is much closer to the approach of anthropologists (Dudeck and Allemann 2016). On top of that, the quality of the images and audio is professional,

27 Interestingly, the example provided in chapter 1 (Erich Kasten) on the life history of the Even elder Nadezhda Barkavtova indicates that different recordings of one and the same story can exist at the different ends of this continuum, which in fact can provide a unique opportunity to compare the "spontaneous" with the "dramatized" version.

and typically much better than that recorded by linguists or anthropologists, who are at best amateur filmmakers. The raw film footage, which is ideally archived and available for research, covers not only the topic at hand, but everything discussed before and after the actual scenes used in the final documentary film, including material on other topics which may also be of interest. In this way, the context of the recordings and potentially even the degree to which the situation was "dramatized" can later be reconstructed. All in all, such recordings undoubtedly have significant potential to be useful sources for research in linguistics and the social sciences. In our specific case concerning the documentary film about the Skolt Saami speaker, we were fortunate because, on the one hand, the filmmaker was well aware of the relevance of her materials for research, and, on the other hand, both the filmmaker and the informant agreed to allow the materials to be archived and made available to researchers.

The following example (13) is an extract from the interview recorded in the town of Kola on the 4th September 2015. The recording took place outdoors, on the street where a former boarding school was situated and where a playground is now there in its place.

(13) *Tä'st leäi internat, mij tä'st mätt'tõõđin. Jiânnai päärnžed le'jje, i sää'm i ruõšš. I le'jje i Muõrmaš- i Tuållâmpäärna i Tuulomapäärna i ru'vddčuâkkaz mie'ldd. Le'jje tâk, Laplandija räjja le'jje i Puljââu'rest. I Loparskast, i Kicast, i Tajbolast. I Šoŋgast. Puk le'jje, i võl le'jje måttam päärna â'lddla puättam. Le'jje måttam ruõššpäärna, sääldatpäärna le'jje.*
"This was the boarding school, here we went to school. There were many children, both Saami and Russian ones. And there were both the kids from Murmashi and from Verkhnetulomsk, and from Tuloma and even those who lived along the railroad. They were, from Laplandiya station and from Pulozero. And from Loparskaya, Kitsa, Taibola. And from Shonguy. From everywhere and there were even kids from far away. There were also a couple of Russian kids, children of soldiers." (sms20150904Kola-Internat-007-013)[28]

Zoya Nosova went to this vocational school between 1956 and 1958, so she was 19 when she started there. Upon being asked whether it was hard for her to live at the boarding school, she answers:

(14) *Lossâd leäi, tõndiõtt što mee'st jee leämma ... Mij to'lko poorin internatpoorrmõõžž. Jååđin bäinnest. Tä'st ij leämma puõ'lli čää'cc. Nu i... jiijj põsslõõjjin. Jiijjân päikka jåå'ttlin to'lko õhttešt, tälvva. Vot, tâk rosttovkanikului i vot, to'lko*

28 As the film project is only in the works, the processing of these recordings is not finished and they are not archived yet. We therefore provide only a translation of the extracts without a transcript of the Skolt Saami original. No specific identifier for the single sentences/utterances is currently available.

kuõ'htt neä'ttel. A nu't pirree'jj tä'st jeälstin. Da, lossâd leäi.
"It was hard, because we didn't … We only ate the boarding school food. They went to the sauna [at home]. But there was no hot water here [at the boarding school]. And … we did the washing ourself. To our families we went only once, in winter. Well, the Christmas holidays, only two weeks. But the whole year we stayed here. Yes, it was hard." (sms20150904Kola-Internat-044-052)

Later in the recording, Zoya Nosova repeats information which she already gave and continues speaking about additional memories from the boarding school. She does this in Russian, and not in Skolt Saami as before, because she is addressing her granddaughter and not the camera.

(15) Холодно. Ветер с залива … есть … На втором этаже … было видно, Кольский залив … Магазин был и залив. Магазин был, вот здесь, вот где [кралечка]. Вот тут магазин был. Насыпи не было. Нет, такой большой магазин был; в основном был рыбный, но и продавленный. Потому что привозили с моря рыбу и прямо выгружали. А магазин высоко к берегам был и … ящиками рыбу. А мы отсюда продукты брали, с этого магазина.
"It is cold. There is wind from the bay … From the second floor you could see … the Kola Bay … There was a shop and the bay. The shop was, well, over there where the Kralechka store is. Well, over there was the shop. The levee wasn't there. No, it was such a large shop, basically a shop for fish, but also for selling things. Because they brought fish from the sea and unloaded the ships here directly. And the shop was a tall building at the shore and … [they loaded] the fish into crates. And we got food from here, from this shop." (sms20150904Kola-Internat-095-100)

Izhva Komi

The Izhva Komi (in Komi *izhvatas*, in Russian *izhemtsy*) is an ethnic group which came into being in the 18th century as a mixture of a number of Komi ethnic subgroups, primarily consisting of speakers of the Vym and Udora varieties in the western and north-western areas of the present-day Komi Republic. These people intermarried while moving northwards along the river Izhma, but also married Russians (mostly from Novgorod and Arkhangelsk) and later also Nenets, a reindeer-herding people in the very north of European Russia. The language spoken by the Izhva Komi is the northernmost variety of Komi-Zyrian, spoken both in the north of the Komi Republic and in a number of small diaspora settlements in a wide swath of territory from the Kola Peninsula in the northwest of European Russia to northwestern Siberia.

Whereas the language is vibrant (and learned by children as their first language) in the majority of places where it is spoken inside the Komi Republic, it is critically endangered in most of the diaspora settlements. On the Kola Peninsula, where they have been existing in close interaction with Kola Saami people for more than a century, the number of ethnic Izhva Komi is at most one thousand. However, according to our estimates much less than half of them speak the language (cf. Blokland and Rießler 2011).

The Izhva Komi Documentation Project began in 2014 and has been collecting speech recordings in all areas where Izhva Komi live and has been systematically annotating legacy data from other projects and archives. In 2016, we launched a multimedia database[29] including the recordings we have annotated so far. Among them are also multiple examples of oral history.

Our recordings from the Kola Peninsula are often interlinked at several layers with the Kola Saami oral histories since both typically mention one another, as in the following extract from an oral history recorded in Izhva Komi with Marfa Maximovna Andreeva (born 1922) from Lovozero. The recording was done by Valentina Filippova, Paul Fryer and Paula Kokkonen in 2000 (cf. Kokkonen 2004) and transcribed and translated by the Izhva Komi Documentation Project in 2014.

> *(16) А сэсся тридцать втором году, кор раскулачитісны, дак сыа муні мамыс доре. Мамыскед оліс. А миян, ми бара код кыче. Митрей дяде муні. Э, мыйке, сылэн вӧлі бабаыслэн вок да сыа пыысянсэ сетіс, сэтэн олісны семьяыс. А ми вот эта лопарскей керкаас, аддьылін тай, эта лёк, дёлиндик – сэтте петім. Сэтте керкаас петім.*
> "And when they were dekulakized in 1932, she moved to live at her mother's place. She lived there together with her mother. But we, [lived] wherever. Grandpa Dmitri passed away. He had a brother-in-law and he [the brother-in-law] gave them his sauna, there they lived with the family. And we, well [we moved] into this Saami house, you have seen it, the small one—over there, we moved to live there. We moved into that house." (kpv_izva20000320-1AndrejevaMM.173-182)

In the next example (17), Marfa Andreeva recollects the period of political repressions during the early 1930s, the so-called dekulakization. When she was a 10 year old girl, her family's property—as allegedly better-off peasants—was expropriated.

> *(17) Ме пӧмнита, ми кор аптека керкаас олім, миян зэй ыджыд эстшем вӧлі этаа джуджджатэм сундук. Сэтэн вӧлі мамелэн пимыыс, сэсся, лёк, маличаясыс, паркаясыс быдсэн сэн куйлісныс. [Interviewer: Ыхы.] Ставсэ босьтісныс. [Interviewer: Код нэ босьтіс? Код сэтшем?] Мун да тӧд. Комиссия босьтіс, а кыче карисныс, ме ог тӧд. [Interviewer: Аха.*

29 http://videocorpora.ru [20.02.2017]

> *А сэсся тіянтэ кыче, керкасьыс вӧтлісны?] Вӧтлісныс. Ми лопарьяс ордэ сэк петім. [Interviewer: Аха.] Ӧтік изба сэтэн обшей вӧлі да сэтте ставнум воим.*
> "I remember, when we lived in the building with the pharmacy, we had such a very big box of this height. Mom's fur boots, fur parkas, parkas, everything was stored inside there. [Interviewer: Aha.] They took everything away. [Interviewer: Who took it away? Who would be like this?] Who knows. The commission took it away, but I don't know who they gave it to. [Interviewer: Aha. And you, you were turned out of the house?] We were turned out. We went to the Saami place. [Interviewer: Aha.] There was a shack we shared, and all of us moved in there." (kpv_izva20000320-1AndrejevaMM.256-270)

Summary of the case studies

These example case studies from Pite Saami, Kildin Saami, Skolt Saami, and Izhva Komi illustrate both the opportunities and the limitations for oral history research using oral histories which were not intentionally collected as such. Here, we have provided a variety of examples from very recent field recordings, legacy recordings and even language recordings done for visual arts rather than primarily for language documentation. Our case studies also provide insight into how language documentation projects can provide useful oral history sources, even inadvertently, and that such data can be accessed by interested researchers, regardless of background, via the international, digital archives. Finally, these examples also demonstrate how various themes are influenced by the zeitgeist of the time of recording (e.g. using propaganda phrases, or the positive attitude towards boarding school), as well as even the selection of topics and texts which are included.

In the following sections, we will present our vision of how oral history and other social sciences can gain to learn from the practices and experiences linguistically informed documentation projects have. Specifically, this covers the use of language technology and metadata, on the one hand, and some best practice suggestions for both archiving and making data available, on the other.

Oral History, Language Technology and "Thick" Metadata Descriptions

Although being multifunctional in principle and including data on linguistic and cultural knowledge, the virtual research infrastructures created by endangered language documentation projects are still predominantly used as databases for structural linguistic investigations. Furthermore, structural linguistically oriented documentation projects typically pick out only one endangered language, or ethnic culture using this language, merely in relation to its geographical location, as if the corresponding language or culture existed separately from its neighbors. But this scarcely reflects social reality. Ethnic and linguistic identity can overlap between people in contact with each other and even between minority and majority groups. Even more so, it is in fact the situation of multilingualism and cultural contacts—combined with a social status asymmetry between different groups—that often leads to one group's assimilation to another group and its ultimate disappearance.

Sociolinguistic approaches, i.e. the study of linguistic variation and change in language structures determined by social variables, have a long tradition in English and other major languages and are becoming more and more popular even in endangered language documentation. Most typically, however, documentary linguists work separately on their own single languages of interest and construct monolingual corpora. This is despite the fact that their speaker informants are almost always multilingual themselves. This is definitely the case for all Arctic cultures and languages dealt with in our chapter. Sometimes, one and the same speaker is recorded by different projects and included in three different corpora, in our own projects for instance in Russian, Kildin Saami, and Izhva Komi or in Russian, Nenets and Izhva Komi. Furthermore, whereas linguists prefer to collect data exclusively in the respective target language(s) under investigation, cultural and social anthropologists or historians often work in the same area and with the same individuals as informants but use the majority language as lingua franca and create a corpus of data *about* a group's culture but without including the target language.

In order to make future qualitative and quantitative sociolinguistic and other cross-disciplinary investigations possible on these and other multilingual situations as well as the cultural-historical contexts in which these situations are embedded, we believe it is imperative to better *interlink* our newly collected data with previously archived data on both linguistic and other cultural practices of the different and ethnically overlapping and or culturally interacting communities in the Arctic. Ideally, our collections can be enriched by and interlinked with non-linguistic legacy data from archives and existing publications (e.g. photographs, biographies, written documents and all kinds of secondary sources already based on such data), as well as speech data not recorded in the target languages specifically (e.g. audio and video interviews exclusively in Russian, rather than in the native language).

The way this could be done is by rigorously applying methods from language technology to automatically create metadata and other annotations for large amounts of data. Language technology can be defined as the applied side of computational linguistics, as it aims at analyzing (and eventually also generating) natural language. Whereas a variety of language technology tools are available for larger languages (including Russian), Saami languages and Komi are still under-resourced in this respect. However, the relevant technologies are available in principle, and could be applied to these small languages as well. Note, that our idea goes far beyond cataloging and digitally publishing searchable data collections. Specifically, we mean the automatization of annotating both textual and non-textual data in order to build ontologies of relevant categories which in turn can be automatically linked to each other across different collections, across different time spans and across different indigenous communities. As a result, a larger amount of data can be browsed and analyzed, ultimately resulting in scientific generalizations with more significant empirical support. Note that computerized work is crucial in our work because our own projects already have hundreds of hours of transcribed interviews, and these cannot be processed manually any longer in an efficient way.

As one example of a technology to be utilized, we want to mention "named-entity recognition", a method applied in linguistic corpus creation. It results in the automatic parsing and tagging of text strings belonging to predefined categories (simple examples are for instance dates, names of persons, places, companies, etc.). Applying named-entity recognition in processing our databases automatically results in a number of searchable cross-database links throughout the corpora. As an example, one can think about the numerous place names mentioned in Zoya Nosova's oral history about the boarding school in (13–15), which also occur in other texts recorded by our projects or mentioned in other documents. Once extracted and tagged as named-entities, these place names can be linked not only to each other across different recordings, but even to external geodata in order to be visualized on maps. Another example is the name of Ivan Osipov, mentioned in the oral history by Lazar Yakovlev (11), which is also relevant to other recordings or various other documents on Kola Saami language teachers, especially concerning the well researched period of Kola Saami language planning in the 1930s.

In a similar way, keywords can be extracted automatically from our data and interlinked between recordings and other documents. The resulting relations can be formalized semantically in order to automatically construct relevant ontologies and then use these in digital catalogs of the data.

The description above is still merely an idea towards a new research approach, combining methods from computational sciences and linguistics with oral history research. The ultimate aim we envision could be described as "thicker metadata description". This is a metaphor which we have borrowed from Clifford Geertz (1973). At first glance, anthropologist Geertz's qualitative approach to interpreting and describing culture seems completely opposed to our quantitative way of working. However, our quantitative methods for data annotation are a tool to attain a better empirical foundation for qualitative interpretation, rather than the interpretation as such. What we aim for is a method for making more and better data available for qualitative analyses. Our "thick (digital) metadata" should therefore be compared to Geertz's preliminary analyses in his field diary, rather than his final interpretations and descriptions.

Whereas the change towards data-driven research has already been accepted by most linguists, we are aware that the methods we are describing here will definitely challenge the field of anthropology, which still relies exclusively on the qualitative-hermeneutic approach and takes a rather sceptical stance in regard to the relevance of "data" and quantitative interpretations. We nevertheless believe that anthropology, other fields in the social sciences as well as linguistics stand to profit significantly from our approach to documentation, archiving and publication (the latter two are treated in more detail below).

Archiving and Publishing Oral History Data

Over the last two decades, documentary linguistics has become more and more established as a subdiscipline of applied linguistics with its own theoretical approaches, methodologies and best practices, as detailed more distinctly in § *Oral Histories in Endangered Language Documentation*, above. Archiving and publication are two aspects of contemporary, digital and data-driven language documentation that are particularly relevant to our discussion. In the following we provide a general outline of these from the perspective of documentary linguistics in hopes of providing not only an example but also an impetus for oral history to consider adopting similar standards, and in doing so improve how oral history data are dealt with. Much of what we discuss here can be found in various scholarly works in language documentation and will sound quite familiar to most documentary linguists, but we particularly want to point out the insightful and thorough discussion and best practice guidelines provided in Bird and Simons' article "Seven Dimensions of Portability for Language Documentation and Description" (2003), as well as the very recent white paper by Ameka et al. (2017). To be clear, we are talking about the archiving of digital data, an essential part of digital humanities, big-data research and e-sciences in general.

First of all, archiving—as we practice it in our projects—is in itself one way to publish data. However, the main function of digital archiving is twofold:

1. *scientific preservation*: guarding and making multifunctional data discoverable and available beyond one's own project, and
2. *scientific reproducibility*: ensuring that the entire dataset still exists in an immutable form in order to enable future replication of an analysis.

Both are basic principles in digital humanities. The first principle is also especially important for oral history researchers who want to make their research and the collected data available to the communities they investigate in the long run.[30] The second

30 Making data available to communities on temporary data media such as DVDs or Flash drives is certainly a legitimate short-term solution, particularly for communities without unproblematic access to the internet. Indeed, this is even an essential solution for moribund languages whose communities should have access to such data before it is too late, in order to be able to utilize them in revitalization efforts, for instance. However, we would like to emphasize that such solutions are not sustainable in the long-term.

principle is not only generally accepted in natural sciences, but also in quantitative linguistics and quantitative social sciences, which believe that true scientific claims need to be reproducible (and thus verifiable or falsifiable).[31]

Archiving is really only useful when the archive itself is likely to survive long-term. In this, we do not only mean that the archive will exist as an institution, but also that all data in the archive will be migrated into new formats as these become relevant before the data are no longer accessible as older formats become obsolete. In other words, "archiving" data by keeping them on DVDs in a box is hardly sufficient for a number of reasons, such as the short life-expectancy not only of the physical disks themselves, but even of the format (as nowadays even blu-ray disks are less frequent as streaming services and cloud-storage become prevalent). For the same reasons, storing data on university servers cannot be considered proper archiving, although the bitstream (i.e., the actual computer data in raw form) may be safe in such cases. Instead, an actual digital archive which takes its archiving practices seriously in the long-term is clearly preferable. Two examples of such digital archives are the ones that we store our projects' data in: the Endangered Language Archive (ELAR),[32] which is part of the library at SOAS/University of London, and The Language Archive (TLA)[33] at the Max Planck Institute for Psycholinguistics in Nijmegen/Netherlands. The latter even hosts the recent social scientist oral history research found in the deposits by Anna Afanasyeva and Lukas Allemann (cf. § *Oral Histories in the Arctic*).

Metadata (as discussed in more detail above in § *Oral History, Language Technology and "Thick" Metadata Descriptions*) should be as extensive and detailed as possible, covering topics beyond simple cataloguing facts such as who, where and when. Rich, detailed descriptions of the interview situation and even interpersonal relationships, as well as details about participants' backgrounds should be included.

The metadata should be structured in a clearly understandable way, ideally in an open-source, plain text standard, and ideally in xml format, such as in the IMDI[34] or CMDI[35] format, two current standards. When metadata are stored in this way, then it is possible for these to be harvested by meta search engines (search engines that search multiple other search engines) such as the Virtual Language Observatory (VLO)[36] or the Open Language Archives Community Language Resource Catalog.[37] Similarly,

31 Social scientists and many linguists who work in a qualitative way only make "data" available as excerpts and as far as these support the argumentation (i.e. by including snippets from oral histories, or example clauses from a language corpus in a published article), but not the data in their entirety. As a result, the analyses cannot be reproduced, and the scientific community is ultimately left with no choice but to either believe the claims or not believe them.

32 https://elar.soas.ac.uk [02.03.2017]

33 https://tla.mpi.nl [02.03.2017]

34 https://tla.mpi.nl/imdi-metadata/ [02.03.2017]

35 https://www.clarin.eu/content/component-metadata [02.03.2017]

36 https://www.clarin.eu/content/virtual-language-observatory-vlo [02.03.2017]

37 http://search.language-archives.org/index.html [02.03.2017]

transcriptions, annotations and similar text-based data should also be structured in a clear and understandable way, using an open-source, plain text standard, ideally in xml format. If possible, recordings are also linked to the relevant annotations (even including time-alignment whenever useful) and to metadata (this can be done for instance using the ELAN tool (cf. § *Case studies*, above).

Any written text should be stored in non-proprietary, plain-text format (note that this does not include Microsoft Word or Microsoft Excel), and using the Unicode standard for encoding text characters. Audio and video files should be recorded in high-quality, open formats (or at the very least standard formats); smaller sized versions can be created for publication (such as streaming or distribution to the native community) if necessary, but higher quality cannot be created if the original data is poor from the very beginning.

Concerning publication, we mean this in the broadest sense, and use the term in reference to very simply making data available to others.[38] In many cases, modern digital archives provide a way to access the data they store, and many of the points presented above are equally valid in this respect (such as using open formats, or including as much descriptive detail as possible in metadata). But in addition to that, a major point concerns ensuring that metadata are available to repositories and catalogues that are used as search engines by researchers looking for data. While keywords are certainly a useful tool in ensuring discoverability, making not only all metadata, but in fact all textual data searchable for search engines increases discoverability even more.[39]

In case some data are sensitive and require restricting access as a result, one should work with archives and publication outlets that have a robust and explicit implementation of access rights. The archives mentioned above employ systems that implement such access restrictions, even on a file-by-file basis.

Conclusion

Language and social sciences, and particularly language documentation and oral history, take significantly different approaches to collecting and analyzing data. One important reason for these differences is the qualitative approach preferred by social sciences compared to quantitative approaches typically used in some sub-disciplines of language sciences, such as language documentation and corpus linguistics. Another reason is the focus on the multi-functionality of collected data (a main goal of language documentation) as opposed to a more focused, research-driven incentive (i.e.

38 While community members should definitely be included when publishing materials, our focus in this chapter is on researchers; for more on communities as a target audience, see chapter 1 [Kasten] .

39 Cf. Nathan et al. 2004 for an insightful discussion on what all can count as metadata.

using oral history for a specific research question and without considering later re-use of the collected data). In this chapter, we have presented our vision of a symbiosis of language documentation and oral history research based on the idea that both disciplines could learn from one another's standard practices, and benefit greatly from each other's data collections (even if these were not collected with the other field's research goals in mind). As documentary linguists, we have focussed on presenting aspects of language documentation that may be particularly innovative for oral history studies, and indeed for social sciences in general.

After determining that currently there is *de facto* no significant interdisciplinary collaboration between the two disciplines, we first outlined some oral history projects concerning Arctic peoples that share a similar approach with our language documentation projects. In this, we also discussed the seemingly contradictory lack of focus on the native languages common in such projects. We then discussed how oral histories can in fact be found in the recordings done by many language documentation projects, and included a number of examples for such data in our Pite Saami, Kildin Saami, Skolt Saami and Izhva Komi documentation projects. We then outlined how language technology and "thick" metadata can be utilized to ensure discoverability of data, and how this can be particularly useful for oral historians. Finally, we presented an overview of some basic best-practice recommendations that we think should be implemented on a wider scale in the social sciences, ultimately aimed at increasing the empirical base; even qualitative research stands to benefit from this. With such practices in place, it is possible for archived materials to become oral again.

In Table 1, we provide a summary of relevant criteria, and how the social sciences and language sciences relate to these in general. While there are certainly numerous counter examples, the trends we observe support these categorizations. Here, we have set up a binary opposition between generally being applicable (+) or not being applicable (–), but this is of course hardly black and white, but rather a continuum.

While language documentation and corpus linguistic projects tend to have large amounts of data which are digitally archived and annotated to various extents, oral history and other social sciences tend to have much smaller collections, and these are only occasionally available to anyone outside a specific project. On the other hand, the quality of social science data tends to be much higher concerning the particular topic being studied in a particular research project, while the contents of linguistics collections tend to be fragmentary and random. However, due to the very fragmentary and random nature of linguistics collections, they tend to be more multifunctional, as they provide a wider variety of topics, while social science project data are less useful for other disciplines because they are more focussed on a single topic. Since language is the core topic of linguistics projects, they have high potential for providing unique insights into the actual contents of collected texts, as this is potentially only accessible through the native language. Many social science projects use majority languages when working with informants, and this may exclude such language-specific insights.

While linguists collect metadata, these typically do not include nearly as many details for the contextualization of a recording, while this is standard fare for, and indeed the core of social sciences. Language documentation projects often include legacy data, and thus cover a greater time-span, which then allows for diachronic comparisons; for social science projects this is less common. Finally, due to the standard practice of archiving materials in digital archives, language documentation and other linguistics data are in general more accessible and sustainable, as well as more easily verifiable (and thus accountable) than social science data that is not publically available in its entirety.

All in all, we hope that the future leads to more interdisciplinary co-operation between oral history and language documentation. At the very least this should be in the form of mutual consultations concerning the advantages that one field may have over another (including the points we have presented in our chapter). Ideally, this would consist of carrying out interdisciplinary projects that include both documentary linguists and oral historians working together on the same team.

		Linguistics	Social Sciences
1.	Large quantity of available original data (digitally archived, transcribed, translated, keyword-tagged and catalogued)	+	–
2.	High quality of available original data (e.g. topic-specific, reflective questions in the interview)	–	+
3.	Multifunctionality (providing potentially different topics)	+	–
4.	Potentially unique insights via native language	+	–
5.	Contextualization (available via metadata)	–	+
6.	Time-span represented (availability of legacy data)	+	–
7.	Accessibility, accountability, sustainability (through digital archives)	+	–

Table 1: A summary of the pros and cons of data from documentary linguistics (and other areas of linguistics) as opposed to oral history (and other social sciences); + = more applicable, – = less applicable.

References

Afanasyeva, Anna 2013. Forced Relocations of the Kola Sámi people. Background and Consequences. M.A. thesis. Tromsø: Universitetet i Tromsø. http://munin.uit.no/bitstream/handle/10037/5241/thesis.pdf [01.03.2017]

Afanas'eva, Nina E., and Michael Rießler (eds.) 2008. Лӣзер кӣллса моаййнас. Кырьха лӣ Ēльцэ Нӣна. Berlin: Humboldt-Universität zu Berlin.

Allemann, Lukas 2010. Die Samen auf der Kola-Halbinsel. Über das Leben einer ethnischen Minderheit in der Sowjetunion. Frankfurt am Main: Peter Lang.

— 2013. The Sámi of the Kola Peninsula. About the Life of an Ethnic Minority in the Soviet Union. Tromsø: University of Tromsø. http://dx.doi.org/10.7557/10.2546 [01.03.2017]

Ameka, Felix, Jonathan Blumtritt, Lissant Bolton, Vera Szöllösi Brenig, Irmgarda Kasinskaite Buddeberg, Brian Carpenter, Hilaria Cruz, Sebastian Drude, Patience L. Epps, Vera Ferreira, Colleen Fitzgerald, Ana Vilacy Galucio, Lauren Gawne, Brigit Hellwig, Oliver Hinte, Gary Holton, Maja Kominko, Manfred Krifka, Susan Kung, Miyuki Monroig, Bhanu Neupane, Ayu'nwi Ngwabe Neba, Sebastian Nordhoff, Brigitte Pakendorf, Kilu von Prinz, Felix Rau, Keren Rice, Michael Rießler, Mandana Seyfeddinipur, Nick Thieberger, Paul Trilsbeek, Hein van der Voort, Tony Woodbury 2017. Public Access to Research Data in Language Documentation. White paper. In *Language Documentation & Conservation*. (in print)

Austin, Peter K. 2013. Language Documentation and Meta-Documentation. In *Keeping Languages Alive. Documentation, Pedagogy and Revitalisation*. M. Jones and S. Ogilvie (eds.), 3–15. Cambridge: Cambridge University Press.

Austin, Peter K. 2013. Language Documentation in the 21st Century. *JournaLIPP* 3: 57–71.

Bird, Steven, and Gary Simons 2003. Seven Dimensions of Portability for Language Documentation and Description. *Language* 79(3): 557–582.

Bjarnson, Donald Einer 1976. A Phonemic Transcription of Lovozero (Kildin) Lappish. M.A. thesis. Bloomington: Indiana University.

Blokland, Rogier, Marina Fedina, Niko Partanen, and Michael Rießler 2009–2017. "Izhva Kyy". In *The Language Archive (TLA). Donated Corpora*. In collab. with Vasilij Čuprov, Marija Fedina, Dorit Jackermeier, Elena Karvovskaya, Dmitrij Levčenko, and Kateryna Olyzko. Nijmegen: Max Planck Institute for Psycholinguistics. https://hdl.handle.net/1839/00-0000-0000-0005-8A34-E@view [01.03.2017]

Blokland, Rogier, and Michael Rießler 2011. Saami-Russian-Komi Contacts on the Kola Peninsula. In *Language Contact in Times of Globalization*. C. Hasselblatt, P. Houtzagers, and R. van Pareren (eds.), 5–26. Amsterdam: Rodopi.

Bowern, Claire 2011. Planning a Language-Documentation Project. In T*he Cambridge Handbook of Endangered Languages*. P. K. Austin and J. Sallabank (eds.), 459–482. Cambridge: Cambridge University Press.

Dudeck, Stephan Johannes, Florian Stammler, Nina Messhtyb, Lukas Allemann, Nuccio Mazzullo, and Roza Laptander 2015. *Nomadic Memories. People and Oral History in the 20th Century along the Shores of the Arctic Ocean.* Rovaniemi: University of Lapland. DVD/USB flash drive.

Dudeck, Stephan, and Lukas Allemann 2016. Indigene Oral History entlang des Eismeeres von Lappland bis zum Lena-Delta. In *Arktis und Subarktis. Geschichte, Kultur und Gesellschaft*. G. Saxinger, P. Schweitzer, and S. Donecker (eds.), 83–102. Wien: New Academic Press.

Evjen, Bjørg, and Marit Myrvoll (eds.) 2015. *Från kust till kyst – åhpegáttest áhpegáddáj. Møter, miljø och migrasjon i pitesamisk område*. Stamsund: Orkana Akademisk.

Forbes, Bruce C., Timo Kumpula, Nina Meschtyb, Roza Laptander, Marc Macias-Fauria, Pentti Zetterberg, Mariana Verdonen, Anna Skarin, Kwang-Yul Kim, Linette N. Boisvert, Julienne C. Stroeve, and Annett Bartsch 2016. Sea Ice, Rain-on-Snow and Tundra Reindeer Nomadism in Arctic Russia. In *Biology Letters* 12.20160466.

Freund, Alexander, Kristina R. Llewellyn, and Nolan Reilly 2015. Introduction. In *The Canadian Oral History Reader*. K. R. Llewellyn, A. Freund, and N. Reilly (eds.), 3–21. Montreal: McGill-Queen's University Press.

Geertz, Clifford 1973. Thick Description. Toward an Interpretive Theory of Culture. In *The Interpretation of Cultures. Selected Essays*. C. Geertz (ed.), 3–30. New York: Basic Books.

Gerstenberger, Ciprian, Niko Partanen, Michael Rießler, and Joshua Wilbur 2016. Utilizing Language Technology in the Documentation of Endangered Uralic Languages. In *Northern European Journal of Language Technology* (4): 29–47.

Halász, Ignácz 1893. *Népköltési gyűjtemény. A Pite Lappmark Arjepluogi egyházkerületéből.* Vol. 5 of Svéd-Lapp Nyelv. Budapest: Magyar tudományos akadémia.

Himmelmann, Nikolaus 2006. Language Documentation. What is it and what is it good for? In *Essentials of Language Documentation*. J. Gippert, U. Mosel, and N. Himmelmann (eds.), 1–30. Berlin: De Gruyter.

Kert, Georgii M. 1961. Obraztsy saamskoi rechi. Materialy po yazyku i fol'kloru saamov kol'skogo poluostrova (kil'dinskii i iokan'gskii dialekty). Moskva: Nauka.

Kokkonen, Paula 2004. Kuolan niemimaan komilaiset. *Suomalais-ugrilaisen Seuran Aikakauskirja* 90: 371–384.

Krauss, Michael 1997. The Indigenous Languages of the North. A Report on their Present State. In *Northern Minority Languages. Problems of Survival*. H. Shoji and J. Janhunen (eds.), 1–34. Osaka: National Museum of Ethnology.

Lagercrantz, Eliel 1957. West- und südlappische Texte. Gesammelt und herausgegeben von Eliel Lagercrantz. In *Lappische Volksdichtung.* Vol. 1. Helsinki: Suomalais-Ugrilainen Seura.

Llewellyn, Kristina R., Alexander Freund, and Nolan Reilly (eds.) 2015. The Canadian Oral History Reader. Montreal: McGill-Queen's University Press.

Manker, Ernst 1947. De svenska Fjällapparna. (STF:s handböcker om det svenska fjället 4). Stockholm: Svenska Turistföreningens Förlag.

Nathan, David, and Peter K. Austin 2004. Reconceiving Metadata. Language Documentation through thick and thin. In *Language Documentation and Description*. Vol. 2. P.K. Austin (ed.), 179–187. London: SOAS, University of London.

Øverland, Indra, and Mikkel Berg-Nordlie 2012. *Bridging the Divides. Ethno-Political Leadership among the Russian Sámi.* Oxford: Berghahn Books.

Rantala, Leif, and Aleftina Sergina 2009. *Áhkkila sápmelaččat.* Oanehis muitalus sámejoavkku birra, man maŋimuš sámegielalaš olmmoš jámii 29.12.2003. Rovaniemi: Lapin yliopisto.

Rießler, Michael 2005–2017. Kola Saami Documentation Project. Linguistic and Ethnographic Documentation of the Endangered Kola Saami languages. In *The Language Archive (TLA). DoBeS archive. Digital language archive.* In collab. with Anna Afanas'eva, Anja Behnke, Svetlana Danilova, Andrej Dubovcev, Aleksandra Erštadt, Dorit Jackermeier, Elena Karvovskaya, Kristina Kotcheva, Jurij Kusmenko, Maryna Litvak, Sergej Nikolaev, Kateryna Olyzko, Niko Partanen, Elisabeth Scheller, Nina Šarshina, Ganna Vinogradova, Joshua Wilbur, Evgenia Zhivotova, and Nadežda Zolotuchina. Nijmegen: Max Planck Institute for Psycholinguistics. https://hdl.handle.net/1839/00-0000-0000-0005-8A34-E@view [01.03.2017]

Rießler, Michael 2013. Towards a Digital Infrastructure for Kildin Saami. In *Sustaining Indigenous Knowledge: Learning Tools and Community Initiatives for Preserving Endangered Languages and Local Cultural Heritage*. E. Kasten and Tjeerd de Graaf (eds.), 195–218. Fürstenberg/Havel: Kulturstiftung Sibirien.

Scheller, Elisabeth 2011. The Sámi Language Situation in Russia. Finno-Ugric Minorities. In *Ethnic and Linguistic Context of Identity. Finno-Ugric Minorities.* R. Grünthal and M. Kovács (eds.), 79–96. Helsinki: Suomalais-Ugrilainen Seura.

Siegl, Florian, and Michael Rießler 2015. Uneven Steps to Literacy. The History of Dolgan, Forest Enets and Kola Saami Literary Languages. In *Cultural and Linguistic Minorities in the Russian Federation and the European Union. Comparative Studies on Equality and Diversity.* H.F. Marten, M. Rießler, J. Saarikivi, and R. Toivanen (eds.), 189–229. Cham: Springer.

Valijärvi, Riitta-Liisa, and Joshua Wilbur 2011. The Past, Present and Future of the Pite Saami Language. Sociological Factors and Revitalization Efforts. *Nordic Journal of Linguistics* 34: 295–329.

Wilbur, Joshua 2008–2017. Pite Saami. Documenting the Language and Culture. In *Endangered Languages Archive (ELAR). Digital Language Archive.* In collab. with Iris Perkmann, Elsy Rankvist, and Peter Steggo. London: SOAS University of London.

Wilbur, Joshua 2014. A Grammar of Pite Saami. Berlin: Language Science Press.

Woodbury, Anthony C. 2003. Defining Documentary Linguistics. In *Language Documentation and Description*. Vol. 1. P.K. Austin (ed.), 35–51. London: SOAS, University of London.

Woodbury, Anthony C. 2011. Language Documentation. In *The Cambridge Handbook of Endangered Languages*. P.K. Austin and J. Sallabank (eds.), 159–186. Cambridge: Cambridge University Press.

Ziker, John, and Florian Stammler (eds.) 2011. *Histories from the North. Environments, Movements, and Narratives.* Proceedings of the Final BOREAS Conference, Rovaniemi, Finland, October 29–31, 2009. (Faculty Authored Books 279). Boise: Boise State University.

3 "OUR ICE, SNOW AND WINDS": FROM KNOWLEDGE INTEGRATION TO CO-PRODUCTION IN THE RUSSIAN *SIKU* PROJECT, 2007–2013

Igor Krupnik and Lyudmila S. Bogoslovskaya[1]

Introduction

This paper explores the story of the Russian SIKU ('Sea Ice Knowledge and Use')[2] project, a local component of the international effort in knowledge documentation and co-production during the recent International Polar Year (IPY) 2007–2008. SIKU project activities in other Arctic areas in Alaska, Canada, and Greenland were covered extensively in scores of international publications (cf. Krupnik et al. 2010a; Aporta 2011; Gearheard et al. 2013). Yet it was not until late 2013 that the full account of the Russian SIKU appeared in Russian, in the book called *Our Ice, Snow and Winds* (hereafter OISW—Bogoslovskaya and Krupnik 2013). Most of its 400 printed copies were shipped to local partners and Russian educational and heritage institutions, while barely a handful books reached western libraries and journals (Trukhanova 2014). In this paper, we share some lessons of the Russian SIKU activities that expand the experience of the larger SIKU team and of other social science projects during IPY.

Fig. 1 Cover of the Russian SIKU book, *Our Ice, Snow and Winds* (2013)

Like other SIKU efforts, Russian SIKU was a collaborative program with the goal to record local ecological knowledge (LEK) related to Arctic sea ice and climate change. It was a collective project of a large team made of scientists, experts from indigenous communities, and staff workers from local

1 Sadly, the second co-author, Lyudmila Bogoslovskaya (17.03.1937–18.02.2015), passed away on February 18, 2015. This paper is dedicated to her lasting legacy in promoting partnership in studies of ecological culture and subsistence practices of the Arctic peoples.

2 The *SIKU* acronym for the project title was deliberately created to match the word *siku*, the most general term for sea ice in all Eskimo languages (Inuit/Inupiat/Inuktitut, Yupik, Yup'ik), from Chukotka to Greenland.

research and environmental agencies. Another task of the Russian SIKU, also common to many IPY 2007–2008 initiatives, was to raise awareness and appreciation of indigenous cultures and knowledge among scientists, agency managers, and science planners. Eventually, the Russian SIKU team included more than 30 people; twenty of them became contributing authors to the summary volume (OISW 2013).

Russian SIKU embraced the ethics and general approach shared by other SIKU activities in Alaska, Canada, and Greenland (Krupnik et al. 2010b: 7–14). It initiated monitoring of ice and weather conditions by local village observers; compilation of indigenous terminologies for ice, snow, winds, and weather-related phenomena; and documentation of elders and hunters' narratives related to the use of sea ice, safety in ice hunting and traveling, and practices of ice- and weather forecasting. Unlike most other SIKU efforts in North America, the Russian team engaged professional climate scientists, ice and weather monitors, and marine biologists. It explored ways to match instrumental ("scientific") data on ice, climate, and marine animals with indigenous observations and ecological knowledge. Thus, the story of the Russian SIKU illuminates many transitions in partnering, sharing, and building relations with northern communities that were critical to knowledge co-production as its eventual outcome.

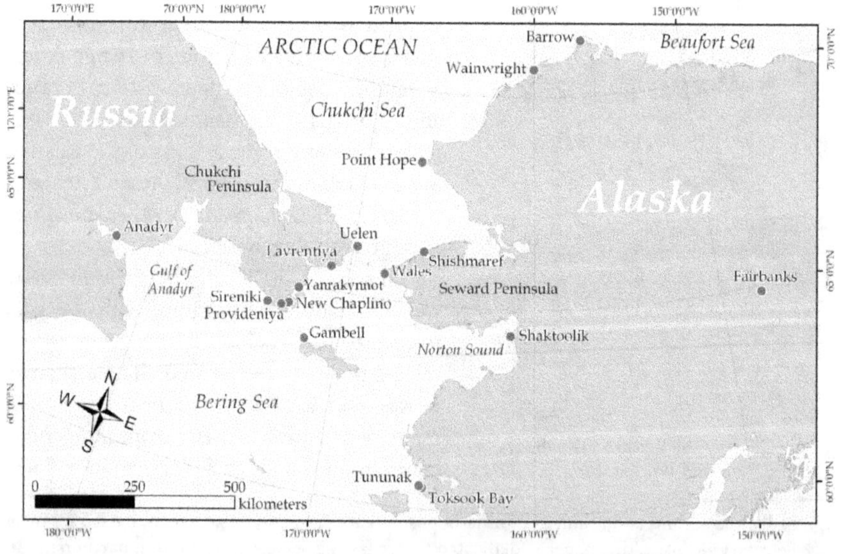

Fig. 2 Map of the Russian SIKU area (by Matt Druckenmiller)

Russian SIKU Activities

The planning for the Russian SIKU started in 2005–2006 (Krupnik and Bogoslovskaya 2007: 77). Residents from five rural communities took part in the project for different time periods in 2006–2010: Sireniki (population 507) on the Gulf of Anadyr shore; Novoe (New) Chaplino (population 440) and Yanrakynnot (population 338), in the southeastern fjord zone of the Chukchi Peninsula; Uelen (population 740) on the Chukchi Sea shore; and Vaegi (population 502), in the interior tundra. The project also engaged senior experts from the former communities of Naukan (Nevuqaq) at East Cape/Cape Dezhnev and Old Chaplino (Ungaziq) at Cape Chaplin that were closed and relocated by the Soviet authorities in the 1950s. Support to the project was provided by the *Shared Beringia Heritage Program* of the U.S. National Park Service, Alaskan Office; the Russian Institute of Cultural and Natural Heritage in Moscow; and local agencies under the Administration of the Chukchi Autonomous Area ('Chukotka,' in Russian). Two small local institutions supplied key staff for the project: the Natural-Ethnic Park Beringia (now Beringia National Park) with its main office in the town of Provideniya, and the Laboratory of Multidisciplinary Studies, Russian Northeastern Research Institute (SVKNII) in the city of Anadyr. Local Chukchi and Yupik researchers and park rangers, including Victoria Golbtseva, Vladislav Nuvano, Arthur Apalu, Alexander Borovik, Natalya Radunovich, Nadezhda Vukvukai, and others, served as prime contributors to the study and to the book (OISW 2013), as its main outcome. Lyudmila Bogoslovskaya was the Russian project coordinator, together with Igor Krupnik, the SIKU project leader; together they also co-edited the Russian summary volume.

IPY 2007–2008 was the first major international initiative in the polar regions that actively sought indigenous peoples' participation in research and viewed their knowledge as a valued contribution to scientific exploration of the global processes (Krupnik et al. 2005; Krupnik and Hovelsrud 2011). In spite of its noble goal, the overall IPY ethos was dominated by physical sciences, such as climate studies, oceanography, glaciology, meteorology and atmospheric research. IPY planners aspired to augment such physical focus of their venture via addition of a certain "human dimension" to promote its inter-disciplinary nature and new inclusiveness in polar research (Allison et al. 2007: 11). Such intellectual format *a priori* favored the "integration" of indigenous peoples' knowledge into the hard-core science structure and datasets in scholarly assessment of environmental dynamics in the polar regions. Several major surveys of the era, such as the *Arctic Climate Impact Assessment* (ACIA 2005), *Snow, Water, Ice, Permafrost in the Arctic* (SWIPA 2011) embraced similar templates, also championed by the two most recent IPCC Assessment Reports of 2007 and 2014.

Russian SIKU, like its parent international SIKU project, advocated a different approach based on several earlier collaborative studies of indigenous knowledge of climate change (i.e., Krupnik and Jolly 2002; Fox 2003; Ozeeva et al. 2004; Huntington and Fox 2005; Gearheard et al. 2006; Laidler 2006; 2008, etc.). It was participatory, multi-focused, and built on data collected primarily by indigenous researchers and monitors with deep roots in their home communities. Russian SIKU also relied on established partnerships forged during prior years of collaboration among Chukotka hunters, knowledge experts, biologists, conservationists, and anthropologists (Ainana et al. 1997; Bogoslovskaya et al. 1982; Bogoslovskaya 2003). Thanks to its strong local connections, Russian SIKU team was able to implement several tasks.

Local observations of ice and weather

Prior to IPY 2007–2008, polar physical scientists paid little attention to Arctic peoples' practices in observing the environment, and systematic records of indigenous ice and weather monitoring existed for no longer than a few-month period (cf. Oozeva et al. 2004).

Fig. 3 *Tekeghin* – ice "point" stretching out into the sea. Good for moving to the ice edge while pulling a boat; dangerous to walk on, as it may crush or break off and float away. Sample entry from the Sirenikski Yupik sea ice "dictionary" by Aron Nutawyi, with pencil drawing by Vadim Yenan, 2008–2009 (OISW 2013: 81).

Observations for the Russian SIKU project started in the fall of 2006. It eventually included five monitors working in their home communities of Uelen (Roman Armaergen, November 2006–June 2009), New Chaplino (Aleksandr Borovik, November 2007–June 2009), Yanrakinnot (Arthur Apalu, November 2007–June 2009), Sireniki (Oleg Raghtilkun, January 2008–May 2009), and Vaegi (Nikolai Nuvano, October–November 2006). Observers' logs covered daily temperature, wind, weather, ice conditions, information on local wildlife and community activities. Entries varied from a few lines and up to 150–200 words per day. The Russian SIKU team also included two experienced non-Native ice monitors in Uelen, on the Chukchi Sea coast (Victor Struzhikov) and in Provideniya Bay (Igor Zagrebin—OISW 2013: 300–307, 309–322). Such combination of indigenous and non-indigenous monitors provided critical insight into the nature of ice and weather watch based on observer's background (see below).

Indigenous ice, snow, and wind terminologies

SIKU was the first scientific program in the Arctic that systematically collected indigenous nomenclatures for ice, snow, and weather phenomena in local languages and dialects. Altogether, the international SIKU team recorded over 30 nomenclatures from today's elders or compiled words for ice from dictionaries and early literary sources in the area from Bering Strait to Labrador and East Greenland (Krupnik 2011: 60–62). The Russian SIKU team produced five dictionaries of indigenous ice nomenclatures in three local languages, one list of snow terms, and several shorter lists of local names for winds, currents, and weather phenomena:

- *Siberian / Chaplinsky Yupik ice terminology* formerly in use in the community of Sireniki—over 60 terms with explanations in Yupik and Russian (OISW 2013: 72–82; see Fig. 3);
- *Siberian / Chaplinsky Yupik ice terminology* used in the former community of Ungaziq (Old Chaplino)—almost 80 terms arranged by major types of ice and ice processes (OISW 2013: 97–99);
- *Siberian / Naukansky Yupik ice terminology* used in the former community of Naukan / Nevuqaq—90 alphabetically arranged terms (OISW 2013: 149–153);
- *Northeastern Chukchi ice terminology* used in the community of Uelen—over 200 terms and expressions (OISW 2013: 172–193; see Fig. 5);
- *Eastern Chukchi ice terminology* used in the community of Yanrakynnot—52 terms (OISW 2013: 125–137);
- *Southern Chukchi snow terminology* used in the community of Vaegi—over 100 terms and expressions (OISW 2013: 197–205).

Documentation of indigenous safety rules, navigation and forecasting practices

Recent climate warming, thinning of ice, and weather instability have increased the risk to people, who travel on ice, snow-covered tundra or ice-chocked waters. It exposes them to new dangers even in their familiar habitat. Several stories collected from local elders on their personal experience were compiled in the Russian volume, with the illustrations by pencil drawings and hunting scenes engraved on walrus tusks (OISW 2013: 216–238).

Fig. 4 Vadim Yenan's pencil drawing to the Elders' stories about traditional ways of traveling on drifting ice (OISW 2013: 219).

Fig. 5 Victoria Golbtseva (right) and Roman Armaergen document Uelen Chukchi terms and expressions for various types of sea ice and ice processes (OISW 2013: 236).

Survey of historical ice and climate records

The Russian SIKU team collected historical data on weather and ice conditions in Chukotka and the nearby seas, including early instrumental weather records, ice charts, published ice and climate overviews, photographs, and ship logs. In Chukotka, such early records have been available since the mid-1800s (in Provideniya Bay—Krupnik 2013c) and, more systematically, since the late 1800s (Mahoney et al. 2011). Instrumental weather observations became common in the 1920s and 1930s (Vdovin, Evstifeyev 2008; OISW 2013: 279–280), and data on ice conditions in the coastal areas of the Bering, Chukchi, and East Siberian Seas have been available since the 1930s (OISW 2013: 287–299).

Public activities

Russian participants used various venues to inform local residents about their activities, climate change, indigenous knowledge and heritage documentation. They organized training workshops for local monitors, elders, and students in participating communities, as well as in the area hubs of Provideniya, Lavrentiya, and Anadyr. The results of the Russian SIKU activities were presented at several *Beringia Days* conferences in Anadyr (in 2006, 2010, and 2013), Fairbanks (2008), and Nome (2011). Several local public and media sessions featured the publication of the Russian SIKU book in 2013. It was the first scientific program in Chukotka that systematically reached out to local audiences via a variety of means.

Russian SIKU Transitions: From Knowledge Integration to Cultural Ice Scapes

As the records generated by the Russian SIKU team kept growing, it expanded beyond the project's original goal to strengthen the scientific documentation of local ice and weather change. The wealth of information covered various aspects of community life, subsistence, use of local languages, and ecological knowledge. Many local partners—experienced hunters, observers, and naturalists—built personal photo archives and carefully recorded seasonal ice formation, animal and bird behavior, and community life. This vast visual archive became another product of the Russian SIKU team; only a small portion of it has been published so far.

With the limitations of the "knowledge integration" paradigm mounting, we were pushed to revisit the template of the data presentation in the Russian SIKU book. Instead of individual chapters structured by geographic areas, types of ice or other environmental components, we eventually arranged our material in seven blocks by participating communities (Sireniki, New Chaplino, Old Chaplino, Yanrakinnot, Naukan, Uelen, and Vaegi). Such structure better reflects how local residents view environmental change: not by natural elements but holistically, by their familiar home habitats.

Next, the very term "integration" was quietly retired, as our local partners expressed little enthusiasm about integrating their observations into the existing scholarly models. We started looking for other terms, such as "knowledge interaction," "matching" (Callaghan et al. 2004) "complement" (Laidler 2006), "combining," etc. Between 2010 and 2012, the overall structure of the Russian SIKU book was reorganized. Initially, it envisioned a large opening synopsis of the scientific data on climate and ice change in Chukotka and the Eastern Russian Arctic to be followed by local observations as supporting and comparative material. In the 2013 volume, that order is reversed: all "scientific" (instrumental) records are summarized in its *last* chapter as a backdrop and large-scale view of the data collected in local communities (OISW 2013: 276–300).

Another critical milestone was a new concept of "cultural ice-scape" (Krupnik 2012; OISW 2013: 10–23) to account for the growing volume of project's cultural data. It introduced a vision of the sea ice as a *cultural environment*, a *cultural space* (or, rather many local spaces) used by individual communities, often for many generations. Such spaces on ice bear several features typical of the land-based "ethnographic scapes," like historical place names, established routes, navigation markers, other physical modifications, safety rules, stories, and myths (Krupnik et al. 2004). Such imprints of human presence and associated knowledge transform the sea ice, a physical body, into a component of human culture, local identity, and heritage.

Created by the forces of Nature, a cultural scape on sea ice is a product of delicate and fluid agents—human memory, people's presence on the ice, and continued transmission of cultural knowledge. Unlike culturally modified spaces on land, human "ice-scapes" are *seasonal* phenomena. They evolve during the wintertime, from the fall freeze-up till spring break-up, and then vanish each year with the summer melt. They leave no physical traces, no archaeological remains, and no records, except in the human mind. Absent in the summer, cultural ice-scapes are restored in the fall by the sheer power of human use and knowledge. If the traditions associated with local ice-scapes cease to be passed or people move elsewhere, the ice once again transforms into a cultural "desert," the endless mass of cracks, hummocks and ridges, a barren frozen sea, the *ultima Thule* of ancient cartographers and early explorers. Yet today's survival of cultural ice-scapes is also threatened by rapid climate change.

It is obvious that the concept of cultural ice scape is a product of social sciences rather than of indigenous knowledge systems that lack such terminology. Nonetheless, "cultural ice scape," an invisible reality sustained by human memory, has many close paradigms in indigenous epistemologies, like "spiritual scapes" (Basso 1996; Fair 2004), "memoryscapes" (Nuttal 1991), "fishermen's scapes" (Maurstad 2004), or "aboriginal dreamlands" (Smith and Burke 2004).

Local people may not call their ice a "cultural scape"; but their known representations of it as a familiar cultural habitat, a space both revered for its power and feared for its danger are intimately tied to this paradigm. It is materialized in Native maps, drawings, and graphic art. People follow established routes across the barren ice by using familiar place names, navigation marks, and age-old stories. They also view the ice as a teaching, training, and spiritual ground, where humans have to co-exist with dangerous creatures, like dwarfs, giant worms, monster polar bears, sea woman, etc. (Heyes 2011; Fienup-Riordan and Rearden 2012; Wisniewsky 2010). The concept of "cultural ice scape" became a valuable tool to encourage the flow of information of importance to local partners and transformed the SIKU data collection into a two-way process driven increasingly by local interests and needs.

Discussion: Insights into Knowledge Co-production from the Russian SIKU

Since the key outcomes of the Russian SIKU have been presented elsewhere (Bogoslovskaya et al. 2008; Krupnik 2009; Krupnik et al. 2014; OISW 2013: 328–339), the section below introduces its contributions related specifically to the knowledge co-production process.

1. Co-Production in Scale and Resolution. Modern scholarly studies of Arctic change increasingly focus on modeling and projections of the polar processes. The goal here is to produce reliable scenarios and forecasts at regional and eventually global scale, and with the ever-advanced precision. Local knowledge has an entirely different purpose: it serves people's practical needs for successful and long-term use of particular habitats. It has the strongest observational and explanatory power at *local scale*, that is, at the level of individual or community knowledge of a certain portion of land, ocean or sea ice. Here, people's intimate connection to the same ecosystems, often for several generations, makes it possible to register even a minute signal of change and at a remarkable speed.

From the diaries of SIKU observers, we learned that they commonly monitor many species of animals, birds, and plants as indicators of natural and man-created shifts; even more so, they usually focus on *combinations* of multiple indicators. People constantly scan the environment for many signals, including wind direction, persistence, and strength; cloud and weather patterns; ice movement; current and tidal cycles; status of the tidal area and of the tundra surface; timing of animal, bird, and fish migration and reproduction, plants' and animal seasonal status, and many more. The most experienced monitors track key sites for certain features year after year to assess the condition of each individual season, as quoted below:

> I took my grandchildren down to school about 9 a.m. and I looked for water and ice near the school side of the shore—whether there is any open water out there (far at sea—IK). I could tell it because there was some dark(ness) in the sky far over there; that dark sky is over open water. I stayed at the store

> for some time to get information from other people, who were there earlier in the morning. We always have a few people of my age gathering at the store, the side that faces the water and the beach—they just stay there for some time, watch the weather and ice, and talk (Chester Noongwook, February 2001—Krupnik 2002: 173).

The strength of indigenous monitoring is also rooted in the large number of seasoned observers, who constantly network in tracking and analyzing any signals of change. Judging from the SIKU monitors' diaries, they always cross-check the information they report against other people's observations and they commonly practice what is called "cross-fertilization," that is, they use indicators from different, often unrelated fields. Here, the lesson for knowledge co-production is that indigenous observations should be treated as reliable and verifiable in their own sense, even if not accompanied by instrumental records. They are highly valuable to our understanding of environmental processes, particularly at local and regional scale.

2. Climate Warming and Observation at Local Scale. Russian SIKU records generally concur with the diverse and quite detailed body of Arctic peoples' observations that points definitively toward the present-day *warming* of the northern circumpolar zone (Hovelsrud et al., 2011; Huntington, Fox 2005; Krupnik, Jolly, 2002; Krupnik et al., 2010). In Chukotka, the diaries of local monitors tracked many signs of recent warming in the area's land-, sea-, and ice scapes; in weather, snow, and ice regime; increase in storm frequency; rapid coastal erosion and degradation of the permafrost layer; shifts in local biota and seasonal cycles of many marine and terrestrial species (OISW 2013: 239–245). Yet this general warming trend is neither a linear nor a uniform phenomenon.

Arctic ecosystems are remarkably diverse. They often have individual microclimates and ice regimes, comprise highly distinct sets of plant and animal species, and display a variety of physical and topographic features. Local people accumulate the knowledge of such local diversity for practical use; scientists just started grasping how to incorporate it in their models.

Indigenous peoples' monitoring of their home habitats is a long-term occupation. It covers myriad sites around northern villages, family cabins and fishing camps, and long transects along hunters and herders' seasonal routes, often for hundreds of miles. Each local community serves as an informational hub, where many knowledgeable observers share and discuss any unusual signals of change. Expanses of ice, land, and sea that are being carefully watched to produce overlapping continuums of individual and community scapes, often for major sections of the seashore or entire river systems. The obvious advantage of knowledge co-production is that it brings many qualified observers and at more sites than scientific programs and government weather services can afford.

3. Co-Production of Visions. The combination of indigenous and non-indigenous observers, often at the same sites, pioneered in the Russian SIKU project revealed significant *cultural* differences in environmental monitoring. For the first time, we may assess how people rooted in local cultural traditions view change in their home habitats compared to outsiders, even skilled monitors. Non-native observers, particularly those working for scientific programs and weather services, follow standardized protocols and concentrate largely on a defined set of environmental features. They have articulated historical approach and eagerly mark individual years along few selected parameters. Yet their focused and number-driven vision is also fragmented. It may track minute changes in ice, clouds and temperature, but it leaves out winds, tides or currents that are integral to indigenous sea and weather watch.

Non-native climate change monitoring is also thin on biological indicators. In Native observers' logs, numerous life forms—birds, beach invertebrates, marine and terrestrial animals, even sled dogs—make a constant presence as important signal of any pending shifts. Yet the most remarkable feature of non-native monitoring is an absence of people and a lack of interest in people's daily activities. An outsider monitor usually stands as a lonely person tasked to document an assigned segment of the environment. Indigenous entries, to the contrary, brim with people's names, remarks, and shared data, as if the observer is always surrounded by fellow villagers, elders, relatives, visitors, even strangers on the road. Such openness to other people's input makes local observers natural partners in knowledge co-production and willing players in any teamwork. To them, co-production is primarily about personal interaction, and is always a learning experience and fun.

4. Indigenous Environmental Terminologies. It is a common saying that the Inuit (Eskimo) have "200 words for snow." It may be an old joke and the number is inflated, but the richness of indigenous terminologies is undisputed. In many Inuit communities, the number of actively used ice and ice-related terms is close to 50–80, and some experts can name up to 100–120 terms and expressions in their native language or dialect (Krupnik 2011: 60–62).

Local terms often carry more information compared to their analogs in the scientific ice, snow, and weather nomenclatures, which is critical to knowledge co-production. Internationally accepted sea ice terminologies are aimed at observers at coastal stations, ship's bridge or a flying aircraft and they commonly refer to all polar seas, both in the Arctic and Antarctic. Indigenous ice terms, to the contrary, were coined by people moving on the ice and they identify ice features according to their safety, age, and formation history (Krupnik 2002; Norton 2002). For example, international ice classification defines *rotten ice* as one of the forms of melting spring ice 'which has become honeycombed and is in an advanced stage of disintegration' (http://www.aari.ru/gdsidb/glossary/p1.htm). A Chukotka Native definition of the similar ice called *aghulleq* in Yupik is 'the old ice thinned by spring warming; extremely dangerous for walking, pulling boats or any work, even dog-driving. While walking on this ice, one always has to use a special ice-stick (*tuvek*) with a sharp iron or bone edge and continuously check the ice thickness and sturdiness for safety' (OISW 2013: 73). The informational and safety message of indigenous definition is obvious, as well as its practical value to anyone moving on the ice.

5. Indigenous Knowledge and Biodiversity. Indigenous knowledge systems with their multiple indicators and detailed terminologies are tuned to accumulate data on the status and trends in local diversity, both environmental and cultural. Overall, people tend to be more caring and thoughtful of Nature within certain set of traditional norms. In spite of decades of predatory harvesting and economic mismanagement by commercial fisheries, whaling and sealing industries, Arctic indigenous users generally sustain a high level of biological productivity in their home habitats. Small communities whose livelihood depended on local "scapes" were naturally concerned about sustainable, long-term use of biological resources.

We may say it otherwise: "the Nature is best secured by Tradition and not by people" (Koulemzine 1999: 450). By preserving their cultural rules, indigenous people acted historically as stewards of their home ecosystems, on which their livelihood and identity was built. To the contrary, the risk of major biodiversity losses increases, deliberately or accidentally, when indigenous knowledge is ignored and people themselves are moved off their home landscape. Another lesson in knowledge co-production is that without indigenous people and their knowledge, the Arctic will quickly transform into an area for resource extraction built on a mixture of modern extractive technologies (cf. Bogoslovskaya 2014). In that case, damage to our common knowledge and to the regional (global?) sustainability would be irreparable.

6. Resilience of Cultural Ice-Scapes. The Russian SIKU project produced a pool of benchmark data to assess the status of local ice scapes and associated cultural knowledge in Chukotkan communities in the early years of the 21st century. It underscored both the resilience and vulnerability of aboriginal ice-scapes in Chukotka of the modern era. Many hunters and Elders still possess the rich body of practical knowledge, are fluent in traditional ice and weather nomenclatures, and abide to traditional safety rules. Even in those communities, where people have mostly switched to Russian as their daily language, certain traditional practices of ice scape use are sustained (OISW 2013: 105–108, 121–123, 170–171). New ice-related activities are sometimes added, like dog-races or winter catch of marine invertebrates through ice holes and cracks (OISW 2013: 109–113). They help support people's use and knowledge of ice, and thus preserve a living ice scape.

7. Knowledge Losses and its Consequences. Yet cultural ice scapes can hardly be immune from the general culture trends. As people switch from their indigenous languages to Russian, traditional nomenclatures for ice, snow, winds, and animals fall out of use. Younger generations operate with "creolized" Russian equivalents for

a few basic terms that fit poorly to the variety of local conditions. Indigenous place names disappear or are replaced by Russianized forms from contemporary maps and everyday vernacular. As Elders and senior hunters continue to use traditional terms not known by the youth, generational cultural gaps, "cracks in the knowledge" (Heyes 2011) expand. Even middle-aged hunters in Chukotka use but a handful of indigenous ice terms and scores of borrowed Russian words for local ice conditions, compared to some 100 traditional terms their grandparents applied to the same ice-scape.

The fading of the old cultural ice scapes and the 'thinning' of the current ones illustrate the vulnerability of cultural knowledge. Here, the value of co-production is critical, as without a sustained effort to strengthen community-based knowledge transmission, we are certain to see a rapid transformation of local cultural ice scapes in Chukotka and its conversion into the Russian language domain by the middle of this century. As this process advances, many components of today's practical knowledge and use of sea ice may be lost.

Conclusion

During its seven-year teamwork, the Russian SIKU partnership has moved from a concept of "integration" of the scientific and indigenous knowledge to "interaction" and, eventually, to "co-production." It adopted a different template for the organization and presentation of project data aimed at new audiences. We eventually opted for a popular and less technical heritage publication called "Our Ice, Snow, and Winds,"[3] one organized in community-based chapters and illustrated not by charts and graphs but by photographs and drawings made by local participants. Textual descriptions were shortened and scientific interpretations of today's ice and climate trends were placed at the very end of the book. In this transition, our trajectory was similar to that of other co-production publications of the post-IPY era (Gearheard et al., 2013; Fienup-Riordan and Rearden 2012; Salamon et al. 2011).

Even more notable was the *intellectual* shift from the "integration" to "co-production" paradigm in course of the project years. It required a new framework, such as the concept of cultural ice-scape, to document the rich information on individual communities' vision of their home ice-scapes. It encompasses patterns of local ice use, the cycle of ice-related activities, ways of observation; specific ice, snow, and weather nomenclatures in local languages; knowledge sharing via people's memories and stories. By viewing local ice through the lenses of cultural scape, we moved it from the

3 In Russian, the words *ice* and *snow* have plural forms; so, the authentic translation of the Russian book's title is "Our Ices, Snows, and Winds," which underlines the diversity of indigenous people's visions of local environments.

realm of climate change assessment to the domain of culture, language, and community lifeways, where it belongs.

In the aftermath of this transformative experience, we view the "integration" and "knowledge documentation" paradigms as almost two opposing ends in the spectrum of participatory LTK/TEK studies. Whereas the former aims at using ("integrating") indigenous data in scientific models and monitoring practices, the latter focuses on recording indigenous knowledge *per se,* albeit with the use of certain scholarly means, such as published books, charts, computer datasets, reports, and others.

We should also emphasize that the terms "knowledge documentation" and "knowledge co-production" are by no means synonymous. It is appealing to view co-production as something "in the middle" of the integration-documentation continuum that strives to incorporate (blend?) multiple perspectives. Even more tempting is to argue that co-production produces *new shared knowledge* (Hegger et al. 2011; Pohl et al. 2011; Stegmaier 2009). We found it difficult to prove. Co-production does generate new paradigms; but they have clear birthmarks of their parental knowledge systems, like the concept of "cultural ice scape" that does not exist in Native epistemologies. An illustrated bilingual lexicon (dictionary) of local ice terms is another example, as it had no place in indigenous culture, yet it appeals to today's hunters, elders, youth, teachers, ice scholars, linguists, and heritage specialists. Rather, *in spite* of different origins, the outcomes of knowledge co-production have value to multiple audiences, as is the very process of collaboration, from which such products originate.

We tend to view knowledge co-production as a dynamic and fluid space, a continuum with the boundaries defined on a case-by-case basis, by intuition rather than by default. Each team in this emerging space may experiment with its own template to achieve a balance based on its goals, composition, and project arrangements. Such legacy of seeking a *balance through respectful coexistence* of various types of knowledge is the most valuable lesson of the Russian SIKU project. It may be of particular importance to those who strive to "integrate" the wealth of indigenous knowledge into scientists' models, charts, and table spreadsheets.

Acknowledgements

We are grateful to our many partners in the Russian SIKU project, as well as in the previous work with indigenous experts in Chukotka for sharing their knowledge, providing insight, hospitality, and emotional support for almost forty years. Marie Roué and Douglas Nakashima initiated the first draft of this paper in 2014 and offered valuable comments, as also did Shari Gearheard and Matthew Druckenmiller.

References

Ainana, Lyudmila, Lyudmila S. Bogoslovskaya, Oleg V. Veter, and Nikolai I. Mymrin 1997. *The Role of Chukotka Eskimo Society in the Development of Traditional Subsistence Practices by Aboriginal People of Chukotka*. Unpublished report to the Department of Wildlife Management, North Slope Borough (in Russian).

Allison I., Béland M., Alverson K., Bell R., Carlson D., Danell K., Ellis-Evans C., Fahrbach E., Fanta E., Fujii Y., Glaser G., Goldfarb L., Hovelsrud G., Huber J., Kotlyakov V., Krupnik I., Lopez-Martinez J., Mohr T., Qin D., Rachold V., Rapley C., Rogne O., Sarukhanian E., Summerhayes C., and C. Xiao 2007. *The Scope of Science for the International Polar Year 2007–2008*. Geneva: WMO. Technical Document no. 1364.

Aporta, Claudio 2011. Shifting Perspectives on Shifting Ice: Documenting and Representing Inuit Use of the Sea Ice. *The Canadian Geographer / Le Géographe canadien* 55(1): 6–19.

Basso, Keith H. 1996. *Wisdom Sits in Places: Landscape and Language among the Western Apache*. Albuquerque: University of New Mexico Press.

Bogoslovskaya, Lyudmila S. 2003. The Bowhead Whale Off Chukotka: Integration of Scientific and Traditional Knowledge. In *Indigenous Ways to the Present. Native Whaling in the Western Arctic. Studies in Whaling* 6. A.P. McCartney (ed.): 209–254. Edmonton: Canadian Circumpolar Institute.

— 2014. Budushchee Rossiiskoi Arktiki: Sistema kul'tur ili summa tekhnologii? [The future of the Russian Arctic: a system of cultures or a sum total of technologies?]. In *Kul'tura Arktiki*. U. Vinokurova (ed.): 127–134. Yakutsk.

Bogoslovskaya, Lyudmila S., and Igor Krupnik (eds.) 2013. *Nashi l'dy, snega i vetry. Narodnye i nauchnye znaniya o ledovykh landshaftakh i climate Vostochnoi Chukotki* [Our Ice, Snow, and Winds. Indigenous and Academic Knowledge on Ice-Scapes and Climate of Eastern Chukotka]. Moscow and Washington: Russian Heritage Institute.

Bogoslovskaya, Lyudmila S., Boris I. Vdovin, and Victoria V. Golbtseva 2008. Izmeneniya klimata v raione Beringova proliva. Integratsiya nauchnykh i tradititsionnykh znanii (SIKU, MPG #166) [Climate Change in the Bering Strait Region. Integration of Scientific and Traditional Knowledge (SIKU, IPY #166)]. *Ekologicheskoe planirovanie i upravlenie* 3–4: 36–48.

Bogoslovskaya, Lyudmila S., Leonard M. Votrogov, and Igor Krupnik 1982. Bowhead Whale Off Chukotka: Migrations and Aboriginal Whaling. *Report of the International Whaling Commission* 32: 391–399.

Fienup-Riordan, Ann, and Alice Rearden 2012. *Ellavut / Our Yup'ik World and Weather. Continuity and Change on the Bering Sea Coast.* Seattle: University of Washington Press.

Fox (Gearheard), S. 2003. *When the Weather is uggianaqtuq: Inuit Observations of Environmental Change*. Boulder, CO: University of Colorado Geography Department Cartography Lab. Distributed by National Snow and Ice Data Center. CD-ROM.

Gearheard, S., W. Matumeak, I. Angutikjuaq, J. Maslanik, H.P. Huntington, J. Leavitt, D. Matumeak-Kagak, G. Tigullaraq, and R.G. Barry 2006. "It's not that simple": A Comparison of Sea Ice Environments, Uses of Sea Ice, and Vulnerability to Change in Barrow, Alaska, USA and Clyde River, Nunavut, Canada. *AMBIO* 35(4): 203–211.

Gearheard, S., L. Kielsen Holm, H.P. Huntington, J.M. Leavitt, A. Mahoney, M. Opie, T. Oshima, and J. Sanguya (eds.) 2013. *The Meaning of Ice: People and Sea Ice in Three Arctic Communities.* Hanover: International Polar Institute.

Hegger, Dries, Machiel Lamers, Annemarie Van Zeijl-Rozema, and Carel Dieperink 2011. Knowledge Co-Production in Climate Change Adaptation Projects: What Are the Levers of Action?
http://cc2011.earthsystemgovernance.org/pdf/2011_colora_0153.pdf [06.10. 2016]

Heyes, Scott A. 2011. Cracks in the Knowledge: Sea Ice Terms in Kangiksualujjuaq, Nunavik. *The Canadian Geographer / Le Géographe canadien* 55(1): 69–90.

Hovelsrud, Grete K., Igor Krupnik, and Jim White 2011. Human-Based Observing Systems. In *Understanding Earth's Polar Challenges. International Polar Year 2007–2008.* I. Krupnik et al. (eds.): 435–456. Edmonton: Canadian Circumpolar Institute.

Huntington, Henry P., Terry Callaghan, Shari Fox, and Igor Krupnik 2004. Matching Traditional and Scientific Observations to Detect Environmental Change: a Discussion on Arctic Terrestrial Ecosystems. *AMBIO* 11(1): 18–23.

Huntington, Henry P., and Shari Fox 2005. The Changing Arctic: Indigenous Perspectives. In *Arctic Climate Impact Assessment* (ACIA), C. Symon, L. Arris, and B. Heal (eds.): 61–98. New York: Cambridge University Press.

Huntington, Henry P., George Noongwook, Nicholas A. Bond, Bradley Benter, Jonathan A. Snyder, and Jinlun Zhange 2013. The Influence of Wind and Ice on Spring Walrus Hunting Success on St. Lawrence Island, Alaska. *Deep Sea II* 94: 312–322.

Koulemzine, Vladislav M. 1999. Traditions et environment. *Sibirie II. Questions siberiennes.* Paris, pp. 447–450.

Krupnik, Igor (ed.) 2000. *Pust' govoryat nashi stariki. Rasskazy aziatskikh eskimosov yupik. Zapisi 1975–1990 gg.* [Let Our Elders Speak. Stories of the Yupik-Asiatic Eskimo, 1975–1990]. Moscow: Russian Heritage Institute.

Krupnik, Igor 2002. Watching Ice and Weather Our Way: Some Lessons from Yupik Observations of Sea Ice and Weather on St. Lawrence Island, Alaska. In *The Earth Is Faster Now: Indigenous Observations of Arctic Environmental Change.* I. Krupnik and D. Jolly (eds.): 156–197. Fairbanks: ARCUS.

— 2009. The Ice We Want Our Children to Know: SIKU Project in Alaska and Siberia, 2007–2008. *Alaska Park Science* 8(2): 97–101.

— 2011. "How Many Eskimo Words for Ice?" Collecting Inuit Sea Ice Terminologies in the International Polar Year 2007–2008. *The Canadian Geographer / Le Géographe canadien* 55(1): 56–64.

— 2012. Sea Ice as a Cultural "Scape" - an IPY Legacy. Unpublished paper presented at the IPY *Knowledge to Action* Conference. Montreal.

Krupnik Igor, Ian Allison, Robin Bell, Paul Cutler, David Hik, Jeronimo Lopez-Martinez, Volker Rachold, Eduard Sarukhanian, and Collin Summerhayes (eds.) 2011. *Understanding Earth's Polar Challenges: International Polar Year 2007–2008.* Edmonton: Canadian Circumpolar Institute.

Krupnik, Igor, Claudio Aporta, Shari Gearheard, Gita J. Laidler, and Lene Kielsen Holm (eds.) 2010a. *SIKU: Knowing Our Ice. Documenting Inuit Sea Ice Knowledge and Use.* Dordrecht: Springer.

Krupnik, Igor, Claudio Aporta, and Gita J. Laidler 2010b. SIKU: International Polar Year Project #166 (An Overview). In *SIKU: Knowing Our Ice. Documenting Inuit Sea Ice Knowledge and Use.* I. Krupnik, C. Aporta, S, Gearheard, G.J. Laidler, and L. Kielsen Holm (eds.): 1–28. Dordrecht: Springer.

Krupnik, Igor, and Lyudmila S. Bogoslovskaya 2007. Izmenenie klimata i narody Arktiki. Proekt SIKU v Beringii [Climate Change and Arctic Peoples. SIKU Project in Beringia]. *Ekologicheskoe planirovanie i upravlenie* 4(5): 77–84. Moscow.

Krupnik, I., L.S. Bogoslovskaya, B.I. Vdovin, V.V. Golbtseva, N.I. Kalyuzhina, and V.N. Nuvano 2014. K itogam proekta SIKU na Vostochnoi Chukotka: Rol' narodnykh znanii v epokhu "global'nykh izmenenii" [Main Outcomes of the SIKU Project in Eastern Chukotka: The Role of Indigenous Knowledge in the Era of Global Change]. *Ekologicheskoe planirovanie i upravlenie* 2(15): 72–88. Moscow.

Krupnik, I., M. Bravo, G. Hovelsrud-Broda, L. Müller-Wille, B. Poppel, P. Schweitzer, and S. Sörlin 2005. Social Sciences and Humanities in International Polar Year 2007–2008: An Integrated Mission. *Arctic* 58(1): 91–97.

Krupnik, Igor, and Diana Jolly 2002. In *The Earth Is Faster Now: Indigenous Observations of Arctic Environmental Change.* I. Krupnik and D. Jolly (eds.). Fairbanks: ARCUS.

Krupnik, Igor, Rachel Mason, and Tonya Horton (eds.) 2004. Northern Ethnographic Landscapes: Perspectives from Circumpolar Nations. *Contributions to Circumpolar Anthropology* 5. Washington, DC: Arctic Studies Center.

Laidler, Gita J. 2006. Inuit and Scientific Perspectives on the Relationships between Sea Ice and Climate Change: The Ideal Compliment? *Climatic Change* 78: 404–444.

Laidler, Gita J., A. Dialla, and Eric Joamie 2008. Human Geographies of Sea Ice: Freeze/Thaw Processes around Pangnirtung, Nunavut, Canada. *Polar Record* 44: 335–361.

Mahoney, Andy, John R. Bockstoce, Daniel B. Botkin, Hajo Eicken, and R. Nisbet 2011. Sea Ice Distribution in the Bering and Chukchi Seas: Information from Historical Whaleships Logbooks and Journals. *Arctic* 64(4): 465–477.

Maurstad, Anita 2004. Cultural Seascapes. Preserving Local Fishermen's Knowledge in Northern Norway. In *Northern Ethnographic Landscapes: Perspectives from Circumpolar Nations. Contributions to Circumpolar Anthropology* 5. I. Krupnik, R.

Mason, and T. Horton (eds.): 277–297. Washington, DC: Arctic Studies Center.
Norton, David 2002. Coastal Sea Ice Watch: Private Confessions of a Convert to Indigenous Knowledge. In *The Earth Is Faster Now: Indigenous Observations of Arctic Environmental Change*. I. Krupnik and D. Jolly (eds.): 126–155. Fairbanks: ARCUS.
Nuttall, Mark 1991. Memoryscape: A Sense of Locality in Northwest Greenland. *North Atlantic Studies* 1(2): 39–50.
Oozeva, Conrad, Chester Noongwook, George Noongwook, Christina Alowa, and Igor Krupnik 2004. *Sikumengllu Eslamengllu Esghapaleghput / Watching Ice and Weather Our Way*. Washington, DC: Arctic Studies Center.
Pohl C., S. Rist, A. Zimmermann, P. Fry, G. Gurung, F. Schneider, C.I. Speranza, B. Kiteme, S. Boillar, E. Serrano, G. Hirsch Hadorn, and U. Wiesmann 2010. Researchers' Role in Knowledge Co-Production: Experience from Sustainability Research in Kenya, Switzerland, Bolivia, and Nepal. *Science and Public* Policy 37(4): 267–281.
Salomon, Anne, Huntington, Henry P., and Nick Tanape, Sr. 2011. *Imam Cimiucia. Our Changing Sea*. Fairbanks: Alaska Sea Grant and University of Alaska Press.
Smith, Claire and Heather Burke 2004. Joining the Dots: Managing the Land- and Seascapes of Indigenous Australia. In *Northern Ethnographic Landscapes: Perspectives from Circumpolar Nations. Contributions to Circumpolar Anthropology* 5. I. Krupnik, R. Mason, and T. Horton (eds.): 379–400. Washington, DC: Arctic Studies Center.
Stegmaier, Peter 2009. The Rock 'n' Roll of Knowledge Co-Production. *EMBO Reports* 10(2): 114–119.
Trukhanova I.S. 2014. (Review) *Our Ice, Snow, and Winds: Indigenous and Academic Knowledge on Ice-Scapes and Climate of Eastern Chukotka*. ARCTIC 67(2): 262–263.
Vdovin, Boris I., and Alexei Yu. Evstifeev 2008. Izmenenie klimata vostochnoi Chukotki za poslednee stoletie po dannym instrumental'nykh nablyudenii [Climate Change in Eastern Chukotak over the past 100 Years, According to Instrumental Data]. In *Beringia – most druzhby*, pp. 17–24. Tomsk: TGPU.
Weyapuk, Winton, Jr., and Igor Krupnik (comps.) 2012. *Kingikmi Sigum Qanuq Ilitaavut / Wales Inupiaq Sea Ice Dictionary*. Washington, DC: Arctic Studies Center.
Wisniewsky, Josh 2010. Knowings about Sigu: Kigiqtaamiut Hunting as an Experiential Pedagogy. In *SIKU: Knowing Our Ice. Documenting Inuit Sea Ice Knowledge and Use*. I. Krupnik, C. Aporta, S, Gearheard, G.J. Laidler, and L. Kielsen Holm (eds.): 275–294. Dordrecht: Springer.

4 FADING MEMORIES AND LINGUISTIC FOSSILS IN THE RELIGIOLECT OF KERALA JEWS

Ophira Gamliel

Introduction

Jewish presence on the West Coast of South India is documented back to the ninth century CE, when the dialects of South-Dravidian assumed their distinctive features marking the beginning of the Malayalam language (Ayyar 1993: 18–9; Sekhar 1951; Krishnamurti 2003: 2). The oldest Jewish compositions in Malayalam are comparable in language and style with Old Malayalam literature and, therefore, predate the fifteenth century (Gamliel 2015: 509). In 1954, Malayalam speaking Jews migrated *en masse* to Israel, gradually giving way to Modern Hebrew. Like other Jewish communities with such a long history, Kerala Jews also developed their own distinctively Jewish dialect or, more accurately, religiolect (Gamliel 2009). Presently, Jewish Malayalam is in a moribund stage with less than 500 speakers in varying degrees of fluency. The chapter describes the documentation of this fading religiolect.

Section 1 discusses the term religiolect and the position of Jewish Malayalam on the spectrum of Jewish languages. Section 2 explains the motives for implementing the approach of language documentation (Himmelmann 1998; Gippert, Himmelmann and Mosel 2006; Messineo 2008; Austin 2014, 2015). Section 3 utilizes historical linguistics based on the audio database of Jewish Malayalam. Section 4 draws upon the database for the study of Kerala Jewish oral history. Finally, Section 5 concludes with the implications of the study of religiolects for the history of religious minorities with Jewish Malayalam as a case study.

Jewish Languages and Religiolects at a Glance

The term "Jewish languages" is based on the definition of languages on religious grounds rather than on structural linguistics. As such, the attribute "Jewish" better fits a dialect or, at best, a language variety. Benjamin Hary (2009: 11–12) defines Jewish languages as religiolects based on their marked religious affiliation with a different linguistic substratum of sacred texts. Seen from this perspective, Jewish languages belong to a broader field of religiolects, namely minority dialects that evolved out of contact between the liturgical language of the minority group and the spoken language of the majority, which may vary greatly in their structure and genealogy. However, as a research field, the study of Jewish languages is unparalleled by a research field concerning for instance Muslim languages in Southeast Asia or Christian languages in the Arab-speaking world that may very well fit the characteristics of dialects differentiated from the majority language by their religious affiliation (Hary and Wein 2013).

The term "religiolect" is a late-comer in the field of Jewish languages. While the study of Jewish languages like Yiddish, Ladino and Judeo-Arabic was already established in the late-nineteenth century, the linguistic analysis of a dialect or a language variety as "Jewish" remains somewhat evasive, oscillating between two contrasting approaches. On the one hand, there is the tendency to view Jewish languages as a sub-category within a broader field of language variation (Rabin 1981). On the other hand, there is a tendency to view Jewish languages as a unique phenomenon related to centuries-long exile, gradually distanced and scattered from a common language substratum, namely Hebrew (Wexler 1981).[1] The term "religiolect" is useful in anchoring the study of Jewish languages in a broader field of religiously-defined language varieties inherently related to dialectology, sociolinguistics and languages in contact. Thus, beyond the confinement of Jewish religiolects to Jewish Studies lies a wide array of religiously-defined language varieties.

The four criteria for defining a Jewish language were first set by Moshe Bar-Asher (2002):

a. Jewish languages are written in the Hebrew script
b. The linguistic tradition contains verbatim translations of sacred texts
c. Hebrew phrases are used as idioms in casual speech
d. Archaic features of the host language are retained

Benjamin Hary (2009: 19–25) adds six criteria to the above, extending the range of the definition "Jewish language" to even include other Jewish languages that do not neatly fit into the paradigm set by Bar-Asher. Thus, even though Jewish Malayalam is mostly conveyed by the Malayalam script, it shows the other three major features as well as much of what Hary considers as defining criteria for a Jewish language (Gamliel 2009; Rubin and Kahn 2015: 3).[2]

Among the better-known Jewish languages are Yiddish, Ladino and Judeo-Arabic; each is affiliated with a different language family: Slavo-Germanic (Kahn 2015), Romance (Bunis 2015) and Central-Semitic respectively (Khan 2015). Jewish

1 Chaim Rabin (1981) suggests the analytic framework of diglossia, where Biblical and Classical Hebrew serve as the "upper"register and the colloquial spoken languages (e.g. Yiddish) serve as the "lower" register. Paul Wexler (1981), on the other hand, suggests the framework of historical analysis attributing Hebrew the status of a common substratum that was diffused into Diaspora languages through a process of shifts.

2 The Hebrew script was used to represent Malayalam words in a limited way in Hebrew documents such as prayer books or marriage-contracts (*ketubah*).

Malayalam is exceptional in its affiliation with the Indian linguistic area, though there are speculations on other Indian-Jewish religiolects (Wexler 1981: 113; Rubin and Kahn 2015: 750). It should be stressed that besides Jewish Malayalam there is no other Indian-Jewish religiolect with a community of speakers whose literature predates the sixteenth century. The contacts between Jews using the Hebrew script and Malayalam speakers were already attested for the ninth century, with signatures in Judeo-Persian found in a royal inscription granting land and privileges to West Asian traders. This Old Malayalam inscription is engraved on copper plates and dated to 849 CE (Narayanan 1972: 31–37; Varier and Veluthat 2013: 113). Moreover, the contacts of Jews with the Malayalam-speaking region are amply attested in Judeo-Arabic letters exchanged between South India, Aden and Egypt between the eleventh and the thirteenth centuries.[3]

In 1954, when Kerala Jews migrated *en masse* to Israel, there were approximately 3 000 Malayalam-speaking Jews, with a few hundred community members left behind. A second wave of migration occurred in the 1970s, leaving behind less than 100 community members. The Jews arriving in the 1970s had their speech standardized by the educational system in Modern Kerala, where the literacy rates are currently nearing 94% according to the 2011 Census of India. In contrast to this, the earlier migrants did not enjoy the educational reforms in Kerala, so that by the 1970s their speech was judged as outdated and incorrect by the later migrants. Even today, when asked about their language, Jewish Malayalam speakers define their language as old (*paẓaya*) or broken (*meʃubeʃet*), often with a sense of embarrassment. It was only in 2008 that the Malayalam spoken by Kerala Jews in Israel was recognized by scholars as a Jewish language variety (Gamliel 2009, 2014).

Remarkably, even some six decades after the detachment from the Malayalam-speaking region in South India, Kerala Jews in Israel still use their religiolect, although fluent speakers are mostly in their sixties and older. The reason may be related to their settlement patterns in the newly-founded state of Israel in the 1950s. Kerala Jews were relegated to agrarian settlements in the border regions and, as a consequence, maintained close communal life and familial relations. Contemporary Jewish Malayalam speakers often attribute their knowledge of Malayalam to their grandparents, who retained the use of Malayalam in the domestic environment many years after the mass migration. Under these circumstances, the Jewish religiolect of Kerala is still maintained by speakers and available for documentation, description and analysis.

3 For the Judeo-Arabic letters related to the Indian Ocean trade, see Goitein and Friedman 2008.

Better Late Than Never: Documenting Jewish Malayalam

Kerala Jews have been the subject of anthropological research and historical study since the 1930s (Mandelbaum 1939; Fischel 1967; Johnson 1975; Walerstein 1987), but it was not until the 2000s that the linguistic heritage of Malayalam-speaking Jews was put in the spotlight. This indifference towards the linguistic heritage of the community stands in stark contrast to the curiosity of Jewish scholars towards this "esoteric" community, ostensibly isolated and having its origins shrouded in mystery. Notwithstanding the scarcity of premodern sources related to the history of Kerala Jews, their origins are traceable to the ninth century in relation to the medieval Indian Ocean trade routes.[4] With such a long history of Jews in the Malayalam-speaking region, it is plausible to assume that a distinctive Jewish religiolect evolved. Nevertheless, Jewish Malayalam remained for a long time a subject for mere speculation. The early 2000s constituted the last moment for salvaging something of the fading linguistic heritage of the community before it is too late.

The first attempt at studying the linguistic heritage of the community was related to hand-written manuscripts containing Jewish wedding songs in the Malayalam script (Johnson 2002). Occasional attempts at translating the Jewish Malayalam songs over the years did not mature into a fully-fledged linguistic description. Thus, all interviews and recordings of community members were conducted either in English or in Hebrew avoiding the challenges involved in translations from Malayalam, an under-researched language, let alone a dialect of Malayalam on the verge of extinction. It was only in 2002 that a scholar of Malayalam language and literature, Scaria Zacharia, was first introduced to the field. He made some public speeches in Malayalam in front of community members in Israel, and received an enthusiastic response. Zacharia began to promote the research and publication of Kerala Jewish literature for rendering the nearly forgotten literary corpus accessible to community members in both Malayalam and Hebrew (Zacharia and Gamliel 2005). However, Zacharia was under the impression that Jewish Malayalam was not a distinct Jewish language as, say, Yiddish or Ladino,[5] possibly because the elderly women and men who migrated in 1954 felt embarrassed to expose their "broken" Malayalam to the venerable scholar.

In 2007, after nearly four years of studying spoken Malayalam in Central Kerala, I moved to Mesilat Zion, an agrarian settlement of Malayalam-speaking Jews near Jerusalem. My elderly neighbors were happy to engage in casual Malayalam conversations, but conversing with them was frustratingly difficult. It was not long before I realized that they speak a non-standard Malayalam variety very different from the one I was familiar with from Central Kerala. Firstly, their Malayalam was outdated in relation to contemporary Kerala dialects. Secondly, it was spiced up with lexical borrowings from Modern Hebrew. Thirdly, it depicted features of a Jewish religiolect which

4 For further discussion on the topic see Gamliel 2013b.

5 Personal communication.

likely predates the migration to Israel. Above all, it became evident that whatever language or dialect Malayalam-speaking Jews in Israel were using, it was in the process of fading away, along with stories, jokes, proverbs, idioms and invaluable ethnographic data that had been left out of the scope of studies on Kerala Jewish history and culture.

Considering the urgency in salvaging whatever is left of the linguistic heritage of Jewish Malayalam, I began documenting casual speech following the principles of language documentation as elaborated by Gippert et al. (2006). At the time, there were already several projects—some completed and some in progress—that focused on Kerala Jews in Israel. None of the projects, however, had anything to do with Malayalam. On the contrary—the interviewers were reluctant to conduct an interview in Malayalam even though many of them were Malayalam speakers themselves. Moreover, the prospects of fieldwork were narrowed down to personal memoires captured on tape by well-intentioned field workers with no technical training in digital recording, archiving and cataloguing.

The initiative for the language documentation project emerged out of the community in an almost arbitrary manner. One of my neighbors in Mesilat Zion asked me whether I would be willing to teach the Malayalam script to Malayalam speakers living in the area. Thus, the project began even before it was officially launched and before any institution offered support. We started a "class" composed of Malayalam speakers in their sixties and above. Everybody was enthusiastic and excited about the opportunity to discuss Malayalam and exchange jokes, stories, anecdotes, etc. I brought in a small and almost unnoticeable digital recorder and began to take notes, archive and catalogue all that was going on in the "Malayalam class". Even though the attempt to teach the Malayalam script was futile, the meetings of the Malayalam "class" turned out to be a language revival group.

In fact, the Jewish Malayalam documentation project emerged out of this group, which provided the essential initial findings behind the argument that Kerala Jews developed their own distinctive Jewish religiolect. The group meetings further served as a platform for recruiting language workers and for campaigning for a broader scale of language documentation within the community and beyond. In collaboration with Jarmo Forsström, a phonetician studying the traditional Hebrew pronunciation of Kerala Jews (Forsström 1997), I applied for funds for the Jewish Malayalam language documentation project. Thus, under the auspices of the Ben-Zvi Institute, the Jewish Malayalam language documentation project was launched in 2008.

Even though the budget was relatively small, the enthusiastic support of several dedicated community members enabled us to collect, archive and catalogue approximately forty gigabytes of digital records, mostly of audio files. Our budget was spent mainly on travel around the country for interviewing elderly community members; except for a high quality digital recorder and a laptop for one language worker, we could not afford more sophisticated tools such as a video camera or video editing programs. Above all, the Jewish Malayalam documentation project could not complete the required tedious work of transcriptions and translations due to the lack of further institutional support in training documentary linguists.[6]

The project was launched with two aims in mind. Firstly, there was the need to establish a corpus of Jewish Malayalam oral literary forms and linguistic data. Secondly, we sought to enrich the repertoire of Hebrew recital traditions for Forsström's research. The method for interviewing was divided between meetings with individuals or couples in their homes, and recordings of community events or group meetings. This fourfold strategy of documentation is reflected in the catalogue of the audio records. Audio files containing Hebrew recitals are catalogued as A for communal events and B for individual interviews. Audio files containing Jewish Malayalam speech are catalogued as C for group meetings and D for individual interviews. Besides these four types of recordings, the archive also contains JPEG files with photos of people and objects catalogued as E for those documented in Israel and F for those documented in Kerala. Lastly, some texts also surfaced during the documentation project; they are catalogued as G in the archive. The archive can be expanded to include any material donated by community members or other researchers.

Regretfully, the Jewish Malayalam documentation project has yet to be utilized for research and study. Merely fragments of the data collected were transcribed, translated and analyzed in casual papers on Jewish Malayalam published by me on different occasions. The bulk of the material still awaits transcription and translation. Moreover, it awaits its inclusion in the wider context of the study of endangered languages beyond the somewhat isolated niche field of Jewish languages.

The importance of the Jewish Malayalam documentation project for the community of Jewish Malayalam speakers cannot be overstated. It has contributed ethnographic, folkloric and linguistic data indispensable for the study of the sociocultural history of the community. In the following sections, I draw upon the database for linguistic and ethnographic data that is transcribed, described and analyzed here for the first time.

Linguistic Fossils and Historical Linguistics

As already mentioned above, evidence for the existence of premodern Jewish communities in the Malayalam-speaking region is scarce and circumstantial (Gamliel 2013b). Based on data recorded in the language documentation project, it is possible to supplement the existing sources and documents with evidence based on a diachronic analysis of archaic forms attested to this day in the speech of Malayalam-speaking Jews in Israel.

---

6 It was not until February 2016 that the first course of documentary linguistics took place at the Israeli academia at the Hebrew University.

The most prominent finding in this regard is the use of the archaic dative form *-ikkə* after the masculine singular *-aṉ*. In standard Malayalam, the parallel form would be *-ə*, which had replaced the dative ending *-ikkə* after the ending *-aṉ* by the fourteenth century (Ayyar 1993 [1938]: 27–8). As in (1):[7]

avaṉikkə	*iṣṭam-bōle*	*atə*	*namukkə*	*koṭukk.ām*
3SG.M.DAT	desired-as	DEM	1PL.INCL.DAT	give.MOD

According to his wish, we can give it [to someone else].

[C6, 07:22–07:25][8]
https://ia601508.us.archive.org/32/items/FMExx6/FM_exx_1.wav

The retention of the archaic dative is a linguistic "fossil" preserved in Jewish Malayalam. It is also recognized as a typical feature of contemporary *Māppiḷa* (Muslim) dialects in Kerala.[9] The retention of the archaic dative is evidence that by the fourteenth century Jewish (and Muslim) communities were already well-established in the Malayalam-speaking region. It is, therefore, not surprising that Jewish literature in Malayalam emerges no later than the fifteenth century (Gamliel 2015).

Another feature differentiating Jewish Malayalam from contemporary spoken Malayalam is the realization of *-a* as the accusative morpheme instead of the Old and Modern Malayalam *-e*, which branched off the realization *-ai* in Middle Tamil (Sekhar 1951: 67; Ayyar 2004: 44), as in (2):

(2)	*paṭikkaṉa*	*ṟābbə*	*allē*	*paṭippikkaṉa*
	study.PRS.PRT	rabbi	NEG.Q	teach.PRS.PRT
	makkaḷ-a	*paṭippikkaṉōṉ-āṉə*		
	kids-ACC	teach.PRS.3SG.M-COP		

The Rabbi studies, right? He teaches. He is the one who teaches the kids.

[D32-ED, 03:05–03:09]
https://ia601508.us.archive.org/32/items/FMExx6/FM_exx_2.wav

The accusative morpheme *–a* is unrepresented in any of the historical phases of evolution of Malayalam. It is retained in some castolects in Kerala, besides the Muslim and Jewish religiolects. However, this retention is more wide-spread in northern

7 The transcripts of the oral samples employ the transliteration guidelines adapted by Roland E. Asher and T.C. Kumari (1997: 406). A more precise transcript is beyond the scope of the present paper.

8 The capital letters with numbers refer to the catalogue number of the recording from where the speech samples are taken. They are followed by the annotation of the time on the recording. The catalogue is available upon request from the author.

9 T.B. Venugopala Panicker in a personal communication. [15.07.2016]

Kerala; it points at historical contacts with the Koḍagu-speaking region bordering the northernmost districts of the Malayalam-speaking region. In Koḍagu, the accusative morpheme is *-a* (Krishnamurti 2003: 227). Further evidence for the possibility of historical affiliation with Koḍagu is attested in the insertion of the increment *-ṉ-* before the accusative morpheme *-a* in words ending in *-a*. Contrarily, in contemporary standard Malayalam *a*-ending words require the insertion of a glide /y/. For example, in (3) the word *āṉa*, 'elephant', is marked by the Jewish Malayalam accusative morpheme *-ṉa*, *āṉaṉa*, as opposed to the parallel Malayalam form *āṉaye*.

(3)	*eŋŋaṉa*	*āṉaṉa*	*frījjiḍaṟilēkkə*	*kēṟṟī*
	how	elephant.ACC	fridge.LOC.DIR	enter.CAUS.NFIN
	[iti]l	*[v]ēkkum*		
	DEIC.LOC	put.FUT		

How will you keep an elephant inside the fridge?

[C12, 04:51–04:56]
https://ia601508.us.archive.org/32/items/FMExx6/FM_exx_3.wav

The affinities with the northernmost dialects of Kerala may be contested by comparable non-standard forms typical of castolects in Central Kerala.[10] However, there is at least one feature that strongly points at affinities with dialects from the northern parts of Kerala and possible archaic retentions influenced by Koḍagu: the phonemic alternation unique to Jewish Malayalam in which the sublamino-palatal /ẓ/ is replaced by /t/ in inter-vocalic position and by /s/ before the dental stop /t/. The first instance, as far as I am aware of, is attested only in writing; it must have fallen out of use before the migration to Israel. Interestingly, in at least one instance in the language documentation data, an interviewee pronounces a voiced sublamino-palatal approximant /ẓ/ instead of a dental stop /t/: *kaẓa* < *kata*, 'story':

(4)	*kaẓa*	*koṟaccə*	*[e]ṉikk'*	*aṟiyām*
	story	some	1SG.DAT	know.MOD

I know some stories.

[D32-ED, 00:55–00:57]
https://ia601508.us.archive.org/32/items/FMExx6/FM_exx_4.wav

Even though the alternation /ẓ/ > /t/ seems to have been "corrected" in contemporary Jewish Malayalam, it is still remembered as a peculiar feature of Jewish Mala-

10 T.B. Venugopala Panicker derives the same form through a different process of syllabic reduction, where the increment *-iṉ-* is inserted before the accusative *-a*, e.g. *āṉa-y-iṉ-a* > *āṉayṉa* > *āṉaṉa*.

yalam.[11] This phonemic alternation is attested also in the speech of Tiyyas from the northernmost districts of Kerala (Subramoniam 2006: 21; cf. Krishnamurti 2003: 152), thereby providing further evidence for historical affiliations with the northernmost parts of Kerala.

While there are many other noteworthy dialectical features in Jewish Malayalam, the three features described above are significant for the study of the history of the community. Coupled with textual evidence found in historical sources, they assist in substantiating the postulation that Jews were settled in the northernmost parts of the Malayalam-speaking region by the fourteenth century. This stands in contrast to the view that Kerala Jews settled first at Kodungallur in Central Kerala and, due to nature- or human-induced calamity, they fled to Cochin and other places in Central Kerala in the fourteenth century. The linguistic fossils found in Jewish Malayalam provide concrete evidence for a better understanding of the premodern history of Kerala Jews and their settlement patterns over the centuries.

The dialectical retentions in Jewish Malayalam are insufficient as evidence for a distinct Jewish religiolect emerging as early as the fourteenth century. It is, of course, possible that the archaic features of the dialect predate the Judaization of its speakers. However, there is further evidence to support the assumption that the linguistic retentions and the Jewish identity of the religiolect belong to more or less the same period. That evidence lies in the religious terminology, which is often related to one of the most prominent features of a Jewish religiolect, namely, the Hebrew component (Gamliel 2013a).

The contacts between Malayalam and Hebrew have been attested since the earliest period in the evolution of Malayalam in ninth- and eleventh-century inscriptions. Jews left signatures in the Hebrew script on the above-mentioned copper-plate inscription dated 849. There are also several Malayalam words found in Cairo Geniza documents and written in Judeo-Arabic.[12] That in itself, of course, does not provide any evidence for a fully-fledged Jewish Malayalam religiolect at such an early stage or for the settling of Jews in the region. It does provide evidence for increased contacts between Hebrew writing people and Malayalam speakers between the ninth and the

11 Thuravoor Vishvambharan, a scholar from Ernakulam, recalled in a personal communication in 2006 that Jewish women were known to pronounce /t/ instead of /ẓ/. He imitated this peculiar pronunciation in the following utterance, where the standard verbal form would be *kaẓiccu*:
bakṣaṇam *katicc-ā*?
food eat.PST-Q
Did you take food?

12 S.D. Goitein and Moredechai Akiva Friedman have identified several South Indian terms in their "India Book". Elisabeth Lambourn (2014) identified more terms borrowed from Malayalam to Judeo-Arabic. I identified three more words: FDY'R < *patiyār*, 'chief merchant', DNGLY < *iṭaṅṅaẓi*, a measurement of grains weighing approximately one kilogram, RWY < *ravi*, personal name. I have also identified terms and names in other Indian languages. I intend to publish my findings in the near future.

fourteenth centuries. We can, therefore, assume that the increased contacts in the aforementioned period served as the ground for the early stages of Jewish Malayalam allowing for the incorporation of the Hebrew component in the emerging religiolect.

Hebrew loanwords appear to have been integrated in Jewish Malayalam literature no later than the fifteenth century, though it is only from the late-sixteenth century onward that Hebrew loanwords are abundant and diverse. Lexical borrowing in early Jewish Malayalam literature is limited to names of Biblical characters, though occasionally some other types of loanwords do occur like *sāddikkə*, 'the righteous one' (referring to Joseph) and *seūda*, 'feast'. In the earliest compositions, we find semantic borrowing more frequently than lexical borrowing, such as calque translations like *konnakoṉ*, 'kings of kings' (in Hebrew: *melek̲ ha-mlak̲im*) or *sattiyam*, 'covenant', to denote 'circumcision' (in Hebrew: *brit*). Based on this textual evidence alone, it is difficult to tell whether the occurrence of Hebrew words and calque translations in literary compositions reflects the occurrence of Hebrew loanwords in actual usage in that period.

At least two religious terms recorded in the casual speech of contemporary Jewish Malayalam speakers suggest that indeed lexical and semantic borrowing from Hebrew in Jewish Malayalam is close to the evolutionary stage of Old Malayalam in the fourteenth century. Both terms are hyphenated words derived through semantic rather than lexical borrowing. Since Hebrew loanwords for religious terms are borrowed from a "timeless" liturgical language, it is difficult to ascertain the period in which they were borrowed into Jewish Malayalam. Contrarily, certain Malayalam elements can be associated with different periods in the evolution of Malayalam language. The first term in this respect is *ʃīṟiya-divasam*, 'Destruction-Day', which I heard several times on different occasions. The term denotes the annual fast commemorating the anniversary of the destruction of the first and second Jewish Temples on the ninth day of the Hebrew month Ab in 586 BCE and 70 CE respectively. The common Hebrew term, *Tiʃ'a Be-'Ab* is often replaced by *Yom Ha-Ḥurban*, 'Day of Destruction', which *ʃīṟiya-divasam* reproduces in Jewish Malayalam.

Notably, the Jewish Malayalam compound is derived from an adjectival participle *ʃīṟiya* traceable to Tamil *cīṟu*-, 'destroy' (Fabricius 1972: 161), while the word *divasam*, 'day', is derived from Sanskrit. In contemporary Malayalam, the verb *cīṟu*- does not denote 'destroy'; the verb *aẓi*- is used in this meaning. Moreover, the verb *aẓi*- is the more common word in later Jewish Malayalam for translating the Hebrew verb *ḥ.r.b.*, 'destroy' and its derivations, especially in the context of the destruction of the Jewish temples. Thus, the adjectival participle *ʃīṟiya* is likely to have been integrated into Jewish religious terminology at a relatively early stage in the evolution of Jewish Malayalam, when Tamil was still a dominant language in the Malayalam-speaking region. The combination of a word derived from Tamil with a loanword from Sanskrit further suggests that the term was created when Sanskrit was gradually replacing Tamil in scholarly and literary expressions towards the late-fourteenth century (Freeman 1998: 41).

Another term of interest is *mayyi-beṟāxa*, 'dusk-blessing', which was recorded during a group session discussing the ceremonial procedures customary after the birth of a male child. In this case, the first element of the hyphenated word is in Malayalam and the second is in Hebrew. The Malayalam element belongs to a relatively old substratum of the language; *mayi* means *iruṭṭə*, 'darkness', in Old Malayalam (Pillai 2006 [1923]: 1384). The more common and modern meanings associated with *mayi* are 'ink' or 'black'. The term is historically related to the verb *mayaŋŋ-*, 'to grow dim or dusk', with several adverbs like *mayyalē* and *mayimbu* derived from it to denote 'dusk' and 'twilight' (Gundert 1995 [1872]: 789–791). The Hebrew element, *beṟāxa*, means 'blessing'. Combined with *mayyi* the compound denotes the blessing over the wine customarily performed after sunset to mark the passage from profanity to sacredness and vice versa on holidays and life-cycle events like weddings.

The recording with the term *mayyi-beṟaxa* given in (5) below is telling because it triggers a meta-linguistic discussion between the participants.[13] The context is the special customs performed after the birth of a male child. The father of the newborn (*āvi-āben*, a Hebrew loanword) is granted an honorary status during the Saturday prayers. Once the Saturday prayer is over, the congregation moves from the synagogue to the house of the newborn for the ritual that marks the passage from the holy Saturday to the profane Sunday (Havdalah), which occurs after sunset. The Havdalah begins with the blessing over the wine.

Notably, Jewish-Malayalam speakers understand the word *mayyi* as derived from the Hebrew word *yāyin*, 'wine'. This may not be far-fetched considering the Hebrew term *birkat ha-yāyin*. However, when compared with other Hebrew compounds borrowed wholesale into Jewish Malayalam (e.g. *āvi-āben* < *avi ha-ben*), the derivation is less convincing; we would have expected the right-branching order of words and the definite article *ha-* to be retained in Jewish Malayalam. Moreover, the phonemic shift from a word-initial /y/ to /m/ is unlikely. However, the meta-linguistic discussion is important because it depicts the speakers' awareness of their religiolect. Note that for discussing the meanings of the term *mayyi-beṟāxa*, the participants shift to Hebrew (marked by braces {} to differentiate it from Jewish Malayalam).

---

13 Since there are several participants, I indicate their initials as follows: Yosi Oren [YO], Milka Daniel [MD], Eli Menahem [EM] and Ophira Gamliel [OG]. When several people talk simultaneously, I mark the utterance as belonging to everybody [EB].

The main speaker is Yosi Oren, who migrated to Israel at the age of nine. He commented several times that he used to listen to the stories and memories of his grandparents. His family settled in Taoz, which to this day is populated exclusively by Kerala Jews. Oren's enthusiastic appreciation of the language documentation project contributed more than his own memories and knowledge of Jewish Malayalam—he became an inspiring model for many others in the community and a great help in interviewing older people in their homes.

(5)

[YO] *ellāvarum vannə ā vīṯṯil vannə ē…*
everyone come.NFIN DEM house.LOC come.NFIN
Everyone comes and… they come to that house and…

pustōm-uḻḻa āvədalā koḻḻunn.atə ellām cellum
book-EXIS.ADJ Havdalah^{H} receive.PRS-NMLZ all recite.HAB
They take up the Havdala which is in the prayer book and recite it all.

mayyi-vəṟāxa vāsttum
dusk-blessing bless.HAB
They bless the wine-blessing.

[OG] *ē…?*
The what?

[EB] *mayyi-veṟāxa {yayyin!}*
dusk-blessing {wine^{H}!}

[YO] *mayyi-beṟāxa {ze kidduʃ! mayyi-beṟāxa birkat ha-yayyin}*
dusk-blessing {DEM sanctification dusk-blessing blessing.GEN DEF-wine}
Wine-blessing, {that's Kiddush! Wine-blessing is the blessing of the wine.}

[OG] {*ma ze ha-mayyi ha-ze?*}
{what DEM DEF-dusk DEF-DEM}
{What is this, this '*mayyi*'?}

[OY] {*mayyī ze yayyin*}
{dusk DEM wine^{H}}
{*mayyi* is wine.}

[MD] {*at ro'a ze eyn ba'areṣ* }
{2SG.F see.SG.F DEM NEG LOC-land}

ze ba-safa ha-hodit}
DEM LOC.language DEF-Indian}
{You see, you don't have it in Israel, this is in the Indian language.}

[YD] {*mayyi-beṟāxa ze ha-kidduʃ*}
{dusk-blessing DEM DEF-sanctification^{H}}
{the wine-blessing is the Kiddush}

[EM]	{*hem*	*hayu*	*kor'im*	*le-ha-kol*	*be-'vrit*	}
	{3PL.M	be.PST.PL	call.PL.M	DAT.DEF.all	INST-Hebrew}	

{They would call everything in Hebrew}

[YD]	{*rak*	*et-ze*	*ṣarix*	*la-da'at*}
	{only	DO-DEM	need	to-know}

{It's necessary to know just this.}

[YO]	{*gam*	*ze*	*mayyi-veṟāxa*	*ze*	*kvar*	*ke'ilu*}
	{also	DEM	dusk-blessing	DEM	ADV	as if}

{That too is 'dusk-blessing'. It's as if it is already,}

{*ze*	*kvar*	*nimṣa*	*be-tox*	*ha-malayalom*}
{DEM	ADV	EXIS.SG.M	LOC.inside	DEF-Malayalam}

{it's already there inside the Malayalam.}

{*ze*	*rak*	*ha-yehudim*	*yagidu*	}
{DEM	only	DEF-Jews	say.3PL.FUT}	

{Only the Jews will say that.}

[C6 08:48–09:44]
https://ia601508.us.archive.org/32/items/FMExx6/FM_exx_5.wav

Oral History and Documentary Linguistics

Guided by the principles of documentary linguistics (Himmelmann 1998; Gipert *et al.* 2006; Austin 2015), the Jewish Malayalam documentation was defined right at the outset as a multi-purpose project. One of the most pressing concerns in many of the meetings and interviews was with the history of the community. Depending on the speakers' memories and personal interests, the recorded conversations and interviews reveal different aspects of Jewish history in Kerala varying between accounts of daily life to historical incidents, anecdotes and legends. In the previous section, the examples were drawn from an account related to daily life in the past. This present section focuses on other examples of oral history.[14]

The first example of oral history is a memoir recorded in English and the second is an etiology recorded in Malayalam. Despite the differences, both center on the community of origin of each narrator: Chendamangalam and Parur respectively. This is notable since the history of Kerala Jews heavily relies on a repertoire of legends, myths

14 Note that in accounts dealing with daily life, the habitual verb form (HAB) is amply used, whereas in historical accounts the past form (PST) is more prominent.

and memoirs drawn almost exclusively from the Paradeśi community in Cochin. As a result, the overall image of Kerala Jews overemphasizes the Jewish heritage of Cochin and, in particular, of the Paradeśi community. Jewish Malayalam speakers hailing from different communities and towns in Kerala are therefore eager to voice their version of history to counterbalance their image of being of lesser pedigree and prestigious origins.

The first story in (6) narrates the rise of the Zionist movement in Kerala. It was recorded in English because one of the listeners was a Telugu speaker who was curious to meet Jews from Kerala in Israel.[15] The interviewee, fluent in English, wanted to share with the Telugu speaker visitor from India his version of the rise of the Zionist movement in Kerala. The language is a non-standard South Indian variety of English. Notably, the speaker uses the place name Cochin as an attributive for Kerala Jews (Cochin Jews), even though his community of origin is Chendamangalam. This is partly due to the aforementioned prominence of Cochin in the historiography of the community; Kerala Jews, when speaking with "outsiders" refer to themselves as Cochin Jews, whereas between themselves the reference would always be to the community of origin. It is also due to the fact that the modern state of Kerala was formed after the implementation of the States Reorganisational Act (1956) two years after the majority of Malayalam-speaking Jews migrated to Israel (1954). Except for Parur, the towns in which Jewish communities were located were included in the princely state of Cochin prior to Indian independence from British rule.

(6) You know, the, the … How the first immigration of the first group? No. The Aliyah[16] from Cochin? It is started from a man called Eliyahu Meir. I am calling him the Herzl[17] of Jews of Cochin. The Aliyah, immigration, from Cochin started from him because this gentleman—he was serving in the army, Indian army, in the air force he was in 1932 to 45, he served in Bangalore air force center. And once he was called by the British officer to punish him for something he had done wrong, he didn't salute somebody or something. And when he entered, the British officer was sitting there. He looked on him, looked at the file and asked him, "What is your name?" He told him, "Eliyahu Meir". "Are you a Jew?" "Yes …" "Then why are you standing? Sit [with] me! Sit here with me!" He invited him to sit. And he asked him […] And he … Eliyahu Meir told, "I am from Chendamangalam. We are the Jews there." Then he said, "Do

15 The recording took place in the southern village Shachar in June 2008 at the home of the narrator, Bezalel Eliyahu (born 1930, migrated 1955). The people present were Miriam Dekel, a Jewish Malayalam speaker, Vimala Katikaneni, a visiting researcher from Andhra Pradesh and the present author.

16 *Aliyah* literally means ascent in Hebrew. It is a special term denoting immigration to Israel, conceived as a movement upwards.

17 Benjamin Zeev Theodor Herzl (1860–1904), one of the founding fathers of the Zionist movement.

you know who I am? I am the deputy manager of Anglo-Palestine Bank in Jerusalem! Every night you come to drink with me beer!" From that day he explained to him and got many [pamphlets] in English, about the Kibbutzim, Moshav all this coming in Israel.[18] And he told him, "In the near future there will be a state of Israel!"

Whenever he come, for, off to Cochin, he collected … we were boys … all the boys, he collected all of us, giving lecture—we, one day, we will go to Israel. I am getting contact, I will write … everybody was very … wonderful to hear, but the important person like […] all told he was … eh … one screw is gone … he says simple, stupid, he is telling what he's telling … Three years he was talking on this, but he finished with war, and he returned back, he started to write.

From that time he started to write here and there. This man helped him to address contact; that way started the movement. Then came … till that time, the Israel state forming, and the Jewish agency people are coming up to Bombay only, not to Cochin. Then, in 1948 … the only place in Kerala hoisting a flag in Iyar, Fifth of Iyar,[19] on Friday evening, this is Chendamangalam. I had arranged the flag hoisting. All the youngsters—they made a rally on through all Chendamangalam street. Our older people advised not to make it because the Muslims will come and kill us. No, we made it, we made a flag and then collected some money and gave to a man in Parur, who is making, repairing radio to hear voice of Kol Israel La-Gola[20] and, we paid him money and we all, some people, are sitting to hear … nothing heard. We lost the money.

Aliyah. From that year, every year, I was arranging celebration of Fifth Iyar in Chendamangalam. Every year I am planning, I am collecting money; I am writing stories, I am directing the people, I am acting. And people coming from Ernakulam, Cochin to see the … the … our drama and everything. Till we migrated there. It was came[21] from Chendamangalam; the migration started from Chendamangalam.

[D6 00:00–04:41]
https://ia601508.us.archive.org/32/items/FMExx6/FM_exx_6.wav

---

18 Kibbutz and Moshav are agrarian Jewish settlements, with the former based on communist ideology and leading a communist way of life (in the past). *-im* is the plural marker in Hebrew. Interestingly, the narrator uses one Hebrew term in the plural and one in the singular.

19 Fifth of Iyar is the Hebrew date for Independence Day for the State of Israel.

20 The narrator refers to a broadcasting service of the Jewish Agency that was launched in 1950 under the name Kol Zion La-Gola, 'the voice of Zion to the Diaspora'.

21 The verbal formation "was came" may reflect contact with colloquial British English, in which the formation "was sat" is acceptable by native speakers, though only with the verb "sit" (as confirmed by my colleague Cathy Cantwell in a personal communication, April 2016).

This narration juxtaposes right at the outset a communal figure, Eliyahu Meir, with Theodore Herzl, an iconic founder figure in the history of the Zionist movement. At first, Eliyahu Meir is associated with Indian identity as he serves in the Indian army. His character is somewhat subversive; he gets in trouble with the British officer, representing the colonial authority. The narrator attributes this to a lack of respect for hierarchical order ("He didn't salute somebody or something"). But, when his Jewish identity is exposed, he gains the favor of his superior, and the relationship between the two transforms into friendship ("come drink beer with me!"). The next step is the revelation of the Zionist national identity through the agency of the British authoritative friendship. The young and somewhat subversive Jew marks the emergence of young and progressive leadership within the Jewish community of Chendamangalam. His Zionist leadership skills attract the youngsters while meeting the opposition of conservative powers ("important person") who mock him at first ("one screw is gone").

Importantly, the narrator stresses that the Zionist leadership and organization was an internal development within the community; the Jewish agency neglected them, they only reached as far as Bombay. This is, in fact, a very painful point in the history of Kerala Jewish migration to Israel in the early 1950s. Even though the Jews of Kerala organized themselves to move *en masse* to the newly-founded State of Israel, the Jewish Agency authorities refused to grant them permission to migrate for two years. The professed reason was the fear of elephantiasis being transmitted to Israel by the migrants, even though the disease is not contagious (Chiriyankandath 2008: 39–41). The narrator obliquely addresses the issue of racial discrimination against his community by stressing the lack of involvement of the Zionist leadership in the rise of Zionism among Kerala Jews.

The Zionist activities carried out in Chendamangalam are described as typical Kerala political activism—there are rallies, hoisting of the flag and even a drama to attract Jews of other communities in Ernakulam and Cochin. The narrator highlights the importance of his own community in the Zionist movement in Kerala. He further prides himself in his personal role as a communal organizer. In this way, he obliquely addresses inter- and intra-communal tensions and rivalries: with the Jews of Cochin and Ernakulam (and to a certain extent even of Parur, which had the largest population of Jews in Kerala), with the Muslim neighbors, as well as with the older conservative generation.[22]

While the narration in (7) below is utterly different from (6) in almost every respect, it is similar in its highlighting the importance of the community from which the speaker hails, in this case—Parur.[23] Note also the reference to Cochin instead of Kerala as a general reference to Jews from the Malayalam-speaking region—*koccikār*, 'Cochinites'. Similar to (6), the narrator turns the spotlight on her own community

22 For the history of the Zionist movement in Kerala see Chiriyankandath 2008.

23 The narrator is Hemda Tiferet, who migrated from Kerala to Israel in the 1970s. She told the story in a communal gathering in the southern settlement of Nevatim in May 2008.

of origin, Parur, by referring specifically to *paṟūkkār*, 'Parurites'. This narration too begins with a question designed to provoke the listeners for their interest. It also ends with the narrator as the focal point and with her first-hand memories as validating the truth of the legend she narrates.

Note that there are Hebrew components embedded in the narration; some of them were in use before migration to Israel, like *bedāmikkadāʃə*, 'House of Holies', i.e. the Jewish Temple. This term is documented in Jewish-Malayalam songs that predate the late-eighteenth century. However, the Hebrew loanword *sīppūr* is likely to have been borrowed after migration to Israel. The older Jewish Malayalam term for a Jewish story is *māssa*, 'legend' (< *ma'ase*, Hebrew).

(7)

eṉṟe	*kūṭṭukāratti*	*paṟaññə ...*
1SG.GEN	friend-F	said

My friend told me …

entu-koṇṭ-ā	*nammuṭe*	*koccikār-iṭayilə*	*kovāṉim-leviyim*	*illāttē*[24]
Q-INST-COP	our.INCL	Cochinites-ADV	priests[H]-Levites[H]	NEG.NMLZ

How come there are no priests and Levites among our Cochinites?

appa	*paṟayaṉ-atə*	*sīppūr*	*paṟaɲɲ-atə:*
then	tells-NMLZ	story[H]	told-NMLZ

Then, what she tells was a story that she told:

oru-bāṭə	*kāʃ'*	*uṇṭāy-irunn-appa*	*paḷḷi...*	*ē...*	*paṟūkkār-uṭe*	*kayyilə*
a-lot	cash	became-PRF-when	synagogue		Parurites-GEN	hand-LOC

There was once a lot of cash money at the hands of the synagogue, eh, the Parur people.

appa	*aviṭe*	*orubāṭə*	*kovāṉim-leviyim*	*okke*	*oṇṭāy-irunnə*
then	there	a-lot	priests[H]-Levites[H]	all	became-PRF

At that time, there were many priests and Levities there,

avar.kkə	*bedāmikkadāʃə*	*paṇiy.aṇo-nnə*	*paṟaɲɲə*
they.DAT	temple[H]	build.DSD-QUOT	said

they wanted to build a temple, they said.

bedāmikkadāʃə	*paṇiy.āṉ-āyiṭṭə*	*sādhaṉaŋŋaḷə*	*okke*	*oṇṭākki-irunn-atə*
temple[H]	build.INF-ADV	things	all	make-PRF-NMLZ

They made all the things required for building the temple.

---

24 < *illātt-atə*

ē…	*ādyattə*	*ēveṉ-piṉa*	*vaikk.āṉ-āyiṭṭə*	*vann-appa*
	firstly	foundation stone[H]	put.INF-ADV	come-when

When they first came to lay down the foundation stone,

atu	*vaccu-pōẓatt-ēkkə*	*aviṭe*	*oru-bāṭə*	*sukha-kēṭ'*	*oṇṭāyi*
that	put-when-ADV	there	a-lot	disease	became

As soon as they laid it down, they were struck by so many plagues.

āḷukaḷ	*oru-bāṭə*	*cattə*	*appa*	*oru*	*karaṇam*	*ippa*	*ceyy.ēṇṭa*
people	a-lot	died	then	one	reason	now	do.DSD.NEG

So many people died, then, "There's a reason, [we] should not do [it] now".

ellām	*mūṭiy-iṭṭə*	*kuṟe-kālam*	*kaẓiɲɲ-iṭṭə*
all	cover-put.NFIN	some-time	elapse-COMP.NFIN

All was covered, some time elapsed,

tiriye	*oru-prāvaʃyam-koṇṭə*	*ceytu-nokki*
again	one-occasion-ADV	do.NFIN-tried

and they tried once more to do [the same].

tiriye	*sukha-kēṭə*	*oru-bāṭə*	*vannə*	*kōlaṟa*	*ṭaifōḍə*
again	diseases	a-lot	came	Cholera	Typhoid

Once more, the plagues hit them: Cholera, Typhoid …

aŋŋaṉatte	*sukha-kēṭə*	*vannə*	*oru-bāṭə*	*pōyi-kaẓiɲɲ-appa*
like that	diseases	came.NFIN	a-lot	went-COMP-when

When plagues hit them like that and so many [people] perished,

avarə	*at-ellām*	*[v]iṭṭu-pūṭṭiy-iṭṭ-uṇṭə*
they	that-all	forsook.locked-COMP-PRF

They forsook everything and locked it up.

ayiṉre[25]	*mōḷēl*[26]	*kāṭ'*	*okk'*	*aviṭe*	*vacci*
that.GEN	top.LOC	forest	all	there	put.PST

On top of that, the forest grew all over.

ippōẓ-um	*ā*	*stalattə*	*aŋŋaṉe*	*oṇṭ'*	*ennə*	*paṟayaṇə*
now-CNJ	DEM	place.LOC	like that	EXIS	QUOT	say.PRS

Even now, that place is still like that, they say.

25 < *atiṉre* (intervocalic /t/ > /y/)
26 < *mukaḷil*

paṭiɲɲāṟattē	*kāṭṭ-arv-atiṉṟe*	*puṟav' iṣṭa-nna*	*stalam*	*uṇṭ'*	*atə*
west.LOC.EMP	forest-edge-DEM.GEN	behind pleasing-AD	place	EXIS	DEM

That's the nice place behind the western edge of the forest.

ɲaŋŋaḷə	*kaḷikkāṉ*	*pokunna*	*samayattə*
we.EXC	play.INF	go.PRS.PRT	time.LOC

When we were going to play there,

aviṭe	*ayiṉṟ'*	*aṭutt-ettum-baẓett-ikk-um*[27]
there	DEM.GEN	near-reach-when-ADV-CNJ

Whenever we got close to that [place] there,

maṟṟuḷḷat'	*ellām*	*piḷḷēr*	*ellārum*	*paṟayum*
other	all	kids	all	say.hab

all the other kids used to say,

aviṭe	*pōvalla*	*pōlla*	*cattu-pōvum*
there	go.NEG	go.NEG	die.NFIN-NVOL.FUT

Don't go there, don't go! You will die at once!

atu-koṇṭə	*ippōẓum*	*ōrmmay*	*uṇṭə*
DEM.INST	now.CNJ	memory	EXIS

Therefore, I still remember it even now.

[C5 00:22–01:59]
https://ia601508.us.archive.org/32/items/FMExx6/FM_exx_7.wav

The story of the failed attempt to rebuild the Third Temple in Parur is suggestive of the stereotype associated with the Jews of Parur as proud and haughty; the Parurites were so rich and affluent in the past that they could afford rebuilding the Jewish temple in their own town. Moreover, their community at the time still retained the Jewish priesthood elite (Kohens and Levites), the loss of whom deprived all Kerala Jews of this prestigious Jewish descent.

Conclusion

The documentation of Jewish Malayalam provides a database for linguistic "fossils" that complement the segmented picture we have of the history of the community during the first half of the second millennium CE. The description and analysis of

27 < *aṭutt-ēttum-bōẓett-ēkk-um*

the database created in the project show that documentary linguistics can be crucial for historical linguistics in particular and for a more comprehensive picture of the history of minority and subaltern communities in general. Additionally, the recorded database guided by a multipurpose approach contains previously untold oral histories that represent communal identities that may differ from often biased notions about such marginal communities. In the case of Kerala Jews, the communal identities that emerge of the untold stories challenge the conventional perception among historians and "outsiders" who differentiated between "White Jews" and "Black Jews" (e.g. Segal 1983), regardless of the local identities sustained by Malayalam-speaking Jews even today.

Language documentation projects usually aim at the preservation of endangered languages. Malayalam is far from being an endangered language, but the dialects typical of religious or communal minorities are often subject to gradually falling out of use due to the rapid changes in the way of life, state education and mass media and, in the case of Kerala Jews, even migration and detachment from the native land of their religiolect. The Jewish Malayalam documentation project exemplifies the contribution that studying a religiolect can have to the study of the history and culture of a minority community. Hopefully, the field of Dravidian linguistics will be enriched by similar language documentation projects among communities at the margins of history and cultural studies on the region.

List of Abbreviations

1=first person; 2=second person; 3=third person; ACC=accusative; ADV=adverb; CAUS=causative; CNJ=conjunctive; COMP=completive; COP=copula; DAT=dative; DEIC=deictic; DEM=demonstrative; DIR=directive; DSD=desiderative; EMP=emphatic; EXC=exclusive; EXIS=existential; F=feminine; FUT=future; GEN=genitive; [H]=Hebrew; HAB=habitual; INC=inclusive; INF=infinitive; INST=instrumental; LOC=locative; M=masculine; MOD=modal; NEG=negation; NFIN=non-finite; NMLZ=nominalizer; NVOL=non-volitional; PL=plural; PRF=perfect; PRS=present; PRT=participle; PST=past; Q=question; QUOT=quotative; SG=singular

References

Asher, Roland E. 2011. Malayalam. Encyclopedia of Arabic Language and Linguistics. Managing Editors Online Edition: E Lutz and R. de Jong (eds.). Brill Online. http://referenceworks.brillonline.com/entries/encyclopedia-of-arabic-language-and-linguistics/malayalam-EALL_COM_vol3_0202 [26.10.2016]

Asher, Roland E., and T. C. Kumari 1997. *Malayalam: A Descriptive Grammar*. London: Routledge.

Austin, Peter 2014. Language Documentation in the 21st Century. *JournaLIPP* 3: 57–71.

— 2015. Language Documentation 20 Years on. In *Endangered Languages Across the Planet: Issues of Ecology, Policy and Documentation*. M. Pütz and L. Filipovic (eds.): 147–170. Amsterdam: Benjamins.

Ayyar, L. Vishwanatha Ramaswamy 1993. *Evolution of Malayalam Morphology*. Trissur: Kerala Sahitya Akademi.

Bar-Asher, Moshe 2002. Aspects of the Study of Jewish Languages and Literatures. *Pe'amim* 93: 77–83. [Hebrew]

Bunis, David M. 2015. Judezmo (Ladino). In *Handbook of Jewish Languages*. A. Rubin and L. Kahn (eds.): 365–450. Leiden: Brill.

Chiriyankandath, James 2008. Nationalism, Religion and Community: A.B. Salem, the Politics of Identity and the Disappearance of Cochin Jewry", *Journal of Global History* 3(1): 21–42.

Fabricius, Johann Philipp 1972. *Tamil and English Dictionary*, (4th ed.). Tranquebar: Evangelical Lutheran Mission Publication House. http://dsal.uchicago.edu/dictionaries/fabricius/

Fischel, Walter Joseph 1967. The Exploration of the Jewish Antiquities of Cochin on the Malabar Coast. *Journal of the American Oriental Society* 87(3): 230–248.

Forsström, Jarmo 1997. The Pronunciation Tradition of Biblical Hebrew among the Jews of Cochin: A Preliminary Survey. *Studia Orientalia* 82: 111–128.

Freeman, Rich 1998. Rubies and Coral: The Lapidary Crafting of Language in Kerala. *The Journal of Asian Studies* 57(1): 38–65.

Gamliel, Ophira 2009. Jewish Malayalam. *International Journal of Dravidian Linguistics* 38(1): 147–175.

— 2013a. Judeo-Malayalam, Hebrew Component in. In *Encyclopedia of Hebrew Language and Linguistics, Vol. 2*. G. Khan (ed.): 410–413. Leiden: Brill.

— 2013b. The Neglected History of Kerala Jews. *Zmanim – A Historical Quarterly* 122: 16–29. [Hebrew]

— 2014. Voices Yet to Be Heard: On Listening to the Last Speakers of Jewish Malayalam. *Journal of Jewish Languages* 1:1:1: 135–167.

— 2015. Jewish Malayalam. In *Handbook of Jewish Languages*, A. Rubin and L. Kahn (eds.): 503–516. Leiden: Brill.

Gippert, Jost, Nikolaus P. Himmelmann, and Ulrike Mosel (eds.) 2006. *Essentials of Language Documentation*. Berlin: De Gruyter.

Goitein, ShlomoDov, and Mordechai Akiva Friedman 2008. *India Traders of the Middle Ages: Documents from the Cairo Geniza*. Leiden: Brill.

Gundert, Hermann 1995 [1872]. *Guṇṭarṭ Nighaṇṭu*. Kottayam: DC Books.

Kahn, Lilly 2015. Yiddish. In *Handbook of Jewish Languages*. A. Rubin and L. Kahn (eds.): 641–747. Leiden: Brill.

Krishnamurti, Bhadriraju 2003. *The Dravidian Languages*. Cambridge: Cambridge University Press.

Hary, Benjamin 2009. *Translating Religion: Linguistic Analysis of Judeo-Arabic Sacred Texts from Egypt*. Leiden: Brill.

Hary, Benjamin, and Martin J. Wein 2013. Religiolinguistics: On Jewish-, Christian- and Muslim-defined Languages. *IJSL* 220: 85–108.

Himmelmann, Nikolaus P. 1998. Documentary and Descriptive Linguistics. *Linguistics* 36: 161–195.

Johnson, Barbara C. 1975. *Shingli or the Jews of Cranganore in the Traditions of the Cochin Jews of India*. Massachusetts (unpublished M.A. thesis).

— 1983. Cranganore, Joseph Rabban, and Cheraman Perumal: On the Theme of the Origin of Cochin Jews according to their Folk Literature. *Peamim* 13: 71–83. [Hebrew]

— 1994. Cochin Jews, and Kaifeng Jews: Reflections on Caste, Surname, 'Community' and Conversion. *Peamim* 60: 32–48. [Hebrew]

— 2002. 'They Carry Their Notebooks with Them': Women's Vernacular Jewish Songs from Cochin, South India. *Pe'amim* 82: 64–80 [Hebrew].

Khan, Geoffrey 2015. Judeo-Arabic. In *Handbook of Jewish Languages*. A. Rubin and L. Kahn (eds.): 22–63. Leiden: Brill.

Lambourn, Elizabeth 2014. Borrowed Words in an Ocean of Objects: Geniza Sources and New Cultural Histories of the Indian Ocean. In *Irreverent History: Essays for M.G.S.Narayanan*. K. Veluthat and D. Davis Jr. (eds.): 363–414. New Delhi: Primus Books.

Mandelbaum, David G. 1939. The Jewish Way of Life in Cochin. *Jewish Social Studies* 1(4): 423–460.

Messineo, Cristina 2008. Fieldwork and Documentation of Speech Genres in Indigenous Communities of Gran Chaco: Theoretical and Methodological Issues. *Language Documentation and Conservation* 2(2): 278–279.

Narayanan, Muttayil Govindamenon Sankara 1972. *Cultural Symbiosis in Kerala*. Trivandrum: Kerala Historical Society.

Pillai, Shreekantheswaram G. Padmanabha 2006 [1921]. *Śabdatārāvali*. Kottayam: National Book Stall.

Rabin, Chaim 1981. What Constitutes a Jewish Language? *International Journal of the Sociology of Language* 30: 19–30.

Rubin, Aaron, and Lily Kahn 2015. *Handbook of Jewish Languages*. Leiden: Brill.

Segal, Judah Benzion 1983. White and Black Jews at Cochin, the Story of a Controversy, *Journal of the Royal Asiatic Society of Great Britain and Ireland* 2: 228–52.

Sekhar, A.C. 1951. Evolution of Malayalam, *Bulletin of the Deccan College Research Institute* XII, 1–2: 1–216.

Subramoniam, Vadassery Iyemperumal (ed.) 2006. *Dialect Map of Malayalam: Ezhava-Tiyyar; Dialect Map of Malayalam: Nayar*. Trivandrum: International School of Dravidian Linguistics.

Varier, Raghava M.R., and Kesavan Veluthat 2013. *Tarisāppaḷḷippaṭṭayam*. Kottayam: National Book Stall. [Malayalam]

Walerstein, Shoshana Marcia 1987. *Public Rituals Among the Jews from Cochin, India, in Israel: Expressions of Ethnic Identity*, Unpublished Ph.D. Dissertation, California.

Wexler, Paul 1981. Jewish Interlinguistics: Facts and Conceptual Framework. *Language* 57 (1): 99–149.

Zacharia, Scaria, and Ophira Gamliel (eds. and trs.) 2005. *Kārkuḻali – Yefefiah – Gorgeous! Jewish Women's Songs in Malayalam with Hebrew Translations*. Jerusalem: Ben Zvi Institute. (in Hebrew and Malayalam)

5 OWLS, SASQUATCH AND TSUN' DYE: UNCOVERING INDIGENOUS ENGLISHES THROUGH ORAL STORYTELLING

Sonya Kinsey

Introduction

As part of a large scale process of language contact and change, one that has been underway in North America since the 15th century, many Aboriginal people[1] in Canada have come to speak English, either mono- or bilingually. This has resulted in a plethora of mostly unstudied varieties, or dialects[2], which I refer to here as First Nations English. These are "shaped by the cultural patterns of communication, by phenomena associated by languages in contact, and by the linguistic features of Indigenous languages" (Ball and Berndhardt 2008: 573). Research into these varieties, their features, origins and setting in society has only barely begun in Canada, partially due to the lack of access and overall difficulty of conducting research in First Nations communities. This difficulty is the result of several circumstances. One major problem is that the dialects are focused on reserves, which are often in remote and isolated areas. Aboriginal peoples have responded to the intrusion of colonialism and the ever-advancing Northern frontier by retreating further and further away (Brody 1981), and many reserves are even now located away from major population centres and suffer from a lack of infrastructure that makes travel to and from them difficult. Furthermore, the status of the history of research on First Nations communities and cultures, as well as the cultural gap between First Nations peoples and the researchers, who typically come from an Anglo-European cultural background, have compounded the difficulty. The history of work in anthropology and linguistics with First Nations in Canada is often fraught with dangers and pitfalls created by a background of colonialist and racist attitudes. Many researchers, even those who were genuinely working for the benefit of their informants, still fell prey to the condescending attitudes of their time.

The history of anthropology and linguistics in this context is one of unfortunate and blatant intrusiveness into other people's lives. Although not every anthropologist and linguist who has worked with First Nations (or other communities) has done

1 Aboriginal is a term encompassing Inuit, First Nations and Métis groups in Canada. First Nations in itself refers to many culturally and linguistically distinct bands, each with their own history.

2 I will use both terms interchangeably here. Some researchers prefer the term "variety", feeling that "dialect" still carries negative connotation. However, I feel that it is important to recognize the validity of the term, along with the validity of the linguistic groupings it refers to.

so solely for personal benefit, research in First Nations communities has very often suffered from the taint of Eurocentrism, as researchers often adopted a position of superior intellectual privilege (Zinga et al. 2009) and worked from the assumption of European culture as the default system (Sterzuk 2011). The fundamental problem was the conducting of research *on*, rather than *with* Aboriginal communities (Zinga et al. 2009). Many Aboriginal communities remain skeptical of researchers and their claims of mutual benefit.

A schism exists between the cultural perceptions of First Nations members and those researchers who have been raised and trained in the norms of Anglo-European cultural standards. The latter values objectivity, empirical evidence and the success of the individual. Although there are, of course, variations from nation to nation and beyond, an overall attitude of industrial production, the desire for progress and finding value in material items, and personal ownership can be seen. While First Nations cultures in Canada are by no means monolithic, and vary considerably across North America, there is overall a series of vital differences between First Nations and white settler cultures. Many First Nations cultures value self reliance, but also see a person as an intrinsic member of the group, and often reach decisions by group consensus (Brody 1981). Indigenous worldviews are increasingly recognized as legitimate knowledge systems by academic institutions (Battiste and Henderson 2009). This growing recognition extends to First Nations epistemology and cultural networks, including oral history.

Authenticity in Fieldwork

I conducted six weeks of fieldwork in Northern British Columbia, studying the history and use of Witsuwit'en English, one of many varieties of FNEs in Canada. The Witsuwit'en[3] have lived in the region now called the Bulkley Valley for over 5500 years (Morin 2011). Their traditional territories straddle two intangible borders. The first is the linguistic border between Dene-Athabaskan languages spoken across the Prairies and a plethora of languages in Western and coastal British Columbia (Morin 2011). The second is the cultural boundary that also helps distinguish the Aboriginal groups on coastal B.C. and the Prairies. The Witsuwit'en originally migrated into the region and adopted many customs from the nearby Gitxsan people. This included survival methods, as well as the northwest coast feast system and many corresponding linguistic items (Hargus 2007). The Witsuwit'en adopted the clan and feast system of the Gitxsan and altered it to suit to their needs (Morin 2011). Just under 3000 Witsuwit'en Band members live throughout the Bulkley Valley, and Moricetown is the largest of

3 The English orthography of this word varies from source to source. I follow the orthography of Sharon Hargus, who has studied Witsuwit'en grammar and phonology extensively and is the leading researcher on the topic.

the six reserves, with around 2000 registered Band members.[4] Less than 140 fluent Witsuwit'en speakers are left in these communities, with under a hundred people having some understanding or are learning (First Peoples' Heritage Language and Culture Council 2016). No children have been able to learn their ancestral language. The entire community has shifted to English over the last three generations.

When preparing for my field work within Moricetown in 2014, I was struck by the contrast between the typical setup of sociolinguistic fieldwork (see below) and the modes of cultural interaction described in publications concerning Aboriginal culture and communication in Canada. The standard format of a Labovian style sociolinguistic interview is very problematic when it comes to working in First Nations communities and is not only likely to be inappropriate, but even detrimental to the interview process and results. A second consideration of mine, one that is more widely problematic in sociolinguistics, was the issue of *authenticity*. The goal of any linguistic interview is to record speech acts that can be considered "real" and "authentic", and can therefore be used for linguistic analysis and to assess various hypotheses about the speaker and the speech community. The veracity of our publications relies heavily on the idea that linguists and their methods can access something that can be considered authentic, real speech. And yet it is acknowledged that truly uncensored, honest speech is not always obtainable, especially when one conducts one's research in an ethical manner (Bucholtz 2003). This leads to the observer's paradox (Labov 1972), an inherent problem created when the researcher needs to be present to observe authentic speech, but through their presence, informants become aware of being observed and alter their speech in both subtle and dramatic ways. So what is meant by the term "authentic", and how can we create situations where informants can give us material that may be considered authentic?

The concept of authenticity "underwrites nearly every aspect of sociolinguistics" (Bucholtz 2003: 398). The idea of *real language* and language use remains a central concept and stands in contrast to the idealism of Chomskyan linguistics (Bucholtz 2003). Sociolinguistics can only claim empirical validity when the research is based on data collected in "authentic contexts by authentic speakers" (Bucholtz 2003). For some researchers, the concept of authenticity is a "conceptual error" that should be set aside, a "pseudo-concept" and even unattainable or illusionary (Coupland 2014). Anthropology has also had its share of struggles over authenticity. Although a single chapter is far too short to deal with the concept in its entirety, there are some things that can be discussed briefly. Certainly, we should avoid ideas of finding one's true self or true data amongst unconquered natives (Theodossopoulos 2013). Western anthropology has already made the mistake of connecting the authentic to the exotic and the

4 More information about the Witsuwit'en can be found on the community's webpage, The Office of the Wet'suwet'en. For information on their history and culture, I rely on their own text book, Niwhts'ide'ni Hibi'it'en: The Ways of Our Ancestors Witsuwit'en History & Culture Throughout the Millennia.

Other (Theodossopoulos 2013). This has a doubly negative effect of de-authenticating Western society and any community that has been influenced by it, further devaluing any people whose culture has been forcibly eliminated or altered by colonialism. By this definition, only cultures uncontaminated by modernity can be authentic (Theodossopoulos 2013). Salvage linguistics carries with it the unfortunate viewpoint that as speakers move away from their ancestral languages or lifestyles, they are shifting away from an authentic past (Bucholtz 2003), and somehow losing authenticity and veracity in the process. Salvage linguistics was concerned with recording as much language as possible from dying languages, a belated reaction to the attempted assimilation of Aboriginal peoples into colonial society (Sterzuk 2011; Villagas 2009), and an attempt to preserve knowledge in the wake of attacks on Indigenous realms of knowledge and traditions (Villagas 2009). Much of this anthropological work was also carried out during or after massive epidemics that severely reduced First Nations populations, when it was assumed First Nations people had no future beyond assimilation and extinction. Material was collected for preservation and study, rather than transmission to the next generation. A culture whose bubble has been popped by Western European contact can never be the same, and salvage anthropologists can only hope to pick up a few remaining pieces for preservation. From this viewpoint, authenticity is equated with purity, isolation and stagnation. A culture's value can only be found in its past life, and the anthropologist's task is to search for the genuine article amidst the junk heap of the modern world. Modern anthropology and linguistics must learn to discard these concepts and begin working with First Nations people in the context of the present and future possibilities.

When we shift paradigms and begin to view authenticity as something that people can claim (Eckert 2014) and perform in order to claim, rather than a state of possession of qualities that define an enduring category (Eckert 2014), we can recognize authenticity as plastic and malleable. Authenticity is not a natural given quality; it is a means by which communities shape their identities in an active fashion (Coulmas 2014). Authenticity is something enacted daily in speech acts performed in social settings. Under this new paradigm, research methodology needs to be altered to include First Nations participants as research partners, and in ways that "respect the communities' culture and goals" (Ball and Berndhardt 2008: 582). Decolonizing research means giving up the title of "expert" and recognizing that "important knowledge and perspectives are held by the people whose behaviour the university-based researcher wishes to understand" (ibid.). The comfort and security of the participant should also be taken into account. We must take "the well-being of the people participating in the research" (ibid.) to heart. The interviewer must be involved in the process, not removed. The idea that "face-to-face contacts need to be made to enable trusting relationships and reciprocal learning about language, culture, knowledge systems, and practices" (Ball and Berndhardt 2008) flies against the concepts of Western scholarly practice, but it is nonetheless necessary for research in linguistics and anthropology to move forward. We should consider the applications of research results, and how we turn can aid the community who has helped us. Data should be shared in a way that is relevant and understandable to the community. In addition to possible indirect or altruistic outcomes, the research results should offer direct benefits to the participants (ibid.). It is no longer enough to research for the mere sake of research. It is also important to identify First Nations community members' perspectives on their English dialect (ibid.).

Storywork and Fieldwork

The primary focus of my interviews was to record oral responses from participants and to give them as much choice as possible in deciding what to tell me. It was emphasized that there were no right or wrong answers, but that participants were free to tell any stories they knew, or give opinions on current events. The authentic narrative thus encompasses the lives of the present, not only the distant and mythological past. Speakers, regardless of their fluency in Witsuwit'en, were given an opportunity to tell me about their lives. Indeed, in regards to investigating Witsuwit'en English, fluency in the ancestral language is no longer the sole index of authenticity. Rather than falling into salvage linguistics and conducting interviews that attempt to save history, reconstructing a time before European contact (Bucholtz 2003), my interviews attempted to acknowledge the legitimacy of both the past and the present.

Many of the assumptions Anglo-Europeans make about speaker interaction ring false in situations dominated by speakers with First Nations backgrounds. The structure of Labovian interviews, with their reading lists and text samples, may be inappropriate for First Nations people. The initial emphasis on reading from a word list may cause difficulty, as many First Nations speakers, especially the elderly, are not literate, or have had very negative experiences in the Canadian school system (Leap 1993). Not only do First Nations Peoples speak a distinct variety of English with unique phonological and syntactic properties, they also have different expectations of social situations and of how a group of speakers will interact with and respond to each other (Leap 1993). One of the primary differences is that First Nations cultures are primarily oral, not literary, cultures. While the medium of print and the ability to read are highly valued in Anglo-American cultures (Coulmas 2014), First Nations cultures remain oriented on the transmission of culture via storytelling and face-to-face communication. The supremacy of the oral word in First Nations communities should not be underestimated, along with accompanying value on face-to-face communication. While written languages can help demarcate boundaries of nationalism (Coulmas 2014), oral languages without written standards remain fluid and dynamic.

Atleo describes how Elders do storywork at the level of principle so that people could imagine themselves in and through the story (Atloe and Fitznor 2010). Storywork—the combination of the story, the storyteller and the listener (Friesen 2009), is also referenced in helping to integrate Indigenous knowledge into Anglo-European education curriculums. Oral story-telling may also be a source of knowledge to scientists. In fact, during the time I was doing my fieldwork in British Columbia, a Parks Canada expedition located the wreck of the HMS Erebus, one of the two ships that attempted to find the Northwest Passage under the leadership of Sir John Franklin. Inuit oral history was instrumental in locating the Erebus (News 2014). Indigenous knowledge has survived colonialism and is increasingly being valued by both Aboriginal people and researchers who are coming from the starting point of an Anglo-European knowledge system (Battiste and Henderson 2009). Iwama's paper on Two-Eyed Seeing notes how researchers reproduce the orality of Elders' narratives, and discusses the usage of puppets in oral story telling to transmit legends and initiate healing in Mik'maq legends (Iwana et al. 2009). Oral histories have played an important role in the healing process for individuals and communities who have suffered through residential schools (Atloe and Fitznor 2010). It has been noted, for instance, that Cree authors' writings often favour the realization of their oral dialect over the rules of written Standard Canadian (Gingell 2010).

While heritage languages and language contact are often considered to be the primary influence on First Nations Englishes (Ball and Berndhardt 2008; Leap 1993), the emphasis on oral information over written sources may also have implications for morpho-syntax. In a study conducted by Ball and Berndhardt on First Nations English speakers, one participant reported that First Nations children in her community would often string together phrases without the use of conjunctions as expected in standard English, and instead used "gestures and vocal emphasis to highlight new information" (Ball and Berndhardt 2008). Storytelling may also be nonlinear and not follow the conventions of Western story-telling (Leap 1993). In Ute storytelling, for example, a nonlinear, non-chronological style of topic development is used, and connections are implied, but not explicit, requiring the listener to make the mental connections themselves (Leap 1993). For the Dene in Alaska, "the best telling of a story is the briefest" (Ball and Berndhardt 2008: 582) and this storytelling works on the assumption of shared community knowledge (Ball and Berndhardt 2008). Many cultures emphasize not the accuracy or detail of the information relayed in the story, but the way that the story is told (Leap 1993).

Witsuwit'en Oral History

Stories are essential to Witsuwit'en culture. *Cin k'ikh*, the Witsuwit'en oral history, "reflects our view that the world is as one, with no divisions between the spirit, animal and human worlds" (Morin 2011). *Cin k'ikh* not only perform the function of transmitting traditions and morals, they are integral to Witsuwit'en society, and were previously acted out at feasts. Masks and costumes were used to make *cin k'ikh* come alive before the community. They were an integral part of the *balhats*, the great feasts where individuals took chief names and acted out the stories pertaining to clan crests, or *niwhnitsiy* (Morin 2011). Story telling is still an important part of preparing to take a chief name and serves as a method of indirect instruction to transmit norms of social behavior and explain the system of reciprocity that is so integral to the societies that use the feast system.

Many stories also reference specific locations in the region, and help to directly tie the people to the unchanging land of the *yin tah*, or territories (Morin 2011). Many of these stories also embody Traditional Ecological Knowledge. Other *cin k'ikh* demonstrate the value of community responsibility, generosity, and the importance of acknowledging the sacrifice of animal lives for human benefit. *C'idede* are teaching stories that focus on the relationships between animals and people and the importance of following through with respect and traditions to prevent disasters (Morin 2011). For instance, the story of the "The Orphan Boy Who Became A Culture Hero" (Jenness 1934) demonstrates the importance of these stories, when a young boy learns the secret of a noblewoman who hunts porcupines, and is successful because he has absorbed knowledge from his grandmother: "She taught him by means of folktales all the ancient lore: to be honest, to observe what was permitted and what was prohibited, and to train himself in all necessary pursuits."

The Stories

The interview began with me explaining my research project and obtaining oral consent to continue. I then asked a series of questions about the region and the town, and linguistic awareness ("Do you think people in Moricetown speak differently than people in Smithers?") as a warm up, which sometimes led to further comments. After this first part, my role shifted to that of a listener. Using the framework of storywork, my strategy was to take the role of the learner: "Tell me a story about your people". Acknowledging my status as an outsider and a learner put me in a more suitable position to ask questions about Witsuwit'en customs. It also gave the participants the opportunity to speak for as long as they wanted, on any topic they wanted. They were not obligated to provide right/wrong answers. By taking this viewpoint, I was able to record long, unbroken sections of spoken text, detailing cultural events such as feasts, ghost stories and spirit sightings. These stories offer relatively unbroken narratives of events held to be true, occurring at various times in the past, concerning individuals, both living and dead. The following stories not only contain important cultural information; they demonstrate the features of Witsuwit'en English in use. Although some individuals did reduce the "opacity" of their dialect for my benefit, and admitted as much, during my fieldwork I was able to attend several community events, and the dialect I heard spoken around me is adequately reflected in the recorded data. It was more difficult to decide how to transcribe select portions of the recordings. A great deal of paralinguistic information, such as gestures, was lost in the recording process, as I was only making audio, not visual recordings. In the end, it may prove impossible to create transcriptions that convey the authenticity of the interview, so removed are they from the reality of their performance as acts of authenticity.

The dialogue has been transcribed verbatim, without any editing for "correctness" a set forth in any written standard for of English. Discourse markers such as *um* and *uh* have been included, along with pauses, indicated by commas. Conventional orthography is maintained, with deleted consonants being marked in curved brackets and substituted phonemes shown in in straight brackets, to maintain textual coherency, while additional phonetic transcriptions will be supplied in text as they are discussed. Shifts in clause structure are marked with commas, and clauses that change topic are separated with a full stop for ease of reading. The choice of where to create full stops is dependent on the pauses in the interviews and whether or not they are continuing from a previous topic. As the transcriber, I try to strike a balance between ease of reading and relaying how the story was told, including real-time amendments from the speaker. Finally, names have been changed to protect the identity of the informants. All the participants below are female, Cora and Laura are Elders.

The following texts describe, like many First Nations stories, interactions between human and animals. First there an encounter with a family of sasquatches, then a talking owl, then *tsun' dye*, or otter spirits, and finally the story of a woman who became a frog. Only the last story involving the frog takes place in the time beyond living memory.

> **Sally:** He took, he like(d) being the father of Moricetown. When he buried somebody he said that in short, he said when he buried somebody they go up there and they notice(d) the bodies were missing, the one that they just buried up in the graveyard there, know what they were missing so what he did, and figured the only way they could find out who was doing it was they buried him, made it so that he could breathe and everything in the box, he took some, like bread crumbs or whatever, but a trail to make sure he could find his way back, sure enough they said that thing dug him out and started draggin(g) him up the mountain here. They said there's a cave up here. Father said he notice(d) that he was being drag by something in the bushes so he'd leave little bread crumbs so if he got away he would know which way to come back so when he got there he notice(d) that there was a family of them, woman little one.

> **Cora:** No no, it's a(n) Indian doctor and then he heard that and then a same area then a owl come to him and uh talk to him in Witsuwit'en. /D/ee owl jump up on the tree but our tradition says you cannot answer back the owl. A Fort Saint James lady told me the same thing, its their tradition too. You

can't talk back to the owl and keep talking, the owl will keep going going going and if you stop the owl beat you, you gonna die, that's why you don't answer the owl no matter where you are. That's what they told us when we were kids. I thought it was fun, we were copying the owl here after that they tol(d) us not to do that answer it back, um, that owl jump(ed) on the tree and dad was under the tree, he was spending the night there fire going col(d) and uh de owl tol(d) him (Witsuwit'en) pass(ed) away back home and then the owl said you got one martin in your trap ahead and dad said sure enough in the morning he was heading out on the trail, (h)ees first trap had martin in it an um dad had to stop this owl from talking, he said to him (speaks in Witsuwit'en) fly away or I'll shoot you. That's in Witsuwit'en that that owl he listen(ed) he flew away cause dad didn't wanna talk back anymore and it did fly away. This is true story of the owl speaking Witsuwit'en to dad telling him someone died back home, and when he got home it was true, the owl was messenger delivered the news to dad while he's out in the bush.

Anna: Well they used to talk about tsun'dyes how they can turn into humans or they can turn into anything what they wanna be, an(d) I remember that as a kid there was me my sister, my brother an(d) a couple of our cousins. We used to run across the bridge over there by the canyon an(d) we used to go down to this house where they'd uh always give us snacks and candies an it was Molly's place that's when she used to be with that Arnold guy. She used to lived (d)own there an I remember as a kid we were makin(g) it home too late, it was dark we got stuck in the middle of the bridge an(d) there's four tsun' dyes. We were all huddled together an(d) I was the oldest one there so I was tryna protect them an(d) they wouldn't let us off the bridge and that was the scariest time, after that we quit going across to the to that house after that. It it was like ol(d) people standing one each corner and /d/ey, /d/ey looked scary to, no no they blocked us on the bridge on the middle of the bridge. No they're jus(t) standing there looking at us and we're all too scared to move. We stood there for like uh maybe an hour or two hours and then we just all huddle(d) together an we're all cryin(g) an(d) finally I looked up an(d) I said they're gone they're gone let's go round so we started running we started running.

Laura: They told me lotta stories, now that I'm getting older I'm forgettin(g). There was a story long time ago I guess you gotta all. Ever tell you did anybody tell you that there were the a young girl turn(ed) into a frog an(d) it happen(ed) right in Moricetown eh? Girl disappeared and year uh the granddaughter she turn(ed) into a frog, a, yeah and they turn(ed) into frog and they use to live in smokehouse. They kick(ed) kicked that frog out, that frog keep coming back they didn't know it was their daughter that vanished turn into frog hmm gee I forgot the rest mhm and /d/ere's another thing that you cannot uh when you alone in the bush you never think of your anybody like a boyfriend that uh what they call it, how do you say tsun' dye in Engli/s/, otter otter that can turn into into anything like could be like your boyfriend standing there that's why they gotta ha/b/e a whip, they always see one down the canyon, yeah sounds like a uh yeah one time uh me and mum were in the bush trapping settin(g) trap and /d/en we heard like a lady cryin(g) somewhere, I said how could somebody got los(t) here and um said that might be the uh otter that turns into tryin(g) to make you go towards them I think.

Analysis

In the above transcriptions, the variation in syntax and morphology that distinguishes Witsuwit'en English from other more standardized English varieties can clearly be seen. In these passages, we can observe how the features of Witsuwit'en English play out systemically. The phonology of this English variety allows more variation than standard Canadian English. Consonant clusters are reduced in coda sequences. In the case of Paula's story, we see the deletion of [d] in consonant clusters [ld]. In all texts, we find that the velar nasal [ŋ], especially, is changed into alveolar nasal [n]. The last is a feature frequently found in non-standard English varieties (Kortmann and Lunkenheimer 2013) and in casual speech world-wide consonant cluster reduction was noted by Leap to be present in every variety of Native American and Canadian English he studied (1993). In Laura's interview, voiced fricatives become plosives, as in [deɪ] for *they*, the [v] in *have*, while the voiceless fricative [ŋ] becomes the voiceless sibilant [s]. Both the onset and the coda consonant in the syllable may be affected. Some of this may be the result of native Witsuwit'en phonology; for instance, the voiced and voiced and unvoiced interdental fricative are not in the phonological system, but [d] and [t] are (Hargus 2007).

In all stories, the verbal phrase is subject to a great deal of alteration. Past tense verbs frequently lose the morphological ending *-ed* and become simple present. Perfective *be* and *have* are deleted and past preterite verb forms may be replaced by their present tense forms. In fact, the whole structure of the verb clause could be described as flexible, allowing for the variation on the clause structure, if the coherency of the story remains intact. Since it was established at the outset of the interviews that these events occurred in the past, the story-teller is free to use present tense interchangeably throughout the story. These passages also show another pattern of deletion often found in First Nations Englishes. Genee and Stiger also report uninflected main verb and participles in their review of Blackfoot English, as well as omission of "to be" (2010). Main nouns and pronouns may be deleted. Both the definite and indefinite article can be subject to deletion, and speakers may not repair this "break" in structure before moving ahead in the story. Although this is, to a degree, a characteristic of spoken speech, work on varieties of Native American Englishes has shown that pronoun deletion is systemic and often related to functions in the Ancestral language grammar (Penfield-Jasper 1977; Leap 1993). The same feature has been observed in Blackfoot English (Genee and Stigter 2010) and is surmised to be the result of unneeded parts of speech are being deleted for the sake of economy. In Witsuwit'en, the personal pronoun is used only for focus and emphasis since first and second person subjects, objects and possessors are obligatory marked on verbs and nouns (Hargus 2007). The result here seems to be the deletion of unnecessary personal pronouns in English.

Conclusion

In the thirty hours of recorded interviews, there exists more information than a single chapter can discuss, but the reader can see from these short transcriptions how much information is available, for the researcher who is willing to take a deeper look at these stories and the idea of authenticity. The focus on storywork allowed me to record long sections of uninterrupted speech. Participants could tell whatever stories they were comfortable with, and to take their time with a natural story structure. The topics ranged from stories about people's lives and their personal histories, how they had come to speak English, the dramatic range of changes they had witnessed in their community, along with descriptions of how their parents and grandparents had lived, supernatural stories both old and new, and current news and concerns in the community. There was no pressure to be "correct" and follow a linear Anglo-European style narrative. I recorded many stories about peoples lives and personal experiences, stories often emphasized as being true. The story-tellers themselves claimed authenticity, along with cultural ownership of these passages. If I am told a "true" story, then I as the researcher should accept that the way it was told to me was also authentic. This is regardless of the externally motivated changes on their culture that people have experienced. It makes no difference whether the story was told in English or Witsuwit'en. These speakers are not inauthentic if they tell me a story in English, and indeed, this concept is integral to my study of English varieties. If the speaker expresses themselves and their personal experiences as authentic, and the story is offered to me as an authentic experience, then I as the researcher should work to mediate that authenticity and transmit a sense of that into my analysis.

Linguistics and anthropologists often work with oral texts, which are intangible forms of knowledge and culture. That very intangibility means that they cannot be judged and weighed as one would a Ming vase, or a Haida cedar mask. They cannot be passed from story teller to story-teller unchanged. They are always, in a sense, imbued in a specific context of speaker and listener. Stories cannot exist without the situation of *storytelling*. Salvage linguistics, which recorded the stories without an expectation of further transmission within the community, assumed the stories would be transmitted via recording or transcription, captured and forever replayed, unchanging in form. We should remember as researchers that this is not truly the way oral storytelling works. It is meant to be flexible and adaptive, just as the storytellers and their cultures are. Researchers must themselves learn to adapt to and accept this instability.

We can see how themes of transformation are at play in these tales. Animals like the *tsun' dye* take on human shape, while a girl takes the shape of a frog. But we can also observe the shift in the interaction between man and nature. We see how animals can speak with and even have terrible power over humans. In the story in which the French priest, Father Morice, appears, nature is tricked, driven back and killed. A human has played tricks on nature, and not simply won the game, but also killed the animals. So what can we as researchers take away from these observations? Perhaps it can be said that here, English is also being transformed and played with, moving back and forth between two worlds. Will we as researchers be willing to accept that and play the transformation game? Are we willing to accept that the "other" can have power over us? Or do we hide and lay trails to trap authenticity, to grasp and hold it, and make it concrete? Perhaps such metaphors become too easily tangled, for there are many interpretations of a story. But we should realize authenticity is not a seal of approval to be placed on objects we deem worthy. Authenticity is a process, created and shared by a people in common as they respond to a changing world. It is something that can be shared between speaker and listener, and can transform as needed. To be sure, accepting this process means accepting a constant state of tension in our research methodology, and the realization that we can never be too sure of our power and control over the interview process. But in this tension, there lies the possibility for real connections and real change.

References

Atloe, Marlene R., and Laura Fitznor 2010. Aboriginal Educators Discuss Recognizing, Reclaiming, and Revitalizing Their Multi-Competences in Heritage/English-Language Use. *Canadian Journal of Native Education*: 13–34.

Ball, Jessica, and May B. Berndhardt 2008. First Nations English Dialects in Canada: Implications for speech-language pathology. *Clinical Linguistics and Phonetics*: 570–588.

Battiste, Marie, and James Y. Henderson 2009. Naturalizing Indigenous Knowledge in Eurocentric Education. *Canadian Journal of Native Education:* 5–17.

Brody, Hugh 1981. *Maps and Dreams.* Vancouver: Douglas & McIntyre Ltd.

Bucholtz, Mary 2003. Sociolinguistic Nostalgia and the Authentication of Identity. *Journal of Sociolinguistics:* 398–416.

Coulmas, Florian 2014. Authentic Writing. In *Indexing Authenticity: Sociolinguistic Perspectives, V. Lacoste, J. Leimgruber, and Th. Breyer* (eds.), 289–303. Berlin: De Gruyter.

Coupland, Nikolas 2014. Language, Society and Authenticity: Themes and Perspectives. In *Indexing Authenticity: Sociolinguistic perspectives, V. Lacoste, J. Leimgruber, and Th. Breyer* (eds.), 12–39. Berlin: De Gruyter.

Eckert, Penelope 2014. The Trouble with Authenticity. In *Indexing Authenticity: Sociolinguistic Perspectives, V. Lacoste, J. Leimgruber, and Th. Breyer* (eds.), 43–54. Berlin: De Gruyter.

First Peoples' Heritage Language and Culture Council 2016. *First Peoples' Language Map of British Columbia.* [Online] Available at: perma.cc/4TBQ-L5TA

Friesen, John B., and Anthony N. Ezeife 2009. Making Science Assessment Culturally Valid. *Canadian Journal of Native Studies:* 24–37.

Gingell, Susan 2010. Lips' Inking: Cree and Cree-Metis Authors' Writings of the Oral and What they Might Tell Educators. *Canadian Journal of Native Education:* 35–61.

Hargus, Sharon 2007. *Witsuwit'en Grammar: Phonetics, Phonology, Morphology.* Vancouver: UBC Press.

Iwana, Marilyn, Murdena Marshall, Albert Marshall, and Cheryl Bartlett 2009. Two-Eyed Seeing and the Language of Healing. *Canadian Journal of Native Education* 32: 3–23.

Jenness, Diamond 1934. Myths of the Carrier Indians of British Columbia. *Journal of American Folklore* 47: 97–257.

Kortmann, Bernd, and Kerstin Lunkenheimer (eds.) 2013. *The Mouton World Atlas of Variation in English*. Berlin: De Gruyter.

Leap, William 1993. *American Indian English.* Salt Lake City: University of Utah Press.

Morin, Melanie H. 2011. *Niwhts'ide'ni Hibi'it'en The Ways of Our Ancestors Witsuwit'en History and Culture Throughout the Millennia.* Smithers: Friesens.

CBC News 2014. *Franklin Find Proves 'Inuit Oral History is Strong:' Louie Kamookak.* [Online] Available at: http://www.cbc.ca/news/canada/north/franklin-find-proves-inuit-oral-history-is-strong-louie-kamookak-1.2761362

Sterzuk, Andreas 2011. *The Struggle for Legitimacy: Indigenized English in Settler Schools.* Bristol: MPG Books Group.

Theodossopoulos, Dimitrios 2013. Laying Claim to Authenticity: Five Anthropological Dilemmas. *Anthropological Quarterly:* 337–360.

Villagas, Malia 2009. This Is How We 'Role': Moving Toward a Cosmogonic Paradigm in Alaska Native Education. *Canadian Journal of Native Education:* 38–56.

Zinga, Dawn, S. Styres, S. Bennett, and M. Bomberry 2009. Student Success Research Consortium: Two Worlds Community-First Research. *Canadian Journal of Native Education:* 19–37.

6 "LA GESTE D'ASDIWAL": A STRUCTURAL STUDY OF MYTH IN THE LIGHT OF ORAL HISTORY AND LINGUISTICS

Michael Dürr

Introduction

"The Story of Asdiwal" was the most elaborate text published by Franz Boas in Coast Tsimshian (Sm'algya̱x) with an English translation (Boas 1912: 70–145). In 1958, Claude Lévi-Strauss undertook a detailed analysis of this narrative, comparing it with another version of the story. Mostly relying on the English translation (Lévi-Strauss 1967) of the study, this analysis was controversially discussed during the heydays of structural anthropology,[1] with the result that "Perhaps no single paper in the study of oral literature has provoked such reaction." (Adams 1981: 379) Although structuralism "is no longer a hot-button topic among scholars" (Anderson 2004: 107), the text is still considered an outstanding example for the structural study of myth, and as a side effect, the Asdiwal story itself has become widely known even beyond the field of cultural anthropology.

Although Lévi-Strauss's study attracted great attention for many years, the reception concentrated mostly either on aspects of methodology or, particularly in (American) Northwest Coast anthropology, on cross-cousin marriage as a central issue in his argumentation. According to Mandelbaum (1987: 32), Lévi-Strauss's concern was "to demonstrate the thought patterns" of myths that are manifested in oppositions which "represent dilemmas of human existence." These oppositions are "repeated endlessly, not all in any one story but through all the sacred narratives within a culture." (Mandelbaum 1987: 32) For Lévi-Strauss this is done unconsciously and structuralist methods can crack the code, a methodology that is neither concerned with "who communicates what specific messages to whom, under what circumstances, and to what effect" (Mandelbaum 1987: 32) nor relies on the content and plot of a narrative. This leads to two central methodological problems of the approach: on the one hand the arbitrariness of any selection and categorization of binary oppositions and on the other hand the determination of the underlying meaning of a narrative:

1 Just to mention some contributions that refer directly to the Asdiwal story: Douglas (1967), Ackerman (1973), Adams (1974), Oppitz (1975), and Thomas et al. (1976). Lévi-Strauss took up the discussion, repudiating most of the criticism (Lévi-Strauss 1973, 1983, 1984). For a more recent evaluation see Anderson (2004) in the volume "Coming to Shore." In the same volume, several articles acknowledge the work of Lévi-Strauss as a source for Northwest Coast ethnology and discuss its influence (Mauzé et al., eds., 2004).

"No criteria are anywhere discussed for making this determination. Discussions of tale topics concern the way the tale handles supposedly focal problems, not how these are identified." (Kronenfeld and Decker 1979: 523, 527)

Among the issues raised by Lévi-Strauss in his analysis are "areas of cultural tension, reconciling people to the contradictions of their society by exploring and attenuating oppositions." (Anderson 2004: 108) The most prominent of these cultural tensions Lévi-Strauss centered on was "the cluster of matrilineal kinship and group membership among the Tsimshianic groups: [...] In this cluster Lévi-Strauss saw a contradiction between the pressures of kinship and residence patterns that was partially resolved through matrilateral cross-cousin marriage." (Anderson 2004: 108) The question of cross-cousin marriage in Tsimshian society became the main topic in the discussion of the ethnographic validity of Lévi-Strauss's claims while other aspects of Lévi-Strauss's analysis have been mostly ignored.

Adams (1974) alone raised other important issues that had been disregarded by Lévi-Strauss,[2] insisting on the legal character of the story that leads to a different type of contradiction:

> "The primary use of these myths as social charters which entitle their owners to be considered legitimate members of a timeless, perpetual society must be juxtaposed to the evidence that their owners are in fact newcomers. In this sense, Lévi-Strauss is right about myths being used to overcome and justify a contradiction, ... The justification is arranged by means of a concept of power, thought to come from supernaturals ..." (Adams 1974: 175)

Adams (1974: 173–174) also treated in some detail the meaning of the main protagonist's name. The first element of *Asdiwaal*, the particle *asdi*, signifies either 'improperly, awkwardly' or 'movement away from the fire from the center toward the doorway,' and the verbal construction *asdiwaal* 'have an accident, make a mistake.' The linguistic dimension of the Asdiwal story was alluded to by Lévi-Strauss (1967), but only in an incidental manner. He commented on the name Asdiwal in a note (Lévi-Strauss 1967: 4, 43) and, in the conclusion at the end of his study, referred to Boas's Tsimshian Grammar, briefly characterizing local particles: "a grammatical construction employing couplets of antithetical terms is present in the Tsimshian tongue as a very obvious model, and probably presents itself as such quite consciously to the speaker, [Note: Boas quotes 31 pairs of 'local particles' in oppositions ...]" (Lévi-Strauss 1967: 42, 46)

Except for such cursory references to the Tsimshianic languages, none of the contributors undertook notable efforts to evaluate the tale topics and binary oppositions chosen by Lévi-Strauss or to develop criteria for such selections referring directly

2 As one of the few authors who based his interpretation on a new, independent summary of the story, Oppitz (1975: 268–273) should also be mentioned here.

to the original Sm'algyax text. The present chapter seeks to initiate this kind of investigation and, by means of a well-known example, also exemplify the benefits of linguistic work on such narrative texts.

Adawx: The Question of Genre

The definition of myth is a matter of long-lasting, ongoing debate. Among the various criteria that have been discussed is the question of genre, which was addressed for the Asdiwal story by Alan Dundes:

> "What about ... the story of Asdiwal (which he cautiously labelled 'geste')? This is not a myth either. If it were believed to be historically 'true' by the Tsimshian, then it would be a legend. ... In no way is the geste of Asdiwal an account of how the world or humankind came to be in their present form. It is not a myth by folkloristic standards." (Dundes 1997: 45–46)

While folklorists like Dundes or Bascom (1965) consider myth as a genre of its own, different from legend or fairy tale / folktale, other researchers define myth as a characteristic of narrations not by necessity restricted to specific genres (Segal 2004: 4–6).

When Lévi-Strauss titled his article "La Geste d'Asdiwal," he adapted the translation of "The Story of Asdiwal" used by Franz Boas to French. Instead of a more general equivalent of 'story' in French like 'histoire,' 'conte,' 'narration' or 'récit,' Lévi-Strauss chose the label for a specific genre of French Medieval heroic epic, the 'chanson de geste.'[3] But, without further reference to the genre question, the first sentence of the article starts with: "Cette étude d'un mythe indigène ..." (Lévi-Strauss 1958: 3) It seems as if the translation of genre between English and French is somehow problematic. This raises the question of the universality of the genres myth, legend and fairy tale or folktale: are they more or less universal or eurocentric concepts of folklorists because narrative genres should be better understood as mere culturally specific classifications? Therefore, it may be of some interest to look at what genre the Tsimshian *adawx* represents.

Boas stated that "The Tsimshian distinguish clearly between two types of stories—the myth (*ada'ox*) and the tale (*ma'łesk*). The latter is entirely historical in character, although from our point of view it may contain supernatural elements. The incidents narrated in the former are believed to have happened during the time when animals appeared in the form of human beings." (Boas 1916: 565) Though labelled "myth" by Boas, the *adawx* should better be understood as a "true history,

3 The English translation of the article (Lévi-Strauss 1967) was titled "The Story of Asdiwal" as in Boas (1912).

true telling" (McDonald 2003: 153) in Tsimshian society that manifests historical and social consciousness negotiated within and between lineages (Roth 2008: 6). Laws and customs were also recorded and illustrated in *adawx* (McDonald 2003: 24). Miller (1998: 657) used the term "epic" and criticized the treatment of the type of narratives represented by the *adawx* as "myths": "Unfortunately, popularly and dubiously regarded as 'myths,' these epics have often been slandered by the insensitive and slighted by scholars seeking to impose their own sense of detail and linear chronology on much more complex narratives." Marsden likewise focused on the historical and legal character of the *adawx*: "Adawx are oral records of historical events of collective political, social, and economic significance, …" (Marsden 2002: 102), but also touched on the integrative and complex character of the *adawx* that quite frequently is understood as a characteristic of myths:

> "These adawx, therefore, have many levels of meaning. They describe specific events in the history of a house while also revealing their importance within the broader context of the geographic and political history of the Tsimshian. As well, they exemplify the inherent laws of Tsimshian society by which charters are established that define relationships among peoples and between people and the living power of the land.
>
> The knowledge contained in these adawx, like the events they portray, moves between the worlds of spirit and matter, reflecting the pervasive worldview of Northwest Coast peoples that all creation is imbued with spirit. From this perspective, the adawx reflect the world itself, where human and spirit realms interpenetrate." (Marsden 2002: 135)

Another aspect of *adawx* is the legitimacy of their telling. In contrast to other narratives, *adawx* as family histories belong to the regalia of a specific noble house. Each *adawx* was accompanied by songs and masks or crests that allude to it. The performance and/or exhibition of such sets of regalia was restricted to particular occasions and to a small number of prominent members of the noble house. And, although Henry Tate, the collector or, better still, author of the text, was a member of the G̲awalaa house of the Gispaxlo'ots (eagle) clan,[4] one may doubt if he ever was in the position to tell or record the story legitimately: "While Tate was doubtlessly in a position to hear many of the *adawx* and other traditions, he probably realized that, as a non-royal *lik'agyet*, he might not be capable of securing the permission from knowledgeable chiefs, matriarchs, and elders to record them for publication." (Roth 2008: 173) And in the case of the Asdiwal story, the access seemed even to be not a matter of descent, but of adoption by which he became a member of the

4 According to Roth (2008: 173). The information on the status of Henry Tate supplied by Boas, Barbeau and Beynon is not fully congruous (Roth 2008: 172–173).

Gispwudwada (killerwhale) clan (Boas 1916: 500) to whose regalia the Asdiwal story seems to belong.[5]

But legitimacy was just one of the problems Tate had to solve, as he had also to respect the guidelines of Boas for collecting and writing down Sm'algyax̱ texts. Another important issue concerns the shifts due to the transmission of narratives that were orally performed to the written medium (see Kasten 2017: 20, *this volume*). Such transmissions cannot fully cope with either the elaborate style of formal public speaking or the transient social agreements the narratives are intended to negotiate. The Asdiwal story, as with the other texts collected by Tate, must be understood as an attempt to reconcile the multiple challenges of an intercultural genesis process. And this process affected the narrations in various respects,[6] as, for example, when Tate inserted some ethnographic information on winter famines or on the bird *hats'a̱naas* into the Asdiwal story (Boas 1912: 70; 72).

To close the discussion of genre, it should be noted that Lévi-Strauss himself raised the issue of genre in a later lecture (Lévi-Strauss 1983: 221–237). In this article he analyzed a Kwakiutl (Kwakwa̱ka̱'wakw) story that shows substantial resemblances to the Asdiwal story. A central argument in his comparison of both texts was that the Kwakiutl narrative is a family history ("histoire de famille") and, therefore, differs in function from the Tsimshian myth. As a family history it is situated between the speculative thinking of myth and political realism. Lévi-Strauss admitted its specific character as the family history[7] of one of the Kwakiutl noble houses, focusing on the legitimation and the prestige of this particular house (Lévi-Strauss

5 Only the 1902 version explicitly attributed the Asdiwal story to the Gispwudwada (Boas 1902: 221, 225–229). It may also be noted that Asdiwal (alias Potlatch-Giver in that part of the story) used carved killerwhales, the main crest of the Gispwudwada, to defeat his brother-in-laws (Boas 1912: 136–141). And, though not mentioned in the narrative itself, the royal house of the Ginaxangiik, the family of Potlatch-Giver's wife, belongs to the Gispwudwada.

6 The list of possible deviations includes, among others, omissions: "there have always been comments that she left out part of the legend. ... By not telling all of the legend on tape, she still owned or controlled the adawx." (Mulder 1996: 158) Another issue is the use of story titles as given by Boas (1912). The first author who raised the topic was Barbeau (1917) in his review of Boas's Tsimshian Mythology, observing that "The demarcation between historic-like traditions or myths belonging exclusively to clans and families and those that form part of the general stocks is not clearly drawn here." (Barbeau 1917: 553) and that "Tate, moreover, relates these stories as if he were speaking to a stranger. For instance, he says (p. 389): '... In olden times, people cleared their land with stone axes ...' Such details on culture perspectives do not enter into the undisturbed Indian narratives." (Barbeau 1917: 562) The collaboration of Tate and Boas was analyzed in some detail by Maud (1993), but quite polemically, and, what is worse, he only consulted the English translations of the texts. But this is not the place to go into detail on this; instead, see Dürr (1992, 1996).

7 Unfortunately, the text (Boas 1921: 1249–1255) is one of the few texts in Boas's immense Kwakw'ala corpus only accessible via its English translation. According to Berman (1991: 121–128), in the Kwakw'ala language stories owned by a noble house are called *nuya̱miɫ*, a subgenre of the *nuya̱m* 'myth, history.'

1983: 219). Although he touched on a clue that might have been important for the understanding of the Tsimshian stories as well, he did not revise his earlier interpretations, but rather contrasted these with the Kwakiutl version.

What's the Story about: Potlatch Feasts, Titles and Names

In this section, a topic of the Asdiwal story will be chosen that was not touched on by Lévi-Strauss. In the light of the function of *adawx*, one might expect that activities which lead to prestige and advancement would play an important role in the plot of the stories. And indeed, this aspect is omnipresent in the story of Asdiwal, although it was totally ignored by Lévi-Strauss (1967) in the summary as well as in the analysis.[8]

Due to his descent from a noble family, his success as a hunter and his marriages with daughters of chiefs, Asdiwal became famous and was promoted to chief himself. The cultural framework for this rise is the potlatch feast in which status was negotiated and confirmed in Tsimshian society. And the most obvious indications for advancement are noble titles and prestigious names.

Feasts (Potlatches)

The narrative, therefore, includes a series of three successive potlatches as pivotal incidents. The wording of each of these short text passages is quite similar. In each passage or in the adjacent text the locality (except for the first potlatch) and the social rank of the protagonists are clarified.

The first potlatch took place after the death of the old "chieftainess" (*sigidmna'ax*). Her daughter at that time was married to a supernatural being called *Hats'a̲naas*, who together had a son. The title "princess" (*łguwaalksm hana'ax*) identifies her as the legitimate heir of the chieftainess. She inaugurated a name-giving potlatch to announce the name of her son "Asdiwal," chosen by his father:[9]

---

8 It can also serve as a good example for the highly selective and subjective, and consequently biased character, of Lévi-Strauss's summary and analysis. Some of the omissions might become comprehensible presuming that Lévi-Strauss relied for his summary mostly on Boas's extensive comparative notes on the individual episodes (Boas 1916: 792–825).

9 In this article, the transcription of Sm'algya̲x tries to follow, as far as possible, the conventions in Anderson et al. (eds. 2013), Dunn (1979), Mulder (1996) and Stebbins (2003). Names of places, clans, etc. are given in the form most common in recent literature. In quotations from Boas (1911, 1916) the orthography remains unchanged. For a discussion on the problems of standardizing Sm'algya̲x orthography see Stebbins (2003).

Barred *ł* stands for the voiceless correspondence of *l*, underlined *k̲* and *g̲* for voiceless and voiced uvular stops. Underlined *a̲* represents the shwa sound, *ü* an unrounded high back

1

Ada	*wil*	*dzak-sga*	*'wiileeks-tga*			
and	then	die-CON	great-DEM			
'niigana	*'wiileeks-m*	*yaawk-sga* [10]	*łguwaalks-m*	*hana'ax-ga*	[…]	
therefore	great-CON	give.potlatch-CON	princess-CON	woman-DEM		
Ada-t	*wil*	*aytg-isga*	*na-waa*	*łguułg-tga*		
and-she	then	call.by.name-CON	POSS-name	child-her		
Asdiwaal	*nahła*	*ky'ilam-s*	*na-gwat*	*adm*	*wadi-yaagwa*	
<name>	PAST	give-CON	POSS-father	so.that	like-hold	

"Then the old (woman) died. Therefore the princess gave a great potlatch, [...] Then she called the name of her son. Asdi-wā'l was what the father gave him to be his name." (Boas 1912: 80, line 33–82, line 4; 81–83)

In the following sentences, Asdiwal is characterized as a great hunter of the woods, whose fame was known by all people and animals. In the same context, Asdiwal is also called a "prince" (*łguwaalks*) for the first time. The place of the potlatch is not mentioned, but it seems still to be the provisional camp where the family lived because, immediately after the potlatch, his mother returned to her relatives in Kitselas with Asdiwal.

The second name-giving feast was also held by his mother, when Asdiwal, although still considered dead, came back to Kitselas with his first wife, the daughter of the Sun Chief. The chiefly character of Asdiwal's new name is explicitly mentioned and, from here on, the hero of the story is no longer called "Asdiwal," but "Potlatch-Giver" (*Waxayeewk* or *Waxayaawk*):

2

Ada	*wil*	*gyik*	*hatsiksm*	*yaawk-dit*	
and	then	again	again	give.potlatch-she	
Ada-t	*wil*	*aytg-a*	*waa-m*	*sm'oogyit-dit*	*Waxayeewk*
and-she	then	call.by.name-CON	name-CON	chief-DEM	Potlatch.Giver

---

vowel. Though not written here, shwa may also be present in some consonant clusters resulting from suffixation of the connective *-m* or the third person *-t*. The glossing follows Mulder (1996), although in a simplified manner owed to the purpose of this article. Abbreviations used: CAUS = causative, CON = connective, DEM = demonstrative, EMPH = emphasis, FUT = future tense, NEG = negation, PAST = past tense, PL = plural, and PREP = preposition.

Connectives help to identify the syntactic function within a sentence. They are only indicated on verbs, nouns, and adjectival forms, but not on particles, prepositions or pronouns. Pronominal elements have been glossed with the most suitable English correspondence to ease the understanding. For example, third person *-t* is translated as 'he,' 'him,' 'his,' 'she,' 'her,' 'they,' 'them,' or 'their' respectively, without glossing the demonstratives sometimes present.

The elucidations of lexical morphemes are quoted or sometimes adapted from Anderson et al. (eds. 2013: sub voce). The glosses present only rough approximations to the rich meanings of the morphemes, especially in the case of particles.

10 Boas (1912: 258) *yā'k*, Anderson et al. (eds. 2013: sub voce) *yaawk*, but Dunn (1979: sub voce) has *yaakw*.

A *wil* *dm* *waal-t* *gisga* *dm* *huk-yaawk-tga*
and then FUT be-he PREP FUT always-give.potlatch-he
"Therefore she gave a potlatch again, and she named him with a chief's name, Potlatch-Giver (Waxayē´°k), for he was to be one to give potlatches;" (Boas 1912: 110, line 2–5; 111)

The third and final name-giving feast mentioned in the narrative took place when Potlatch-Giver, leaving behind the Skeena River and his family, went to Ginadoiks. Once again, from here to the end, the hero of the story is referred to consistently by his new name "Stone-Slinger" (*Dahukdzan*):

3 *Ada* *k'a* *gyik* *wil* *'wiileeks-m* *yaawk-tga*
and for.a.while again then great-CON give.potlatch-he
Ada *gyik* *hatsiksm-t* *aytg-a* *gyik* *waa-m* *sm'oogyit-it*
and again again-he call.by.name-CON again name-CON chief-DEM
Dahukdzant-k[11] *su-waa-tga*
<name>-DEM new-name-his
"There he made again a great potlatch. Then he took again a chief's name. Stone-Slinger (Da-huk-dza´n) was his new name." (Boas 1912: 142, line 8–11; 143)

Titles

Most protagonists are referred to either by family relations or by social rank. The narration pays minute attention to the status of the protagonists. Asdiwal's mother is introduced referring to her mother's chiefly rank (*sigidmna'ax*). She shifts from "noble-woman" (*łguyaaksm hana'ax*) to "princess" (*łguwaalksm hana'ax*) when her mother, the chieftainess, consented to the marriage to Hats'a̲nas. Asdiwal, after being named for the first time in a potlatch, is labelled "prince," i.e. heir of a chief. Only his father Hats'a̲nas lacks any designation as a nobleman or as a supernatural being. He is referred to either by his name or as "young handsome man."

Both wives are introduced as daughters of an important chief (*sm'oogyit*), the Sun Chief and later the chief of the Ginaxangiik. While his first wife is referred to as "princess" from the beginning, his second wife starts as a "noble-woman" and advances to "princess" only when her father, the chief, consented to the marriage with Asdiwal. In the narrative his mother and his second wife change from "noble-woman" to "princess" without explicit explanation. The relevance of marriage for the title is inconclusive here because both Asdiwal's mother and his first wife had been married before.

---

11 Unclear, *huk-* 'one who always does something' (Anderson et al., eds. 2013: sub voce)

When Asdiwal stays with the Sea-Lion-People and cures them from an epidemic, the interaction focuses on the chief of that people termed "chief" (*sm'oogyit*) or "master of the sea-lions" (Boas 1912: 133) (*miyaan t'iibn*). He is the only non-relative of some importance mentioned in the story.

The attention to the titles of the protagonists, thus, is characteristic for passages that cope with the establishing or confirmation of higher status by noble marriage or potlatch feasts. It can also be found in some encounters that have the potential to lead to higher status like the first meetings with his future wives or with the chief of the Sea-Lion-People. This brings about a high concentration of the explicit use of titles in the substantial passages of the narrative while in most other contexts kinship terms are preferred when identifying the protagonists.

Names

Even more important than titles are chiefly names. The concept of names is quite specific in Tsimshian society. As a Tsimshian depicted it: "People are nothing. They're not important at all. It's the names that are really real." (quoted in Roth 2008: 30). Miller wrote: "Tsimshian say that people are given to the names rather than the reverse became [sic![12]] the names are immortal and each can convey benefits to its 'holder,' who treats it with respect ..." (Miller 1998: 670) In this respect, "Tsimshians ... are embedded in cycles of transmigrating names: bodies in a lineage shift from name to name, ... so that social advancement and changes in status are inseparable from becoming the new person reified in the new name." (Roth 2008: 4)

Therefore, names seemed to be so loaded with meaning and power that explicit reference by name is restricted to two persons only in the Asdiwal story: to the main protagonist Asdiwal (= Potlatch-Giver = Stone-Slinger) and to his father Hats'a̱nas.[13]

Hats'a̱nas, the name of a bird similar to a robin, is a pun on *hats'a̱naas* 'good luck' (Boas 1912: 72, line 29–32; 73). As mentioned before, the name Asdiwal puns on the verb *asdiwaal* 'making mistakes.'[14] Names like Asdiwal which indicate bad characteristics had been common at least in Gitksan culture to honor the bearer's overcoming of that bad characteristic (Adams 1974: 174).

Like titles, names are used as landmarks for social advancement. Every time a new name was approved in a name-giving feast, the main protagonist is referred

---

12 Should be: because.

13 I exclude two more names mentioned in direct speech only when the master of the sea-lions sent messengers to borrow canoes from "Self-Stomach" / "All-Stomach" (Boas 1912: 132, line 18) and "Self-like-Sea-Lion" (Boas 1912: 138, line 24).

14 A related name Asiwaalgit is used to denominate a specific crest (*dzepk*) depicting a large supernatural bird in possession of the Kitsumkalum G̱anhada house Xpilaxha (McDonald 2003: 85).

by this new, chiefly name in the story. Thus, he is first called "Asdiwal" (Boas 1912: 82–110) and later two names that were explicitly labelled as chiefly names in the text (see examples 2 and 3 above): "Potlatch-Giver" (*Waxayeewk* or *Waxayaawk*; Boas 1912: 110–142) and "Stone-Slinger" (*Dahukdzan*; Boas 1912: 142–144).

Locative Particles in the Story of Asdiwal

While all observations treated up to this point could have also been detected by a careful reading of Boas's translation of the Asdiwal story, the following section will focus on the role and use of specific spatial orientation systems that are deeply inscribed in Sm'algya̲x and in the languages of the North Pacific Rim in general.[15]

Sm'algya̲x locative particles

The Tsimshianic languages possess an elaborated system of particles for specifying the locational aspects of objects or actions. This set of locative particles is by far the largest subgroup of particles in the Sm'algya̲x language. About sixty morphemes either refer to place or position of objects or actions or they indicate motion of objects or actions in relation to place or position (Dunn 1979: 41–45, Boas 1911: 300–312). Semantically, locative particles cover a wide range of meanings within the domain of spatial reference—these include rather abstract concepts as well as concrete ones. Some particles like *bax* 'ascending' vs. *'yaga* 'descending'[16] form pairs of opposites. Movement particles are mostly used adverbially preceding the verbal predicate, e.g.

4	*Ada*	*wil*	***bax**-yaa-t*	*a*	*lax-sga̲'niis-t*
	And	then	up-walk-he	PREP	on-mountain-DEM

"and he [Stone-Slinger] went up the mountain." (Boas 1912: 142, line 24; 143)

In addition, the orientation system of Sm'algya̲x comprises a number of specific particles for geographical and even for in-house movements (Dunn 1979: 43–45, Boas 1911: 300–312, Fortescue 2011a: 33–38), including:

15 Such orientation systems are found in most languages of the Pacific Northwest Coast and seem to be an areal characteristic of the North Pacific Rim (Fortescue 2011a, 2011b).

16 There is also a second pair *man* 'ascending (without surface contact)' vs. *tkyi* 'descending (without surface contact),' distinguished from *bax* 'ascending (with surface contact)' and *'yaga* 'descending (with surface contact)' by the semantic dimension of surface contact (Dunn 1979: 44–45).

1. geographic, coast-oriented

dzagm	'towards the shore (from the water)'
uks	'towards the sea'

2. geographic, river-oriented

k'ala	'upriver'
gyisi	'downriver'

3. domestic, settlement-oriented

na	'out of the woods behind the houses'

4. domestic, in-house[17]

t'm	'from rear to middle of the house'
asdi	'from the middle to the front of the house'
lagawk	'from the side of the house to the fire'

Although only few of the geographical particles, like *k'ala* 'upriver' vs. *gyisi* 'downriver,' can be categorized semantically as true opposites, a number of them verge on a sort of culturally oppositional understanding.

The movement particles *bax* 'up' and *'yaga* 'down'

The particle *bax* 'up' and its opposite *'yaga* 'down' occur frequently (18 and 24 times, respectively) throughout the text. Apparently they are used to describe the movements of the protagonists, in particular that of the main protagonist Asdiwal / Potlatch-Giver. For instance, when Asdiwal moves up into the mountains for hunting:

5					
	Ada	*wil*	***bax**-yaa-t*	*gisga*	*sga'niis-tga*
	And	then	up-walk-he	PREP	mountain-DEM

"and [Asdiwal] went up the mountain." (Boas 1912: 88, line 29; 89)

He went to the mountains, because his father-in-law desired mountain-goat meat:

6							
	daał,	*meł-a*	*hasag-ayu*	*da*	*dm-t*	***bax**-goo-da*	*łams-u*
	dear(female)	say-CON	want-I	PREP	FUT-he	up-go.somewhere-CON	son.in.law-my

mati	*hu-waal-da*	*da*	*gyilhawli,*
mountain.goat	PL-be-CON	PREP	in.the.woods

awil	*n-k'oomtg-a*	*sami-m*	*mati*	*dił*	*yeey-a*	*mati*
because	I-wish-CON	meat-CON	mountain.goat	and	fat-CON	mountain.goat

"'My dear, say that I wish my son-in-law to go up for the mountain-goats there

17 In relation to this specific set of particles, it should be mentioned that, with the exception of hunting, during winter most activities took place inside the houses, including potlatches.

in the woods, because I desire mountain-goat meat and mountain-goat tallow.'" (Boas 1912: 88, line 20–22; 89)

His wife had warned him before about going to the mountain, so that the *bax* movement to the mountains is repeated four times in this short passage until Asdiwal finally decided to go up into the mountains for hunting. And on the next page *bax* is once more used when the heavenly throng wanted to see "who had gone up" (Boas 1912: 90, line 9; 91) (*bax* + *dawł* 'leave, depart').

The next concentration of *bax* can be found when Potlatch-Giver was invited by his brothers-in-law to go mountain-goat hunting. They left together:

<table>
<tr><td>7</td><td>ada</td><td>wil</td><td>bax-waalxs-tga</td></tr>
<tr><td></td><td>and</td><td>then</td><td>up-walk.PL-they</td></tr>
</table>

"They [i.e. Potlatch-Giver and his brothers-in-law] went up;" (Boas 1912: 116, line 21; 117)

Potlatch-Giver succeeded in this contest. Therefore, in the next episode, the brothers-in-law wanted to go hunting in the sea while Potlatch-Giver still preferred to hunt in the mountains, once again moving *bax*:

<table>
<tr><td>8</td><td>ada</td><td>aldi</td><td>wila</td><td>bax-yaa-s</td><td>Waxayaawk-ga</td><td>lax-sga'niis-tga</td></tr>
<tr><td></td><td>and</td><td>EMPH</td><td>then</td><td>up-walk-CON</td><td><name>-DEM</td><td>on-mountain-DEM</td></tr>
<tr><td></td><td>asga</td><td>naa-ktga</td><td></td><td></td><td></td><td></td></tr>
<tr><td></td><td>PREP</td><td>snowshoes-his</td><td></td><td></td><td></td><td></td></tr>
</table>

"Then Potlatch-Giver, on his part, went up the mountain on his snowshoes." (Boas 1912: 118, line 25–26; 119)

<table>
<tr><td>9</td><td>ada</td><td>gyik</td><td>wil</td><td>bax-yaa-s</td><td>Waxayaawk</td><td>gisga</td><td>txal-hawli-tga</td></tr>
<tr><td></td><td>and</td><td>again</td><td>then</td><td>up-walk-CON</td><td><name></td><td>PREP</td><td>touching-woods-DEM</td></tr>
<tr><td></td><td>ada</td><td>gyik</td><td colspan="2">t'apxaad-a</td><td colspan="3">sa-ol-dit.</td></tr>
<tr><td></td><td>and</td><td>again</td><td colspan="2">two.flat.objects-CON</td><td colspan="3">CAUS-hunt.bear-he</td></tr>
</table>

"Then Potlatch-Giver went up again into the woods, and he killed two bears." (Boas 1912: 122, line 6–7; 123)

It turned out that once again Potlatch-Giver was more successful, bringing back bears from both of his hunting trips. Later, when he joined his brothers-in-law hunting in the sea, they left him alone in a critical situation. After his rescue, he once again went into the mountainous inland:

<table>
<tr><td>10</td><td>ada</td><td>wila</td><td>bax-yaa-tga</td><td>asga</td><td>gyilhawli-ga</td></tr>
<tr><td></td><td>and</td><td>then</td><td>up-walk-he</td><td>PREP</td><td>in.the.woods-DEM</td></tr>
</table>

"Then he [Potlatch-Giver] went inland." (Boas 1912: 134, line 29; 135)

Later his wife also came inland (*bax* + *goo* 'go somewhere') (Boas 1912: 136, line 12) and both went further inland (*bax* + *waalxs* 'walk,' the suppletive plural of *yaa*) (Boas 1912: 136, line 18) to reach a lake.

One would expect that the particle *'yaga* 'down,' in contrast, refers to the act of coming back to the village and to the family from a hunting trip. But such incidents are not mentioned. One of the few occurrences of *'yaga* associated with a returning to a village can be found when Asdiwal, after courting the chief's daughter, went to Ginaxangiik:

11 *da-t wila* ***'yaga**-stuul-sga hana'ax-ga*
and-he then down-accompany-CON woman-DEM
"he [Asdiwal] accompanied the woman down (to the village)" (Boas 1912: 116, line 4–5; 117)

In the second example, Potlatch-Giver, after having killed his elder brothers-in-law, returned to stay with the last remaining, youngest brother-in-law:

12 *ni'nii da wil* ***'yaga**-yaa-s Waxayaawk*
that and then down-walk-CON <name>
"Then Potlatch-Giver went down …" (Boas 1912: 140, line 34–142, line 1; 141–143)

The following two examples demonstrate the use of *bax* 'up' and *'yaga* 'down' as a stylistic bracket for episodes. The first example connects the starting point of Asdiwal's relation with the Sun Chief's daughter to the first return to his new wife from a hunting trip, while the second example frames Potlatch-Giver's creation of supernatural killer-whales:

13 *ada wil* ***bax**-yaa-t gisga sga̲'niis-tga*
and then up-walk-he PREP mountain-DEM
ada wil sm-baa-s Asdiwaal-ga
and then very-run-CON <name>-DEM
hoygyigad-a wil gyipaayg-a ts'u'uts'-it
be.like-CON that fly-CON bird-DEM
"and [Asdiwal] went up the mountain. Verily, Asdi-wā'l ran like a bird flying." (Boas 1912: 88, line 29–30; 89)
Ada wil ***'yaga**-baa-s Asdiwaal gisga nagoox-tga*
and then down-run-CON <name> PREP before-CON
wadi-wil gyipaayg-a ts'u'uts'-it
like-that fly-CON bird-DEM
"Then Asdi-wā'l ran down as before, like a bird flying." (Boas 1912: 94, line 12; 95)

14 ada   gyik   wil   **'yaga**-dog-a   n-sa̱'naaxɫd-it   [...]
    and   again   then   down-take.PL-CON   which-make.killer.whale-DEM

"Then he took down again the killer-whales [...]" (Boas 1912: 138, line 18; 139)

    da   wila   **'yaga**-yaa-s   Waxayaawk-ga
    and   then   down-walk-CON   <name>-DEM

    ada   **uks**-huutg-it   gisga   n-dzoog-sga   aks-ga   a   xswa̱t'a̱xg-dit
    and   to.sea-call-he   PREP   POSS-edge-CON   water-DEM   PREP   whistle-he-DEM

    ada   wil   **dza̱gm**-hap-da   'naaxɫ-a   awaa-tga
    and   then   ashore-go.in.group-CON   killer.whale-CON   near-DEM

    ada   wila-t   wulagm-**bax**-dox-tga
    and   then-he   out.of.water-up-take-them

"After a while, Potlatch-Giver went down, stood near the water on the shore of the lake, and whistled. Then the killer-whales came ashore to him, and he took them up ashore." (Boas 1912: 138, line 25–29; 139)

The last example can also serve to demonstrate that the use of *'yaga* is not restricted to motion of the protagonists, but includes in addition verb constructions like *'yaga-gaa* 'take down.' In the first part of the story, Asdiwal's mother repeatedly brought back edible animals. At first, the supernatural Hats'a̱nas supplied her with small animals (Boas 1912: 74, line 5–15), but when greater animals showed up—consecutively a large porcupine, a beaver, and a mountain goat—this is expressed three times by the same *'yaga-gaa* 'take down' (Boas 1912: 74, line 20–76, line 2).

Concentrations of *'yaga* correlate with important incidents in the story, sometimes combining both aspects of motion and food placement. This can be seen in the sentences adjacent to Hats'a̱nas marriage; here, the last sentence emphasizes the role of Hats'a̱nas as the provider of the family:

15 Da   wila-t   **'yaga**-stuul-tga   hana'ax-ga   sup'as-m   'yuuta-ga
    and   then-he   down-accompany-CON   woman-CON   young-CON   man-DEM

    Ada   wil-t   naks-gisga   ɫguwaalks-m   hana'ax-ga
    and   then-he   marry-CON   princess-CON   woman-DEM

    dat   wila-t   **'yaga**-dox-tga   sup'as-m   'yuuta-ga   na-yets'isk-set
    and   then-he   down-take.PL-them   young-CON   man-DEM   POSS-land.animal-DEM

"and the young man accompanied the women down. Then he married the princess, and the young man took down the animals." (Boas 1912: 78, line 29–32; 79)

When Asdiwal / Potlatch-Giver took over the role of the provider of the family, verbal expressions including *'yaga* are used repeatedly when he brings back venison to his family, e.g.:

16 *Ada-t* *k'a-'**yaga**-t'ał-ditga* *gu* *smgal-yikyeey-m* *semi-t*
and-he for.a.while-down-put-them who very-fat-CON bear-DEM
aam *k'a-'**yaga**-ts'nł-doo-ditga* *gana* *'**yaga**-xhuup'ltg-itga*
good for.a.while-down-leave.behind-put.down-them therefore down-until.night-he
"Then he [Potlatch-Giver] carried them [bears] down, those which were fat bears; and he left some behind. Therefore he carried them down until night …" (Boas 1912: 118, line 33–120, line 2; 119–121)

Once, Potlatch-Giver requested something of his wife:

17 *ndo'o* *ma̱* *'**yaga**-goo-ł* *wineey-a*
go.ahead you down-go.somewhere-CON food-DEM
"'Go down for food.'" (Boas 1912: 136, line 20; 137)

His wife left down (*'yaga-dawł*) for food, returning with much food (Boas 1912: 136, line 21–22; 137). In total, more than ten occurrences of different verbal expressions with *'yaga* refer directly to providing food.

A final concentration of *'yaga* 'down' can be found when Potlatch-Giver created killer-whales with his supernatural powers to defeat his brother-in-laws. This new usage starts immediately after the sentence quoted above, which still refers to providing food:

18 *Ada-t* *wil* *'**yaga**-dox-t* *gisga* *ts'm-t'aa-ga*
And-he then down-take.PL-them PREP in-lake-DEM
"Then he took them [the killer-whales] down into the lake." (Boas 1912: 136, line 29–30; 137)

14 *ada* *gyik* *wil* *'**yaga**-dog-a* *n-sa̱'naaxłd-it* […]
and again then down-take.PL-CON which-make.killer.whale-DEM
da *wila* *'**yaga**-yaa-s* *Waxayaawk-ga*
and then down-walk-CON <name>-DEM
"Then he took down again the killer-whales […] After a while, Potlatch-Giver went down," (Boas 1912: 138, line 18–26; 139)

The particle *'yaga* is also interspersed to indicate motions or activities of minor protagonists, as in the case of the brothers-in-law who "took down their canoes" (Boas 1912: 138, line 29) (*'yaga-* + *txoo* 'take a canoe to water') which also helps to augment the concentration of the particle in specific passages.

In summary, the use of the pair of opposite particles *bax* and *'yaga* correlates with hunting. Game is attained in the mountains (*bax*) and, when the hunt was successful, the distribution (*'yaga*) of venison becomes an instrument of prosperity and fame.

Particles describing geographical movement

As mentioned above (: 130f.), particles indicating geographical movements group along several dimensions. For reasons of descriptive economy, river-oriented locative particles will be discussed first, followed by settlement-oriented ones and, at last, coast-oriented particles.

At the beginning of the narrative, the young noble-woman, who later became Asdiwal's mother, and her mother, a chieftainess, lived in different villages along the Skeena River described by the nouns *gyigyaani* 'place up the river' and *gye'ets* 'place down the river.' One of the respective directional particles is only used once, when the noble-woman says:[18]

19	*Dziła*	***gyisi**-yaa-i*
	when	downriver-walk-I

"when I shall go down the river" (Boas 1912: 70, line 17; 71)

When Asdiwal followed a bear to reach the Sun Chief, the particles *gyisi* 'downriver' and *na* 'out of the woods in rear of the houses' are quite prominent. The bear went down the river (*gyisi-yaa*), ran down the river (*gyisi-baa*) three times, but also came out of the woods (*na-baa*) twice (Boas 1912: 82, line 12–84, line 1). Later, Potlatch-Giver left the village of his mother after her death downriver (*gyisi*):

20	*Ada*	*wil*	*sta̱-**gyisi**-yaa-s*	*Waxayaawk*	*a*	***gyisi**-Ksiyaan-ga*
	and	then	steadily-downriver-walk-CON	<name>	PREP	downriver-<name>-DEM

"Then Potlatch-Giver continued to go down Skeena River." (Boas 1912: 114, line 17; 115)

There are no other occurrences of river-oriented particles that seem to be of relevance for the plot of the story.[19]

From the subset of settlement-oriented locative particles, only *na* 'out of the woods behind of the houses' is used in the text. It indicates several returns of Asdiwal/Potlatch-Giver from mountain-goat hunting, the first time when he returns to his first wife:

21	*Ada*	*ła*	***na**-baa-t*	*gisga*	*awaa*	*naks-tga*
	and	PAST	out.of.woods-run-he	PREP	near	wife-his

"(Asdi-wā'l) went to his wife." (Boas 1912: 94, line 15; 95)

18 The context of this sentence reads: "'I remember (think) when I meet my mother when I go down the river, … then I shall eat food …'" (Boas 1912: 71).

19 The only occurrences of *k̲'ala-* 'upriver' refer to the people of *k̲'ala-Ksiyaan* "upriver Skeena" (Boas 1912: 80, line 14) and to Potlatch-Giver's brothers-in-law (Boas 1912: 120, line 28).

The particle *na* can be found next when Potlatch-Giver meets his future second wife for the first time:

22 *ada wila* ***na**-baa-t* *gisga k'üül-da*
and then out.of.woods-run-he PREP one.object-CON
wil-dzox-sga g̲a̲lts'ab-a Ts'msyen-t
where-live-CON village-CON Tsimshian.people-DEM
a wil-dzog-a Gyinaxangyiig-it
PREP where-live-CON <name>-DEM
ada ła dm ***na**-baa-dit*
and near.FUT out.of.woods-run-he
da txa̲l'waay-da k'üül-da łguyaaks-m hana'ax
and meet-CON one.object-CON noble.person-CON woman
gisga txa̲-stuup'l-sga hu-walp-ga
PREP place-rear.of.house-CON PL-house-DEM
"He [Potlatch-Giver] came out at a camp, a town of the Tsimshian, G·inaxang·i'´gɛt. When he came out of the woods, he met a noble-woman behind the houses." (Boas 1912: 114, line 18–20; 115)

The third and last occurrence takes place when Potlatch-Giver returned from a hunting trip to mountains while his brothers-in-law had come home empty-handed from their hunting trip to the sea:

23 *ada-t sa-**na**-baa-t* *gisga na̲-wil-dzox-tga*
and-he suddenly-out.of.woods-run-CON PREP POSS-where-live-their
"He [Potlatch-Giver] came of the woods at their camp." (Boas 1912: 120, line 3; 121)

This particle, therefore, is not used often, but at important junctions of the narrative. Its use can also explain the asymmetry mentioned above (: 131ff.) between *bax* 'up' and *'yaga* 'down' with reference to hunting in the mountains, because the departure for the trip with *bax* is paralleled by *na* instead of *'yaga* 'down.'

As might be expected, the coast-oriented locative particles *uks* 'towards the sea' and *dzag̲m* 'towards the shore' occur quite frequently in the passages narrating the hunting trips to the sea of Potlatch-Giver and of his brothers-in-law.

The particle *uks* 'towards the sea' is used several times to describe the direction of some of the minor participants in the story. Potlatch-Giver is only associated with *uks* 'towards the sea' in the context of sea-lion hunting (Boas 1912: 122, line 21; 132, line 8; 138, line 27–140, line 23):[20]

20 There is also a 2x2 repetitive pattern when Asdiwal is first advised to summon the winds and later follows the advice (Boas 1912: 134, line 5–26). In the case of the East wind, the particle *uks* is used twice: "'*Am-uks-gwaatk.*' '(East wind,) drive it seaward.'" (Boas 1912: 134, line 13, 26; 135)

24 Ada   wagayt-**uks**-moxg-s   Waxayaawk   asga   łguk'a̱laan-tgitga
    and   far-to.sea-go.aboard-CON   <name>   PREP   brother.in.law-his

"Then Potlatch-Giver went out to sea aboard (the canoe) of his little brothers-in-law" (Boas 1912: 122, line 21; 123)

The particle *dza̱gm* 'towards the shore' often describes the activities of Potlatch-Giver's brothers-in-law (Boas 1912: 126, line 1–18; 132, line 8; 138, line 27–140, line 23). The repeated use of *dza̱gm* also includes requests when Asdiwal bids his brothers-in-law to go ashore:[21]

25 Ndo'o,   **dza̱gm**-ga-dawł-sm   ła   aam   wil   'li-t'aa-yut
    go.ahead   ashore-PL-leave-you.PL   PAST   good   where   on-sit-I

"'Go ashore and let me stay here!'" (Boas 1912: 126, line 7; 127)

naat,   ndo'o   **dza̱gm**-dawł-nt
dear(male)   go.ahead   ashore-leave-you

"'My dear, do go ashore!'" (Boas 1912: 126, line 14–15; 127)

Due to Potlatch-Giver's own request, his brothers-in-law leave him alone in a critical situation on a rock in the sea from which his father rescues him. Later in the story, they are killed by Potlatch-Giver by means of supernatural killer-whales—and in this episode *dza̱gm* shows up again frequently. The use of *'yaga* 'down' in the same context was mentioned above in section 4.2.

Particles describing in-house movement

As set out before (: 126 ff.), the Sm'algya̱x text is predominantly concerned with noble status and social advancement. This concern is manifested by repeated stereotypical references to potlatch feasts and to the confirmation of chiefly names, but also includes marriage. The first meetings with his future wives occur behind the house,[22] thus shifting the location from the hunter's domain, the uninhabited wilderness, to the space of social interaction and life, the village and the houses. Marriages create new alliances between noble families, thus ensuring status and regulating the access to new resources and noble regalia. In this respect they must be considered hotspots of status manipulation. While the first encounters with his future wives take place outside the house, the stage for family life is set inside the house of the chiefs. It

---

21 In the first sentence Potlatch-Giver addressed his brothers-in-law, in the second only the youngest brother-in-law who left him unwillingly: "*Ada sm-hagwil-dza̱gm-dawł-ga*—He left him, slowly going towards the shore." (Boas 1912: 126, line 18–19; 127)

22 In the first case (Boas 1911: 86, line 21; 87), the locative particle *gyil* 'behind' is used, in the second (Boas 1911: 114, line 20; 115) *na*- 'from out of the woods behind the house.'

may therefore be of interest to close the discussion with the set of domestic locative particles, and particularly with *t'm* 'from rear to middle of the house' which implies (pro)motion to the most privileged place in the rear of a noble house.

The first occurrence of *t'm* relates to the Sun Chief's acceptance of Asdiwal as his daughter's husband. While Asdiwal was sitting down at the place of the guests on the other side of the fire, the Sun Chief asked his daughter to sit near Asdiwal:

26 *łguułg-i suuna **t'm**-yaa-n*
child-my better rear.of.house-walk-you
ada t'aa-n a awaa wil t'aa-ditga łguwaalks-aga gwa'a
and sit-you PREP near where sit-CON prince-DEM this
ada dm-t naksg-n
and FUT-he marry-you
*ada wil **t'm**-yaa-sga łguwaalks-m hana'ax-ga*
and then rear.of.house-walk-CON princesss-CON woman-DEM
ada wil-t sil-t'aa-t gisga sup'as-m 'yuuta-ga
and then-she together-sit-CON PREP young-CON man-DEM
"'My child, you may come towards the fire and sit down where this prince is sitting. He shall marry you.' Then the princess went towards the fire and sat down with the young man." (Boas 1912: 86, line 29–33; 87)

The next occurrence marks the culmination point of the test motive. Asdiwal has already proven a successful hunter in several tests, when his father-in-law initiated a final test: sitting on hot stones in the chief's house. Asdiwal's wife refused her father's request to order Asdiwal to the dangerous seat. He asked his daughter twice, finally asking Asdiwal himself to go near the fire:

27 *daał, gun-**t'm**-yaa naks-n, ła lamk-a loop* [...]
dear(female) CAUS-rear.of.house-walk husband-your PAST hot-CON stone
"'My dear, order your husband to go to the fire, the stones are hot.' [...]"
(Boas 1912: 102, line 20–27; 103)
ada gyik hatsiksm haw-sga sm'oogyit
and again again speak-CON chief
*asga-t **t'm**-huutg-isga łams-tga*
PREP-he rear.of.house-call-CON son.in.law-his
"Then the chief spoke again and called his son-in-law to the fire."
(Boas 1912: 102, line 31–104, line 1; 103–105)

In the third and final occurrence, the Sun Chief, finally, allocated Asdiwal the prestigious seat in the rear of the house in admittance of Asdiwal's superior power. The Sun Chief said to his entourage:

28 ***T'm**-yaa-n* *łams-utga*
rear.of.house-walk-CAUS son.in.law-my
Ada ma̲ dm t'aa-n-t gisga stuup'l-a
and you FUT sit-CAUS-him PREP rear.of.house-DEM
*Ada wil **t'm**-yaa-s Asdiwaal-ga*
and then rear.of.house-walk-CON <name>-DEM
Ada t'aa-t gisga stuup'l-ga dił naks-tga
And sit-he DEM rear.of.house-DEM and wife-his
"'My son-in-law shall go to the fire. Make him sit in the rear of the house.' Then Asdi-wā'l went to the fire and sat down with his wife in the rear of the house." (Boas 1912: 106, line 17–20; 107)

In the sentence immediately following, the chief admits that Potlatch-Giver had "really greater supernatural power" than he himself, and the text continues: "Now he liked his son-in-law much, and he respected him." (Boas 1912: 106, line 20–24; 107)

The message to the audience of these highly repetitive sections of the story is that Asdiwal has proven powerful enough to withstand the dangers of a chiefly position. The fire and hot stones and Asdiwal's position relative to the fire can be considered symbolic for the perils of such a position.

There is another passage in the text that refers to the placement of Potlatch-Giver in the house. Although *t'm* is not present because no motion was involved, the sentence describes the preparations of the Sea-Lion-People for the invitation of Potlatch-Giver. They indicate his status as a specially honored chiefly guest who sits on mats in the most privileged place in the house:

29 *Ada-t wil baał-a sgan-tga*
and-they then spread-CON mat-DEM
adm-t t'aa-d-it a nastoo walp-t a dzoga-lag-it
so.that-they sit-CAUS-him PREP side house-DEM PREP edge-fire-DEM
"Then they spread out mats for him to sit down on one side of the house close to the fire." (Boas 1912: 128, line 30–31; 129)

There are also three occurrences of *lagawk* 'from the side of the house to the fire.' The first and the last seem obviously to refer to some sort of magical / ritual practice expressed by the verb *lagawk-huutk* 'call, summon towards the fire.' The first request leads to the resurrection of a slave by the chief's daughter stepping over the bones (Boas 1912: 98–101). The latter describes a sacrifice of Potlatch-Giver's wife:

30 *ada wila-t **lagawk**-huutg-itga sm'oogyit-ga naks Asdiwaal-ga*
and then-he to.fire-call-CON chief-DEM wife <name>-DEM
"Then the chief called towards the fire the wife of Asdi-wā'l," (Boas 1912: 98, line 31; 99–101)

31 *ada al ła sga'nag-a* ***lagawk****-huutg-a wineey-t dił yee-t* [...]
and EMPH NEG long.time-CON to.fire-call-CON food-her and fat-her
adm wila da'axłg-da naks-da dzabdzab-dit
so.that then be.able-CON husband-her make.PL-he
"and (his wife) did not stop for a long time putting food and fat [...] into the fire as a sacrifice, that her husband might succeed;" (Boas 1912: 138, line 13–17; 139)

In the second occurrence, cited above in 31, the text repeats the chief's request, shifting from *t'm* and the daughter's perspective ("your husband" *naks-n*) to *lagawk* and the chief's perspective ("my son-in-law" *łams-u*). One may speculate that *lagawk* alludes to the magical / supernatural purpose of the chief's order:

32 *daał, gun-****t'm****-yaa naks-n, ła lamk-a loop* [...]
dear(female) CAUS-rear.of.house-walk husband-your PAST hot-CON stone
gun-lagawk-yaa łams-ut wa lamk-a loop-t
CAUS-to.fire-walk son-in-law-my when hot-CON stone-DEM
"'My dear, order your husband to go to the fire, the stones are hot.' [...]
'Order my son-in-law to go to the fire while the stones are hot.'"
(Boas 1912: 102, line 20–27; 103)

All passages showing *t'm* are concerned with the placement of Asdiwal in a chief's house.[23] Starting from the position as a guest, Asdiwal / Potlatch-Giver achieves a chiefly seat in the respective houses which is repeatedly expressed by the particle *t'm*. The use of *t'm* most frequently correlates with the first marriage when the main protagonist still bore the name Asdiwal. It seems therefore obvious that the frequent use of the particle *t'm* has been triggered by implicit association with its opposite *asdi* that can be used for motion in the front part of the house. The only occurrence of the particle *asdi*, however, is in a non-locative meaning when his first wife advises Asidwal

33 *ma asdiwaan-gn adzi da waa-n*
you make.a.mistake-possibly if then do-you
"'You will make a mistake if you do.'" (Boas 1912: 88, line 24; 89)

The punning with the particle *asdi*—either in the name Asdiwal or in the verb *asdiwaal* 'to make a mistake'—, can consequently not been considered as an explicit binary opposition.

23 There is one more occurrence that does not fit into this line of argumentation, when the Chief of the Sea-Lion people said: "'*t'm-gaa na-lip-xsoo-yut*'—'Take my own canoe to the fire.'" (Boas 1912: 132, line 29)

Implications for an interpretation based on locative particles

Lévi-Strauss acknowledged the relevance of locative particles in the Tsimshianic languages (Lévi-Strauss 1967: 42, 46) and identified geographical movement as part of a scheme of binary oppositions in the story (Lévi-Strauss 1967: 17–20). But the findings originating from the text itself, based on the locative particles, do not fit many aspects of Lévi-Strauss's analysis. Of course, this cannot be understood as a refutation of his analysis, because he explicitly denied the relevance of the content and the plot of a narrative for his kind of more general analyses (Lévi-Strauss 1955: 85–86).

The obvious main concern of the text is social advancement that can be achieved by successful hunting and by marrying women of supernatural or royal ancestry. Although several locative particles would be well-suited for this purpose, no explicit binary oppositions seem to be at work via these particles. Nevertheless, some particles help to orchestrate central issues of the plot of the story. Furthermore, it seems plausible that the repetitive and clustered use of selected particles was the intentional choice of the author / narrator as, in comparison with the other texts in Boas's 1912 collection, locative particles of the geographic and house-oriented subtype are almost twice as frequent in the story of Asdiwal.

The opposite particles *bax* 'up' and *'yaga* 'down' both serve to highlight hunting in the mountains, the former used when Asdiwal / Potlatch-Giver leaves for a hunting trip, the latter when he distributes the resulting venison. The opposites *uks* 'seaward' and *dzagm* 'ashore' help to illustrate the conflict between Potlatch-Giver (*uks*) and his brothers-in-law (*dzagm*).

In the social domain, the particle *'yaga* 'down' serves as a marker for the distribution of venison. The particle *na* 'from the woods to the rear of the houses' characterizes the return of the successful hunter from the wilderness to the social domain, but also his appeal as a potential spouse. The in-house locative particle *t'm* 'from rear to middle of the house' indicates the achievement of chiefly status, and, in the episode of Asdiwal's test by hot stones, also the dangers of that status. The particle *asdi*, although used sometimes as some sort of opposite of *t'm*, does not occur in this locative function in the text, but only once in *asdiwaal* 'making a mistake.' This punning with the name Asdiwal can well be understood as a reference to the overcoming of the characteristics of *asdi* by establishing a *t'm*-like position in the rear part of the house, the place for the highest members of a noble family.

While most locative particles seem inconspicuous, more investigation is needed to achieve a fair understanding of the text, the more so as spatial configurations are also expressed by some nouns as, e.g., *stuup'l* 'rear of house' or *gyigyaani* 'upriver location; the interior' or by the various verbs of motion. Moreover, spatial metaphors most probably are not the exclusive source for culture-specific narrative symbolism.

Conclusions

Using the well-known Asdiwal story, I have tried to demonstrate the usefulness of studies of narratives that rely on a linguistic analysis of the text in the source language. If one approaches texts in such a way, the analysis will focus on the peculiarities of the respective linguaculture and on the specific situation of elicitation as well as on the author or narrator. A careful look at the structure, wording and grammar of the original text reveals narrative mechanisms which may be overlooked in the translation. It also minimizes the risk of biased summaries and interpretations. All operations can be uncovered via direct grammatical representations of the intentions of the author or narrator in a way that leaves little room for arbitrariness. As a linguist I trust in the original Sm'algya̱x wording and, therefore, based my selection for interpretation from this source. Therefore, I appraise the social role of the *adawx* as the key to the interpretation and consider locative particles like *t'm* and others as intentional indicators for the focal points of the Asdiwal story.

Of course, the present study offers a quite literal type of partial interpretation. It is not intended to cast doubt upon the relevance of universalistic myth analyses or upon the decisive impulse to this field that originated from Lévi-Strauss. Not only are binary oppositions an important aspect of narrative structure, but it would also be unwise to ignore that there are many stories within a story and, of course, from a universalist mythographer's point of view behind or beyond all stories. And the story of Asdiwal is far from having being told to its end. Therefore, nothing could be more adequate than closing this article with the modesty formulated by Anderson, taking up the punning on the name Asdiwal: "It is ironic that the name of the hero in the text that has so captivated our discipline puns on 'making a mistake,' because we have certainly made a lot of mistakes in trying to understand it." (Anderson 2004: 120)

References

Ackerman, Charles 1973. A Small Problem of Fish Bones. In *The Logic of Culture. Advancement in Structural Theory and Methods.* I. Rossi (ed.), 113–126. London: Tavistock Publications.

Adams, John W. 1974. Dialectics and Contingency in "The Story of Asdiwal": An Ethnographic Note. In *The Unconscious in Culture. The Structuralism of Claude Lévi-Strauss in Perspective.* I. Rossi (ed.), 170–178. New York: E. P. Dutton.

— 1981. Recent Ethnology of the Northwest Coast. *Annual Review of Anthropology* 10: 361–392.

Anderson, Margaret Seguin 2004. Asdiwal. Surveying the Ethnographic Ground. In *Coming to Shore. Northwest Coast Ethnology, Traditions, and Visions.* M. Mauzé, M. E. Harkin, and S. Kan (eds.), 107–126. Lincoln: University of Nebraska Press.

Anderson, Margaret, et al. (eds.) 2013. *Sm'algyax Living Legacy Talking Dictionary.* Last updated April 2013.
http://web.unbc.ca/~smalgyax/ [30.05.2016]

Bascom, William 1965. The Forms of Folklore: Prose Narratives. *Journal of American Folklore* 78, No. 307: 3–20.

Barbeau, Marius 1917. Review of Tsimshian Mythology by Franz Boas. *American Anthropologist, New Series* 19: 548–563.

Berman, Judith 1991. *The Seals' Sleeping Cave: The Interpretation of Boas' Kwakw'ala Texts.* Ph. D. dissertation, University of Pennsylvania.

Boas, Franz 1895 [1992]. *Indianische Sagen von der Nord-Pacifischen Küste Amerikas.* Berlin: Asher. [Nachdruck 1992: Bonn: Holos.]

— 1902. *Tsimshian Texts.* Washington: Government Printing Office. (Bureau of American Ethnology, Bulletin 27)

— 1911. Tsimshian. In *Handbook of American Indian Languages.* Franz Boas (ed.), part I, 283–422. Washington: Government Printing Office.

— 1912. Tsimshian Texts (New Series). In *Publications of the American Ethnological Society*, vol. III, 65–285. Leyden: Brill.

— 1916. Tsimshian Mythology. Based on texts recorded by William Tate. In *Bureau of American Ethnology, Annual Report* 31, 1909–1910: 27–1037. Washington: Government Printing Office.

— 1921. Ethnology of the Kwakiutl. In two parts. In *Bureau of American Ethnology, Annual Report* 35, 1913–1914: 43–1481. Washington: Government Printing Office.

Douglas, Mary 1967. The Meaning of Myth, with Special Reference to "La geste d'Asdiwal." In *The Structural Study of Myth and Totemism.* E. Leach (ed.), 49–69. London: Tavistock Press. (Association of Social Anthropologists Monographs, 5)

Dundes, Alan 1997. Binary Opposition in Myth: The Propp / Levi-Strauss debate in retrospect. *Western Folklore* 56: 39–50.

Dunn, John Asher 1978. *A Practical Dictionary of the Coast Tsimshian Language.* Ottawa: National Museums of Canada. (Mercury Series, Canadian Ethnology Service, paper 42)

— 1979. *A Reference Grammar for the Coast Tsimshian Language.* Ottawa: National Museums of Canada. (Mercury Series, Canadian Ethnology Service, paper 55)

Dürr, Michael 1992. Nachwort. In Franz Boas, *Indianische Sagen von der Nord-Pacifischen Küste Amerikas*, 389–403. Bonn: Holos.

— 1996. Warum man sich Stachelschweinen vorsichtig nähern sollte – Anmerkungen zur Neuausgabe der "Original Tsimshian Texts of Henry Tate." *Anthropos* 91: 230–236.

Fortescue, Michael 2011a. *Orientation Systems of the North Pacific Rim.* Copenhagen: Museum Tusculanum Press.

— 2011b. Where "Out to Sea" Equals "Toward the Fire": Macrocosm-Microcosm Relationship in Languages of the North Pacific Rim. *Anthropological Linguistics* 53: 1–14.

Kasten, Erich 2017. Documenting Oral Histories in the Russian Far East: Text Corpora for Multiple Aims and Uses. In *Oral History Meets Linguistics.* E. Kasten, K. Roller, and J. Wilbur (eds.), 13–30. Fürstenberg/Havel: Kulturstiftung Sibirien.

Kronenfeld, David, and Henry W. Decker 1979. Structuralism. *Annual Review of Anthropology* 10: 503–541.

Lévi-Strauss, Claude 1955. The Structural Study of Myth. In *Myth. A Symposium.* Th. A. Sebeok (ed.), 81–106. Bloomington: Indiana University Press. (Bibliographical and Special Series of the American Folklore Society, 5)

— 1958. La geste d'Asdiwal. *Annuaire 1958–1959 de l'École pratique des hautes études, Section des sciences religieuses*: 3–43. Paris: Sorbonne.

— 1967. The Story of Asdiwal. In *The Structural Study of Myth and Totemism.* E. Leach (ed.), 1–47. London: Tavistock Press. (Association of Social Anthropologists Monographs, 5)

— 1973. Post-scriptum to the Reprint of La geste d'Asdiwal. In Claude Lévi-Strauss, *Anthropologie structurale deux,* 223–233. Paris: Plon.

— 1983. *Le regard éloigné.* Paris: Plon.

— 1984. *Paroles données.* Paris: Plon.

Mandelbaum, David G. 1987. Myths and Myth Maker: Some Anthropological Appraisals of the Mythological Studies of Levi-Strauss. *Ethnology* 26: 31–36.

Marsden, Susan 2002: Adawx, Spanaxnox, and the Geopolitics of the Tsimshian. *BC Studies* 135: 101–135.

McDonald, James Andrew 2003. *People of the Robin. The Tsimshian of Kitsumkalum.* s. l.: CCI Press and Alberta Acadre Network.

Miller, Jay 1998. Tsimshian Ethno-Ethnohistory: A "Real" Indigenous Chronology. *Ethnohistory* 45: 657–674.

Mulder, Jean Gail 1994. *Ergativity in Coast Tsimshian (Sm'algya̲x).* Berkeley: University of California Press. (University of California Publications in Linguistics, vol. 124)

Oppitz, Michael 1975. *Notwendige Beziehungen. Abriß der strukturalen Anthropologie.* Frankfurt am Main: Suhrkamp.

Roberts, Donny May 2009. *Dictionary of Shm'algyack.* Juneau, Alaska: Sealaska Heritage Institute.

Roth, Christopher F. 2008. *Becoming Tsimshian. The Social Life of Names.* Seattle: University of Washington Press.

Segal, Robert A. 2004. *Myth. A Very Short Introduction.* Oxford: Oxford University Press.

Stebbins, Tonya 2003. *Fighting Language Endangerment: Community Directed Research on Sm'algyax (Coast Tsimshian).* Osaka: ELPR. (Endangered Languages of the Pacific Rim, Publications Series A2-026)

Thomas, Lynn L., Judy Z. Kronenfeld, and David B. Kronenfeld 1976. Asdiwal Crumbles: A Critique of Lévi-Straussian Myth Analysis. *American Ethnologist* 3: 147–173.

7 ON PITS, PROGRESSIVES AND PROBABILITIES OF USE: MEMORIES FROM WALES AND THEIR IMPLICATIONS FOR CORPUS-LINGUISTIC (AND HISTORICAL) RESEARCH

Katja Roller

Introduction

We was, we was all working in the colliery
(FRED, 87-year-old from Swansea, recorded in 1973)

This quote, taken from an interview in the Freiburg Corpus of English Dialects (FRED), can be read from several perspectives. If we focus on the content, the quote may function as a symbol of the importance of coal mining in the history of Wales. Up to some decades ago, the coal mining industry was among the biggest employers in Wales. And to the present day, the work in pits—especially in the southern Welsh Valleys—is seen as a vital part of Welsh working-class culture and identity (cf. Williams et al. 1996). If we focus on linguistic structure, the utterance contains two non-standard grammatical features: a plural pronoun combined with a singular verb form of past tense *be* ('we was', cf. Kortmann and Lunkenheimer 2013) and the non-standard habitual progressive ('was all work**ing**'). This progressive construction is used in Welsh varieties of English to mark habitual, i.e. regularly occurring, actions or events. It is employed in addition to Standard English habitual markers as *would* and *used to* (*we all used to work in the colliery*). The quote thus provides a first tiny glimpse into how oral histories can contribute to structural investigations of Welsh English. But why Welsh English and why should one explore it using oral histories?

English and Welsh, the two official languages of Wales, have been in close contact for centuries. The indigenous Welsh language developed from Brythonic, a branch of the Insular Celtic languages, between 400 and 700 CE (cf. Davies 2014: 13). The first larger-scale uses of English in Wales trace back to the Anglo-Norman invasion in the late 11th century AD (cf. Aitchison and Carter 1994: 23). Despites the presence of English, Welsh remained the majority language of Wales up to the mid to late 19th century (cf. Davies 1994: 437). The Industrial Revolution as well as measures in governmental and educational policies, however, brought about a shift to English. Nowadays, despite the dominance of English, one fifth of the Welsh population is still able to speak Welsh (cf. Williams 2014: 242). Moreover, various contact features can be found in Welsh English dialects. In addition to characteristic phonetic features such as the monophthongs [e:] and [o:] in words like *great* [gre:t] and *road* [ro:d], Welsh English grammar also shows traces from the Celtic substrate. An example of such a grammatical feature would be the non-standard habitual progressive, which will be described in more detail below. Clearly, this variety of English has a lot to offer for e.g. dialectologists, sociolinguists and typologists. Somewhat surprisingly, however, only few studies have investigated occurrences of Welsh English features (corpus-linguistically), and even fewer studies have focused on Welsh English grammar. The paucity of studies goes hand in hand with the scarcity of—especially present-day—Welsh English corpora available to researchers. This chapter argues first that oral history interviews from Wales can fill this gap by providing data which can yield quantitative and qualitative insights into morphosyntactic variation in Welsh English. Furthermore, it is then shown how these linguistic insights may contribute to oral history research.

The chapter is structured as follows. First, the non-standard habitual progressive in Welsh English is introduced and exemplified through instances from two oral history databases: the Millennium Memory Bank (MMB) and FRED. Second, a corpus-linguistic approach to MMB data is presented, centering on ascertaining what corpus frequencies can tell us about salience in Welsh English grammar. Are salient Welsh English features (as perceived by Welsh people and Londoners) more frequent in the corpus than less salient structures? The non-standard habitual progressive is used as an exemplary feature here. Third, how such a corpus-linguistic approach can yield insights for oral history research is determined. The section compares oral histories from the 1970s (FRED) with corresponding data from the 1990s (MMB) to see whether historico-cultural changes in Wales are reflected in interviewees' memories of habitual actions.

Non-Standard Habitual Progressives in Welsh English

In English, there are several ways of referring to actions or events that took or take place habitually. In the past tense, Standard English possibilities of denoting habituality include *used to* (*I used to take the bus to school every morning*), *would* (*We would go there on Sundays*) and the use of the simple past (*We were paid every fortnight*). In the present tense, the simple present is used (*She visits her grandmother on Wednesdays*). Welsh English features an additional way of referring to such repeated actions, namely by means of the progressive (cf. Paulasto 2006; Penhallurick 2008; Roller 2016). This use of BE + verb ending in *-ing* is illustrated in the following example from the Millennium Memory Bank, where an informant from Mid Wales shares her memories on growing up with several siblings under cramped housing conditions.

(1) <Interviewer>: ...where would you all sleep? Do you, were you in one bedroom or two bedrooms...?

<Interviewee>: Yeah, like we was three girls, so we had to sleep in one room and then sort of the boys **were sleeping** in another, that's how you did it like…

In the next example, taken from the FRED corpus, an interviewee talks about his job as a dock worker in South Wales.

(2) <Interviewee>: So I **was steering** with a man from Clydach, he was a deacon in Moriah Chapel, old (name). He was the man and I was the boy. You'd have to eat your food in the boat while travelling. There was no hours and half hours for breakfast…

It is fairly likely that non-standard habitual progressives emerged in Welsh English due to language contact with Welsh (cf. Paulasto 2006; Penhallurick 2008). In Welsh, the same present tense construction can be used for referring to events which are on-going as well as habitual events. For example, the following sentence translates to both "He goes to the cinema" and "He is going to the cinema", and thus can, but does not necessarily, denote a habitual action (cf. Brake 2004; Thomas 1997).

Mae	*e*	*'n*	*mynd*	*i'r*	*sinema*
be.PRS.3SG	he	ASP[1]	go	to the	cinema

He goes/is going to the cinema

The structure and distribution of the feature in Wales have been addressed in previous publications (e.g. Parry 1999; Paulasto 2006), and the non-standard habitual progressive is arguably a "salient" Welsh English feature among scholars. It remains unclear, however, how the feature is perceived by people from Wales (and other parts of Britain). Are speakers aware of using it? And if so, is their level of awareness connected to the feature's frequency in Welsh English? The following section approaches these questions, focusing on how and why oral history interviews from Wales can help shed light on the interplay of usage frequency and perception.

A Corpus-Linguistic Approach to Oral Histories from Wales

Introduction to the project

The research presented here formed part of my Ph.D. project and was carried out between 2012 and 2015. A central objective of the project was to identify factors that determine *salience* in Welsh English grammar. Salience in this study denoted the

1 ASP in this example refers to the category of aspectual marker (cf. Brake 2004: 21).

degree to which linguistic features were perceived consciously by listeners, i.e. insiders from Wales and outsiders from London, and considered as "typically Welsh". One potential determinant of salience investigated in this context was frequency. It was hypothesised that features with higher frequencies of occurrence in Welsh English would be perceived more consciously (possibly due to higher levels of familiarity and entrenchment) than less frequent constructions. To test this hypothesis, the frequencies of different grammatical features in spoken Welsh English had to be determined. Oral history interviews from the Millennium Memory Bank (MMB) proved to be valuable sources for these analyses.

The Millennium Memory Bank (MMB)

The following introduction to the MMB is based on Gallwey (2013), Perks (2001) and Roller (2015), who provide detailed accounts of the database. The MMB is Europe's largest oral history archive, comprising 6 069 interviews from England, Northern Ireland, Scotland and Wales, recorded between 1998 and 1999. A collaboration between the British Library and the BBC, the project aimed to "produce a 'snapshot' of Britain at the turn of the millennium" (Perks 2001: 95). Forty local BBC radio stations were involved in carrying out the interviews—with radio producers and researchers working closely—and many recordings later formed part of the radio series *The Century Speaks.*[2] The interviews circle around personal memories of growing up and living in Britain in the 20th century as well as hopes and/or beliefs for the new millennium. Sixteen topics served as guidelines for structuring the interviews: where we live, house and home, who are we, belonging, living together, crime and the law, growing up, getting older, technology, eating and drinking, money, playtime, going places, life and death, beliefs and fears, and what's next? The interviewees, 44 percent females and 56 percent males, were aged between five and 107 and had diverse occupational and educational backgrounds (e.g. college students, farmers, teachers, police officers).

As discussed by Roller (2015), the MMB has a lot to offer for (corpus-)linguistic approaches to British English. The archive involves a vast amount of spoken language in conversations that do not centre around linguistic topics. Sharing life memories and personal experiences may have led many speakers to focus on *what* they were saying rather than on *how* there were expressing themselves, probably resulting in (relatively) natural language use (cf. Anderwald and Wagner 2006: 38). Moreover, the interviewers in the Welsh section of the MMB—the section used for my research —had usually grown up in Wales themselves. According to Anderwald and Wagner (2006: 36–37), being interviewed by such "insiders" may "relax the interview situation considerably". An example of an "insider" would be Anita Morgan, who conducted many MMB

2 *The Century Speaks* comprises 640 half-hour radio documentaries. It was broadcast on local UK radio stations across Britain between September and December 1999 and, in the form of eight programs, on BBC Radio 4 in the autumn of 2000 (cf. Perks 2001: 103).

interviews in Wales. A Welshwoman herself, she spoke English with a clearly audible Welsh accent, which might have encouraged her dialogue partners to use their local dialects, too.

However, there are some challenges that need to be taken into consideration when approaching the MMB linguistically (cf. Roller 2015). Since the subjects were not selected on the basis of language-related criteria, speakers from a specific region do not necessarily speak that region's local dialect. In approaching the data, it is thus important to take a closer look at individual interviews and/or the metadata provided for all MMB recordings (available at http://cadensa.bl.uk) to learn about a speaker's linguistic background. Also, since the oral narratives focus on past events, past tense constructions (e.g. verbal inflection, temporal adverbs) are likely to outnumber present tense forms. This needs to be kept in mind when determining the usage frequencies of specific features, since they may be skewed towards past tense occurrences simply due to the text genres represented. Limitations with regard to research logistics are that the full-length MMB interviews are currently only accessible in person at the British Library in London and that most of the data have not been transcribed yet due to limited funding (cf. Perks 2001: 100).

To me it was clearly worth taking on these challenges, as the MMB appeared to be a rich source providing valuable insights into dialect morphosyntax. For my own research on Welsh English grammar, I thus transcribed nine hours of MMB interviews from Wales (during a research stay at the British Library).[3]

Data and findings

To approach the usage frequencies of the habitual progressive (and other grammatical features) in Welsh English, the total numbers of occurrence in the corpus texts were determined. As for salience, questionnaires were collected from 150 Welsh people (insiders) and 150 Londoners (outsiders). In the questionnaires, subjects had to assign a range of grammatical features to regions in the British Isles. It was then determined which features had been assigned to Wales most frequently, i.e. which were seen as most characteristic (or *salient*) of Welsh English. To find out about a potential relation between salience and frequency, the values from the questionnaires and the corpus frequencies were then compared. Generally, the data suggest a positive correlation between frequency and salience (both for insiders and outsiders), with more salient features being, on average, more prevalent in the corpus data (cf. Roller 2016). The non-standard habitual progressive covered middle ground with regard to

3 The MMB was not the only source used for my corpus-based analyses of Welsh English. I also worked with the Welsh section of the *BBC Voices* project, which however will not be discussed in detail in the present chapter. The *BBC Voices* interviews were carried out between 2004 and 2005 all over Wales and the UK and centre around e.g. subjects' attitudes to language and local terms, but also contain general life stories and anecdotes (cf. Elmes 2013).

both salience and frequency. The feature was assigned to Wales by 27 percent of the Welsh subjects, while the most salient Welsh English feature was correctly located by 60 percent, and the least salient one by 9 percent of participants. In the corpus data, habitual progressives occurred 2.64 times per 10 000 words, as compared to 4.58 per 10,000 words for the most frequent construction and 0.15 per 10 000 words for the least frequent feature (plus, one feature from the salience questionnaire could not be found at all in the corpus).

While these data provide some insights into perceptions of average speakers, it seems necessary to take a look beyond the corpus means and salience percentages to learn about interindividual differences in salience perceptions. In my research, it was thus also determined to what extent salience ratings differ between subjects with different social and personal backgrounds. And it was found that, for example, in the group of participants from Wales, older people were considerably more likely to identify the Welsh English features. This may be connected to the fact that—with current processes of dialect levelling going on in Wales (cf. Paulasto 2006)—older speakers are more likely to still *use* the non-standard features in their speech, which becomes apparent in the MMB data. This use may result in them being more familiar with some non-standard forms than the younger generations. Also, (Welsh and London) subjects with more positive attitudes to dialectal diversity were significantly better at recognising the Welsh English features. Overall, this shows that data based on oral history can both provide general quantitative accounts of grammatical patterns in a dialect, but also point to individual speakers' experiences with language. It seems extremely worthwhile to exploit both aspects in approaching representations of language in people's minds.

From Corpus-Linguistic Analyses to Insights for Oral History

Moving away from structural-linguistic aspects of habituality and towards the content of utterances involving habitual markers can have some interesting implications for oral history research. An in-depth look at habitual actions can, for example, offer insights into daily routines and practices at different times of (remembered) history. In the following, a pilot study is presented involving a comparison of contexts of habituality in oral histories from the 1970s (FRED) with interviews from the 1990s (MMB). The aim of the pilot study is to determine to what extent societal changes and developments in Wales are reflected in Welsh people's memories of everyday practices.

FRED vs. MMB

The Freiburg Corpus of English Dialects (FRED) was consulted for the study of oral narratives from some decades ago. The corpus consists of 300 hours of oral history interviews from diverse locations. In contrast to the MMB, these interviews were collected by and are stored in many different archives and museums in England, Scotland, Wales and the Isle of Man (cf. Hernández 2006). The majority of the FRED interviews were carried out in the 1970s and 1980s and involve non-mobile elderly rural speakers. In the MMB, the interviewees have diverse social backgrounds and the age range is large. Consequently, for the present analyses, only MMB interviews with rather non-mobile speakers aged 60 or older from rural locations were selected. The transcription conventions are identical for the two collections since I transcribed the MMB data using the FRED transcription standard.

Data analysis

For the sake of comparability, I analysed subsets of FRED and MMB transcripts totalling around 36 000 words each. It should be noted that the research presented here is just a starting point for more in-depth analyses with larger amounts of data to follow in the future. In both databases, which verbs are used in the habitual progressive form (e.g. *work* in *He was **working***) was determined. The aim was to find out about similarities and differences in daily practices in the life stories collected in the 1970s vs. the 1990s. To be able to work with more data, not only were non-standard habitual progressives analysed, but also the standard past habituals *used to*, *would* and simple past. For the MMB and the FRED data, lists with the "habitual verbs" were compiled and sorted by frequency of occurrence. Diachronic changes, i.e. changes over the course of time, were then approached by identifying those verbs that only occurred either in FRED or in the MMB. These verbs are shown in figures 1 and 2. The larger the font size, the more often the verbs appeared in the respective corpus data.

A range of words only occurring in the FRED data (cf. Figure 1) are used in the context of descriptions of working in the coalmines, such as *bind, carry, fill, hook up, line, wheel, tip, wind, peg, emery* and *weigh.* In the following example involving the verb *to wheel*, a southern Welsh speaker shares his memories of his first job in a coalfield:

(3) <Interviewer>: What was your first job?

<Interviewee>: Oh on the surface, wheeling ashes from the boiler and all the rest of it. Hard work. You **were wheeling** the ashes up these old planks and tipping them, you and the barrow in half the time, you got used to it you know. You would be in the truck with the barrow, and unleading small coal after, ten tonners to the boilers.

Work appears frequently in habitual constructions in both datasets; it is the second most frequent "habitual verb" in FRED and the third most frequent in the MMB. Verbs relating to work in pits, however, are much more prevalent in FRED. This may be connected to the fact that the Welsh coal mining industry, "once the biggest single

Fig. 1: Verbs used in habitual contexts in FRED but not in the MMB.

Fig. 2: Verbs used in habitual contexts in the MMB but not in FRED.

employer in Wales" (BBC 2008), experienced a steady decline in the latter decades of the 20th century. While the 1920s saw the largest number of Welshmen working in coal mines (271 000, i.e. ten percent of the Welsh population), many pits closed after WWII, probably due to the growing importance of the oil industry and overseas coal production (cf. BBC 2008). The miners' strikes of 1984/85 could not prevent southern Welsh coalfields from closing, so that only 4 000 miners and seven pits were left at the end of the decade (cf. Davies 1994: 685). "At the end of the 1980s, with more Welshmen working in banks than in pits, one of the most remarkable chapters in the history of the Welsh had closed" (Davies 1994: 685). While the subjects in my MMB sample had witnessed this change, it had not yet taken place to this extent for the FRED speakers. Born around the turn of the 19th to 20th century, they had lived through the heyday of Welsh mining and times when collieries were not only the prime employers in the area, but also constituted integral parts of everyday life in mining communities.

Apart from these dynamic aspects, the analyses of habitual constructions also point to stability in the data, i.e. to habitual practices described by speakers both in

FRED and in the MMB. The following verbs occur four times or more in habitual contexts in both datasets: *be, call, come, do, get, go, have, play, say, take, walk, work.* Not very surprisingly, some (genre-independent) stability is caused by verbs such as *be, do, have* and *say*, which are among the most frequently used verbs in English (cf. Leech et al. 2001).[4] These verbs are thus highly expectable across different text types. In addition to that, however, words such as *work, play, walk* and *call* (as in *we used to call them flower pots*) might hint at some genre-dependent stability and reflect typical and potentially timeless daily routines commonly reported in oral histories.

In a similar study with oral history recordings from Birmingham, Sealey (2009) investigated which words occur across all stories, i.e. in 144 narratives by local people with diverse backgrounds. Apart from a great deal of grammatical words, the items shared by all texts suggest "a glimmer of the 'genre' of 'life history' […]: *good, home, know, like, old, school, see, still, things, think, time, way*" (emphasis in original; Sealey 2009: 218). In addition to that, *I used to* was among the 3-word strings occurring in at least 130 texts, indicating that references to habitual actions are characteristic parts of oral histories. Overall this points to some commonality and stability in the stories' themes.

While the narratives in Sealey's (2009) work, as well as those in my study, show some similarities in topics, they are

> "nevertheless unique; each interviewee demonstrates the ever-present potential for linguistic creativity while simultaneously contributing to the collective entity that emerges as 'the discourse of life histories'. […] [E]ach interview is a record of a specific social interaction, and each interviewee interprets this in his or her own way." (Sealey 2009: 2015–17)

These interindividual differences in oral histories are also mirrored in type frequencies in the MMB and FRED data. Of all verbs in habitual constructions (153), 56 percent (87) occur only once in the speech of a single narrator. To name just a few, such verbs hinting at unique life experiences include *amuse, cuddle, dress, manicure, peel, recite* and *harmonise*, the latter being presented in context in example (4) from FRED.

(4) <Interviewee>: Well I 'll tell you how it started. I was in the army in the First War, and marching along you know how they go, marching along and there was a lot of Lancashire boys with us and there was one of them a pretty decent singer, a pretty decent tenor, and he used to sing that old song "Thora", and I **used to harmonise** it. That was the first time I found out that I had a pretty good voice.

4 The frequency lists provided by Leech et al. (2001) are based on the British National Corpus (BNC). The BNC includes spoken and written language samples totalling 100 million words. Most of the samples are from the 1980s and early 1990s.

In sum, these glimpses of habitual practices and routines reveal both general and much more nuanced and fine-grained aspects of remembered life in Wales. The quantitative diachronic approach points to broader historical and economical changes in Wales, reflected to some extent in the collective memories of informants who grew up at different times. But as with the linguistic approach presented in the previous section, individual stories necessarily differ from such group averages, and particular verbs may function as gateways to unique and very personal memories. In developing a richer understanding of the past, and in keeping it alive, a combination of both approaches may prove helpful, giving "the people who made and experienced history, through their own words, a central place" (Thompson 2000: 3).

Conclusion

Using the example of Welsh English, this chapter has shown how a corpus-linguistic approach to oral history data can yield linguistic and historical insights. Non-standard habitual progressives (and other habitual markers) in Welsh English were chosen as objects of study. To explore them linguistically, a corpus of oral history interviews from the Welsh section of the Millennium Memory Bank (MMB) was compiled. The corpus frequencies of non-standard habitual progressives helped strengthen the hypothesis that the salience of Welsh English features is related to the features' frequencies in language use. Subsequently, habitual markers were analysed with regard to their meaning, i.e. the actions and events they refer to, in order to determine whether they reflect historical changes in Wales. Contrasting FRED interviews from the 1970s and MMB interviews from the 1990s, it was suggested that the downfall of the Welsh coal mining industry is mirrored in the differing topics referred to by the two groups' descriptions of habitual actions. In addition to this diachronic change, the habitual markers also point to commonalities between the older and the newer oral history interviews. Stories constructed with verbs like *work, play* and *walk* seem to constitute general common parts of oral narratives.

Both the linguistic and the content-related approach show how quantitative corpus-based studies can provide insights into *average* language use and memories, but at the same time that this is not the full (life) story. As exemplified by habitual actions only described once in FRED and the MMB, is important to move beyond these group averages and zoom in on variation to account for *individual* language use/stories. Needless to say, language use includes stories, and stories necessitate the use of language. Linguistics and oral history are per se closely linked, and the present chapter has tried to use this link to show how both disciplines can profit from each other.

Future research could explore past habituality in oral histories in more detail. Besides larger amounts of data, group differences concerning how habitual actions are remembered and shared could be analysed more closely. It would be interesting to learn more about potential differences between, for example, female and male speakers and informants from different age groups. Furthermore, it might be worth investigating how body language is used to portray or underline such memories of recurrent actions. "Memories are recounted in more than words. Transcripts can indicate laughter, sobs, finger pointing, or fist shaking. But some expressions and gestures are too complex and subtle to reduce to words." (Ritchie 2014: 137) In exploring narrations of daily practices and routines, it may thus prove fruitful to go beyond the aural and include the visual as well, for example by using corpora based on videos. Such a multifaceted approach may unearth additional stories in the stories, point to patterns they have in common, but also reveal more about the unique colourings of each individual's life memory.

References

Aitchison, John, and Harold Carter 1994. *A Geography of the Welsh Language 1961–1991.* Cardiff: University of Wales Press.

Anderwald, Lieselotte, and Susanne Wagner 2006. FRED – the Freiburg English Dialect Corpus: Applying Corpus-linguistic Research Tools to the Analysis of Dialect Data. In *Using Unconventional Digital Language Data. Vol. 1: Synchronic Corpora*, J.C. Beal, K.P. Corrigan, and H.L. Moisl (eds.), 35–53. Basingstoke: Palgrave Macmillan.

BBC. 2008. *The 20th Century*. URL: http://www.bbc.co.uk/wales/history/sites/themes/society/industry_coal03.shtml [09.07.2016].

Brake, Phylip 2004. *An Introduction to Welsh*. Munich: Lincom.

Davies, Janet 2014. *The Welsh Language: A History*. Cardiff: University of Wales Press.

Davies, John 1994. *A History of Wales*. London: Penguin.

Elmes, Simon 2013. Voices: A Unique BBC Adventure. In *Analysing 21st Century British English: Conceptual and Methodological Aspects of the 'Voices' project*, C. Upton and B.L. Davies (eds.), 1–11. London: Routledge.

Gallwey, April 2013. The Rewards of Using Archived Oral Histories in Research: The Case of the Millennium Memory Bank. *Oral History* 41(1): 37–50.

Hernández, Nuria 2006. *User's Guide to FRED: Freiburg Corpus of English Dialects.* https://www.freidok.uni-freiburg.de/data/2489/ [09.07 2016]

Kortmann, Bernd, and Kerstin Lunkenheimer 2013. *The Electronic World Atlas of Varieties of English.*
http://ewave-atlas.org/ [14.11.2016]

Leech, Geoffrey, Paul Rayson, and Andrew Wilson 2001. *Word Frequencies in Written and Spoken English.* Harlow; Munich: Longman.

Parry, David 1999. *A Grammar and Glossary of the Conservative Anglo-Welsh Dialects of Rural Wales.* Sheffield: The National Centre for English Cultural Tradition.

Paulasto, Heli 2006. *Welsh English Syntax: Contact and Variation*. Joensuu: Joensuu University Press.

Penhallurick, Robert 2008. Welsh English: Morphology and Syntax. In *Varieties of English 1: The British Isles*, B. Kortmann and C. Upton (eds.), 360–372. Berlin: De Gruyter.

Perks, Rob 2001. The Century Speaks: A Public History Partnership. *Oral History* 29(2): 95–105.

Ritchie, Donald A. 2014. *Doing Oral History.* 3rd edn. Oxford: Oxford University Press.

Roller, Katja 2015. Towards the 'Oral' in Oral History: Using Historical Narratives in Linguistics. *Oral History* 43(1): 73–84.

— 2016. *Salience in Welsh English Grammar: A Usage-based Approach.* Freiburg: NIHIN Studies.

Sealey, Alison 2009. Probabilities and Surprises: A Realist Approach to Identifying Linguistic and Social Patterns, with Reference to an Oral History Corpus. *Applied Linguistics* 31(2): 215–235.

Thomas, Alan R 1997. The Welshness of Welsh English: A Survey Paper. In *The Celtic Englishes I*, H. L. C. Tristram (ed.), 55–85. Heidelberg: Winter.

Thompson, Paul 2000.[3] *Voices of the Past: Oral History.* Oxford: Oxford University Press.

Williams, Angie, Peter Garrett, and Nikolas Coupland 1996. Perceptual Dialectology, Folklinguistics, and Regional Stereotypes: Teachers' Perceptions of Variation in Welsh English. *Multilingua* 15(2): 171–199.

Williams, Colin H. 2014. The Lightening Veil: Language Revitalization in Wales. *Review of Research in Education* 38(1): 242–272.

8 A DIFFICULT TERM IN CONTEXT: THE CASE OF FRENCH *STO*

Annette Gerstenberg

Oral history and (socio-)linguistics have profoundly different approaches and as a result, the textual data gained differ in many aspects. However, facing the challenge of combining sources from these two disciplines is very rewarding. Reading and hearing interviews with contemporary witnesses to historical events can sharpen the tools of discourse analysis; awareness of historical discourse can raise our understanding of how individuals deal with topics embedded in collective memory and how they encode their experiences linguistically. Furthermore, in this chapter, we illustrate the core research questions applicable to these different types of corpus: while oral history resources are designed to reconstruct the meaning and the sense attributed to historical events by different individuals and social groups, linguistic audio data allow for analysis of the details and the process of formulation (see section 1).

In order to illustrate the possibilities that such an integrated approach offers, we analyze the linguistic corpus LangAge, which is comprised of biographical interviews with French men and women aged between 70 and 94 (in 2005) concerning how the historical topic of Forced Labor is dealt with. We then compare our findings with the French section of the large oral history project Zwangsarbeit / Forced Labor 1939–1945. The French section is made up of interviews with 19 participants (aged between 81 and 86 at the time of the interviews in 2006) who were forced to work in the program *Service du Travail Obligatoire*, as it was called in French. We present these two resources considering the participants, the interview methods and the resulting types of interaction. We then look at the different methods of exploitation, based on the conventions of transcription, digitization, and word-audio-video alignment (see section 2).

Using the example of the historical term *Forced Labor* with the special meaning of the French term *Service du Travail Obligatoire* (hereafter sto), we show how the historical dimension, the reference to a collective discourse, and the speaker's role as (contemporary) witness can be combined with the analysis of the context, taking the oral processing of spoken language seriously. We formulate our research question exploring how the historical term *Service du Travail Obligatoire* / sto is used in the interviews, and what meaning can be attributed to it in the different linguistic contexts; additionally, we compare the co-occurrences appearing in our data with keyword-in-context searches in French newspaper archives. Comparing extracts from both resources, we show how the denotation of the historical term is specified and at the same time how individual evaluations emerge in discourse (see section 3).

Portelli (1997: 6) observes that "the issue of what is private and what is public in a person's narrative is often uncertain, especially if we are after the elusive theme of the history of private life". We draw our conclusions suggesting that oral history sources and corpus linguistics methods, allowing for the comparison of different witnesses, can help shed new light on these uncertainties (section 4).

Introduction: Oral History and Linguistics

Both in oral history and in linguistics (corpus linguistics, sociolinguistics and discourse analysis), the building of archives and databases forms the basis for systematic and detailed analysis. The mutual benefit of sharing resources and experiences has recently attracted new attention (Roller 2015; for earlier approaches see Löffler 1988; Schiffrin 2003). We follow this approach and specify what we hold to be preconditions, in both theoretical and methodological perspectives. Then we focus on the semantics of historical terms in order to introduce our research question.

Oral history meets linguistics: preliminary remarks

The title of the Freiburg workshop, organized in 2015 by Katja Roller, one of the editors of the present volume, uses the metaphor of an encounter which, by its very definition, takes place between different sides—in a certain sense, they are opposed to each other.

The role of the interviewee in oral history is that of a witness, and the interviews are thematically-oriented, in a more or less broad sense, depending on the subject of the inquiry. Oral history focuses on meaning as it emerges in the strategies and dynamics of individuals dealing with historical experiences. The systematic and comparative evaluation of these strategies and dynamics helps to discover their regularities and patterns ("Erfahrungsgeschichte"; Niethammer 1985: 433). The shaping of theories built on oral history samples is a process of continuous control of one's own assumptions (Thonfeld 2009: 61). Oral history is also, in a very cautious way, focused on the reconstruction of facts: this is one of the results of the Slavery and Forced Labor Project. While originally the focus was on the reconstruction of ways to deal with traumatic experiences and their long-term effects, the evaluation of testimonies' narratives revealed the precision of remembered facts (Plato 2007: 279–280). The linguistic disposition and its properties are considered seriously in some oral history approaches, paying attention to the dialogic structure of the interviews (Bories-Sawala 1996, vol. 1: 87). In addition, the very formulation process has attracted the attention of the historian:

> Between the fluid textual experiments and the frozen formulaic material, the 'archived' discourse breaks through and floats like a moving island, the tip of

> an iceberg. In order to understand how the narrative is shaped, we must not limit ourselves to these moments of fulfilment; we need to consider also the formulaic materials, the apparently formless connecting and supporting matter, and the dialogic directive role of the historian (Portelli 1997: 5).

Still, the evaluation of these linguistic details remains, in oral history, one detail among others. On the one hand, in linguistic approaches to the data of spoken language, the formulation process and the way language is used are at the center of interest. So, the facts or the historical credibility of what is said are, generally speaking, less important. It seems not by chance that in her discussion and application of historical experiences as the subject of discourse analysis, Schiffrin (2003: 84) slightly shifts from *oral history* to *oral histories*; in this linguistic view, the strategies of storytelling are more important than the reconstruction of historical processes. In another field of discourse analysis, Interactional Sociolinguistics (IS), social/cultural issues are at the center of interest insofar as they "tend to arise in today's social environment" (Gumperz and Cook-Gumperz 2007: 483). Potentially, we are at the crossroads of individual, daily communicative exchanges and the production of meaning in the larger context of communities, where the social practices allow for analyzing "conventions and ideologies of interpersonal relations" (Gumperz and Cook-Gumperz 2007: 483). But usually, the (re)construction of meaning is done on the basis of a small part of speech which is analyzed with a fine-grained tool set that includes universal or language-specific traits of spoken language (see Koch and Oesterreicher 2011): details such as prosodic traits (pauses, loudness, lengthening of syllables; see Morel and Danon-Boileau 1998), the way in which speakers start and stop speaking, and how communicative exchange is organized (turn taking; see Sacks, Schegloff and Jefferson 1974).

In the gathering of sociolinguistic data, the subject matter is mostly of minor interest, as it is simply a vehicle to make the interlocutor talk in the most spontaneous way possible. The aim is to create a relaxed atmosphere where the speaker is involved, with the result that no "attention [is] paid to speech" (according to the classical definition of "style" provided in Labov 1972: 188).

Forced Labor / *STO* as a historical term

Taking the example of *Forced Labor*, French *travail forcé*, in the special context of STO, we are dealing with a linguistic sign representing, in public discourse, Vichy France under German occupation and the totalitarian structures affecting private life in a systematic way.

The first group of French men forced to replace the workforce in industrial production (including military production, against the Geneva Convention), agriculture and handcraft and to fill the gap left by Germans serving as soldiers in the war, was comprised of about 1.5 million prisoners of war (Bories-Sawala 1996: 215–244). Starting in June 1942, French prisoners of war were repatriated, after negotiations between Fritz Sauckel and Pierre Laval, in an exchange of one prisoner for three civilian 'volunteers'. This program was called 'relief', in French *la relève* (Bories-Sawala 1996: 265; Durand 2011: chapter 2.1). The negotiated exchange rate, however, was not upheld by the Germans, as fewer prisoners were sent home than was promised and those with higher qualifications were made to stay in Germany (Paxton 1997: 423).

The German recruitment offices for French civilians opened in 1940; intensive propagandistic activity accompanied the efforts to "invite" qualified specialists, craftsmen and technicians to work in Germany and to contribute to the *relève* 'relief'. Placed on colorful posters, slogans addressed national solidarity ('You have the keys to the camps, French workers, you will free the prisoners—working in Germany!' *Vous avez la clef des camps / travailleurs français / vous libérez les prisonniers / en travaillant en Allemagne*) or promised personal benefit ('Hard days are over, Daddy earns money in Germany', *Finis les mauvais jours! Papa / gagne de l'argent / en Allemagne!*). In the France of 1942/1943, the historic hostility towards its adversary Germany was counterbalanced by the possibility of earning money and, at the same time, liberating French prisoners of war and thus fulfilling a patriotic service. At the same time, the negative connotation of (obligatory) service for the enemy was mitigated by the use of slogans in active voice, and the complex compound was put into terms of common usage. One example is the verb phrase *travailler en Allemagne* 'work in Germany' (Figure 1; cf. Savoie Archives, chapter 10).

As the number of volunteers recruited was not sufficient to fill the huge gaps in the German Labor market, the Forced Labor program was launched in 1942 by the Council of Ministers (*Conseil des ministres*), named *Service Obligatoire du Travail* (Le Petit Parisien, February 16th 1943, p. 1). This name would have

Fig. 1
'If you want to earn more money... come and work in Germany!' Propaganda of Vichy regime, undated (Affiche de propagande en faveur de la Relève, 1941/1942, André Deran, Musée Carnavalet Paris).
ullstein bild - Roger-Viollet.

been morphologically more convincing, as it is an 'Obligatory Service' of work, not a service of 'Obligatory Work'. But the related acronym S.O.T. evoked the French adjective *sot* 'stupid', and therefore the name *Service du Travail Obligatoire* and the acronym STO were chosen (Bories-Sawala 1996: n. 286; Harbulot 2003: 269). This law, issued in February 1943 by the Vichy government, required young men older than 20 (age groups 1940, 1941, 1942) to take part in Forced Labor for two years (Journal Officiel, *Loi du 16 février 1943 Portant institution du Service du Travail Obligatoire*). The French Resistance, the *Maquis*, established networks to hide and organize the 'rejectionists', in French *réfractaires,* who refused to perform STO (Paxton 1997: 425). But the risk of non-participation did not only concern individuals; if conscripted young men did not participate, members of their families were held responsible.

On the level of the lexicon, *Service du Travail Obligatoire*, STO, 'Forced Labor' is a term with a precise definition, referring to the historical period in which it was valid, the legal responsibilities, the labor to be done in Germany, the age groups of the young French men concerned, and so on. The double mention of 'duty' (*service, obligatoire*) and the acronym STO fitted well into Nazi terminology, where acronyms played an important role (one of the first observations made concerning LTI; see Klemperer 1949: 15 who coined the sarcastic abbreviation for *Lingua Tertii Imperii*, the 'Language of the Third Reich'). More or less morphologically transparent, they could then enter into common usage (determinologization, Fraas 1997: 437).

The official propaganda with its euphemistic slogans may have contributed to the complex reasons why people forced to participate in STO had a hard time when they returned to France. Only in the 1980s did a revision of the Vichy regime and related topics—like STO—begin (Bories-Sawala 1996: 245). Still, related conflicts were visible until fairly recently, especially during the *querelle du titre*, which was the debate on what to call the forced laborers and if they could be called *déportés* 'deportees'. This debate put into sharp contrast the members of the national organization of deportees, i.e. the former members of STO, with the survivors of concentration camps (Spina 2012: 19). Witnesses in oral history projects report that they were confronted with serious doubts concerning the forced character of STO (Thonfeld 2014: 77). The experience from the French oral history collection documented in FORCED LABOR shows that the number of refusals from potential participants was "far greater than in other projects"; the initiators observed "a memory tainted by shame, a memory of guilt and, finally, a painful memory":

> the collective memory of that period in history has overlooked it, placing it on the dark side of the anti-heroes, or at best of those who had made (or been forced into?) the wrong choice or, more precisely, had failed to choose the right path (Granet-Abisset 2010: 115; 122).

In recent Paris demonstrations (23 June 2016), the slogan *Bientôt le STO* was used, meant to draw public attention to the pejoration of conditions of employment (Blog LSP). In this use, one could recognize a feeling of solidarity with the victims of the historical STO, but at the same time a cynical belittlement. In any case, the slogan manifests the presence of the term in public discourse.

Research question: historical terms at the crossroads

Being a legal term, the denotational meaning and the legal impact of STO are clearly defined. On the level of connotation, the picture is less clear. Speaker connotations can express a position between two extremely different poles: on the one hand, the concepts of cooperation or even collaboration with Germans can be evoked, with the idea of distance and betrayal, or, on the other hand, the meaning of 'victim', or even 'deportee', with the idea of solidarity and empathy.

When individuals talk about STO, they have to deal with the challenge of making sense of this difficult term. Fragments of historical knowledge, the experiences of family members, public discourse and current debates are activated in many different ways. So, as Stubbs (2001: 147) states, "[s]peakers usually do not express themselves 'in their own words' but in words which are endlessly recycled in their speech community". On the other hand, in a single communicative situation and regarding individuals with their very own points of view, meaning and evaluations are emerging in current discourse, and denotations as well as connotations are specified in the individual interaction (Gerstenberg 2009: 155).

In the following, we propose an approach which, in our view, can help to bridge the gap illustrated above between the more holistic oral history approach to linguistic data and the very detailed, local and interactional perspective that dominates in linguistic research on spoken language. We will have a closer look at the use of STO as a historical term. This lexical item has a precise propositional meaning and is found in numerous encyclopedia entries. Following Blank (1997: 29), terms or keywords (German *Begriffe*) are not part of the "normal lexicon" with its usage-based evolutions. The observation that STO is not part of the "normal lexicon" is confirmed by the simple fact that it has no entry in the standard dictionaries of contemporary French. The term STO is mentioned in the French definition of *réfractaire*: 'participant of resistance movement who refused to perform Forced Labor' ("Résistant (1941–1944) qui refusait le travail obligatoire en Allemagne pendant l'Occupation", PRob s.v. *réfractaire*).

In the case of non-terminological words, unconscious and collective dynamics shape new meanings (Burkhardt 1991: 16–17). In contrast, individual texts and authors as well as highly intentional directions of semantic change must be taken into consideration in order to reconstruct the different meanings of cultural and political terms in the course of history (Gerstenberg 2010). The linguistic domain of research on historical keywords focuses, in different traditions, on socio-historical contexts, mentalities or on the performative aspect of political language ("Begriffsgeschichte", Bödeker 2002).

We hold that there is a continuum between the widespread use of historically loaded words and intellectual debates on the precise, legally relevant understanding of the very same words. Taking the case of STO, we see that people talked about it with families and friends, in everyday discourse, when relating to wartime experiences (while not necessarily reporting details about STO, see above), but this term was also the subject of ardent academic and journalistic debates on the subject of STO being a deportation. In this continuum, we see the LangAge corpus nearer to the common usage than the French texts found in the Forced Labor archive.

Data

In the LangAge corpus, wartime witnesses tell their life stories and occasionally report episodes of STO; only one case was based on personal experiencing STO. In Forced Labor, participants are invited as witnesses, as experts, to talk about their own experiences, to reveal their own points of view, and to report on dates and facts, conditions and responsibilities. Some of them are members of associations of former STO and make explicit reference to the debates and terminological discussions mentioned above.

Transcription standards differ between oral history, where the main target is to give and facilitate access to the propositional meaning, and linguistics, where the form and the linear process of formulation are significant as well, and the transcription includes repetitions, interruptions, interjections and pauses, without using punctuation. Still, in both databases, aligned audio (video) files are available.

LangAge corpus

The data from the LangAge corpus stem from a collection of interviews put together in order to perform research on the sociolinguistics of later life. The first series of data for LangAge was collected in 2005 from French speakers in Orléans (and surrounding area). Interviews were conducted and recorded on audio tape; the mean length of these interviews is 45 minutes. The data were orthographically transcribed and aligned to the digital audio tapes (for further information, see LangAge). The French regional center of Orléans, some 100 km south of Paris, is the site of a major sociolinguistic project (Orléans-Corpus, Étude Sociolinguistique à Orléans/ESLO: Baude and Dugua 2011), an advantage for research in age-related issues.

The interview style took the form of an open questionnaire comprising biographical topics such as family, school, experiences in wartime and under the German occupation of Orléans 1940–1944, professional activity, May 1968—and some points concerning lifestyle and opinions in their current life stage. The interview technique is based on the principles of narrative interview (Schütze 1983), encouraging the interlocutors to use a monologue form of free, self-directed, spontaneous and personal speech; the interviewer's role was to suggest topics and listen attentively. Participants were contacted with the explicit mention of oral history topics, so they took part with the motivation of sharing historical experiences with the German interviewer. The 48 older participants of LangAge 2005 were born between 1911 and 1935. In some cases, personal experiences with sto, either interviewees' own episodes or narratives of family members, were reported.

From what has been said above, it is clear that the LangAge interviews are oral history data in a very broad sense; the thematic focus is much larger than in interview settings originating from historical surveys.

The Forced Labor project

Under the label of Zwangsarbeit Archiv, a huge collection of oral history data has been put together at Freie Universität Berlin (see Pagenstecher and Tausendfreund 2013; Pagenstecher 2017). French interviews originate from the French project AAM-RDI Grenoble (Granet-Abisset 2010: 115). Some witnesses told interviewers that prior to the interview they had not talked about their experiences and had not even shown their families the diaries they kept during the sto (Granet-Abisset 2010: 116).

The interviews were conducted in 2006 by two French historians; all are more than one hour in duration (1h20–4h46, mean length 2h26) and are thematically centered on the interviewees' experiences of sto in Germany. The 18 men and one woman were born between 1920 and 1925, most were in the 1921/1922 age groups, and most were lower middle or working class. The oral history interviews of the Forced Labor project are video- and/or audiotaped and aligned to the video-/ or audiofiles. They are prepared for historical research with thematic annotation, normalized orthographic transcriptions and German translations.

What kind of interaction is reflected in oral history interview data?

In his discussion of "interview as text vs. interview as interaction", Deppermann (2013: [6]) summarizes criticism concerning the "non-naturalness" and the low "ecological validity" of interview data which distinguishes situational factors from everyday routines and behavior. Ecological validity is restricted not only because of the non-occurrence of interviews outside of the elicited research context, but also because of the communicative exchange's organization: in everyday talk, the length of statements is restricted; biographical background, in everyday life, is never revealed to strangers without explicit feedback, Deppermann argues (2013: [6]). He proposes an analytic approach based on the precise sequences of answers and the questions or utterances of the interviewer, and of the fine structure of the utterances, the phonetic realizations, potentially meaningful in terms of regional identity, and the formulation process with its hesitations, pauses and false starts (Deppermann 2013: [25]; see also Mondada 2001). In what follows, this view on interview as interaction will be the starting point. In the analysis of data extracts, different levels will be examined: the wider context, the interactional dimension, and the oral realization with a closer look on the linguistic traits. But at the same time we want to underline the observation that the pure fact that interviews do not happen in the participants' daily lives does not make them less natural. Following our observations of the interview situations, most of the interviewees seemed to show a certain familiarity and a natural attitude in telling their life stories.

The oral telling of life stories is a very human trait, and biographical storytelling, even in the form of a monologue, without feedback, is not as rare as one might think—as everyday experiences on trains or in doctors' waiting rooms reveal. The preparing of inner stories or of "endophasic" discourse (without an interlocutor, without phonic realization; Bergounioux 2004: 28) can emerge silently as a more or less urgent need develops to explain one's own point of view. These silent activities can include writing diaries, keeping secret notebooks, and explaining a complex situation to somebody who is not there. Furthermore, listening to other people's stories evokes one's own experiences and makes new stories come into existence ("A particular telling inspires distinct and only partially overlapping narratives, as interlocutors link the telling to their particular lived and imagined involvements in the world", Ochs and Capps 1996: 21).

Sketching these elements of inner monologues, we want to argue that the monologues stimulated in oral history interviews may never have been told before, but are still nothing less than natural or authentic. The opportunity to relate a life story without restricting oneself to the snippets that family and friends happen to endure is, in terms of ecology (see above and Mühlhäusler 2010), a kind of habitat for highly sensitive material.

Historical Terms in Context: *STO*

In the LangAge questionnaire, no question directly concerned Forced Labor. When participants talked about it, it was in the context of related topics like resistance or military service, or memories of friends and siblings. Consequently, the topic was self-introduced and spontaneously developed.

In the statistical analysis, we used the indicator of keyness[1] in order to compare

1 Keyness was measured using Log-likelihood. AntConc, Laurence Anthony, ‹www.laurence-anthony.net/software.html›. For lexical statistics, we used the transcripts of only the witnesses, a corpus of more than 13 500 types in about 322 500 tokens. The statistical keyword analysis

the content of both textual resources. The keyness analysis identifies lexical items which show significant differences between the different linguistic corpora taken into consideration. In our case, it turned out that together with some function words, the nouns *camp* 'camp' (443 vs. 45), *russes* 'Russians' (308 vs. 15), *usine* 'factory' (348 vs. 53), and *prisonniers* 'prisoners' (292 vs. 38) show the greatest keyness difference between FORCED LABOR and a LANGAGE sample of equal size. The term STO (83 vs.12) is less frequent than these nouns and did not appear in the upper ranks of most the important keyness items.

Even it's less frequent, the usage of STO is worth to have a closer look at: in the French texts of FORCED LABOR, there is one form not present in LANGAGE, that is, the use of STO designating 'a person doing Forced Labor'. In these occurrences, the plural form and the indefinite article are used: *(nous,) les STO* (15), *des STO* (5), *un STO* (1). This use of STO is a regular process of word formation and a regular process of semantic change, and more specifically of metonymic change: where a noun designating an institution is used to refer to the person working there. The semantic trait HUMAN ([+HUM]) allows for new morphosyntactic features. While STO 'institution' is exclusively used with the definite article, and has no plural form, the new form which has the semantic trait [+HUM] allows for indefinite use and plural forms: 'a/the person; (the) persons doing Forced Labor'. This usage is not attested in LANGAGE.

In order to have more evidence for this observation, we searched for more discourse contexts. In the catalogue of the French National Library (BnF), six books, published between 1991 and 2013, use *un STO* 'a man having done Forced Labor' on the cover, and three books published between 2007 and 2014 have *les STO* in the title. All of them take the perspective of the young men and their painful experiences. This quite recent perspective is confirmed by the rare occurrences of *un/des/les STO* when searching the sites of the biggest French newspapers, including blogs and discussion forums: only 11 examples with STO meaning 'a person who was obliged to do Forced Labor' could be found, as opposed to nearly four hundred occurrences of STO with the meaning 'the institution of Forced Labor'.[2]

A difficult term

In LANGAGE, the very term STO and the full compound *Service du Travail Obligatoire* seem to be, for some participants, quite hard to find. So, in interview extract A018m76 (4), the participant first looks for the right word and then builds the pleonastic noun

is an indicator of a text's content, its "aboutness" (Baker et al. 2008: 278) of a text.

2 We used the six biggest (by outreach) daily newspapers, according to ACPM: *Le Figaro*, *Le Monde*, *Les Échos*, *La Croix*, *La Libération*, not taking into account newspapers without any occurence of *STO* (*L'Équipe Édition Générale*, *Aujourd'hui en France*). As all of the websites of all six newspapers were searched, forums and blogs were also included. The dozens of hits for *le STO* ('the STO') make it clear that there is still ongoing discussion about related subjects.

phrase *STO obligatoire.* This is an indicator that the content of the acronym is bleached, i.e., the O is no longer transparent as the short form of *obligatoire.* As we have seen above (1.2), the noun phrase *service obligatoire* would have been more logical; so one of the participants somewhat corrects the use, first speaking of *service obligatoire,* then actively remembering the correct term and quoting it (A015f78, 4)—or not recalling it (A009m80, 5; A013f83, 4). Even in FORCED LABOR[3], whose participants are former members of STO, the logically more adequate variant *Service Obligatoire* is sometimes used: 'we heard about it in in the small newspapers that were published at the time, about Forced Labor' (*on en entendait parler dans les petits journaux qui paraissaient à l'époque, du service obligatoire du travail*; za074).

The fact that the compound is morphologically not very convincing may contribute to the use of a paraphrase, with the verb phrase 'work in Germany', *travailler en Allemagne* (A009m80, 4; A045m80, 3; A013f83, 4; A025f84, 3; *travailler dans les usines allemandes* 'work in German factories': A031m85).

In FORCED LABOR, the verb phrase *travailler en Allemagne* is often used as a citation, in order to underline the offensive atmosphere where Forced Labor was understood as a voluntary service. This usage is critically mentioned by the participants: 'no, but in my case, the integration [repatriation] was fine, but well there were always people criticizing me for having gone to work in Germany' (*non mais moi l'intégration s'est assez bien faite mais enfin il y en a toujours qui ont critiqué parce que l'on est allé travailler en Allemagne*, za077; see other similar occurrences of *travailler en Allemagne* FORCED LABOR, in za074, and also by the interviewer M. B.).

Semantics

The extracts from LANGAGE also shed some light on the semantic field that is made up of different groups of young men under the German occupation as partisans, prisoners of war, and people fulfilling the STO. For some of the participants, no difference is made between STO and prisoners (A015f78, 3); as the enumeration of 'those put on a train, conscripted, brought away' (A014m83) shows, the different kinds of obligation (deportation, forced Labor) are all placed at the same level. By contrast, concerning the destiny of men in STO vs. prisoners of war, the difference is clearly marked by one participant who makes clear that 'those people' (*ceux-là*), creating a deictic distance, usually came back; they were held apart from the battlefields of World War II (A024f84, 10). In many different contexts, also in FORCED LABOR, a clear difference is made between 'deportees' and men participating in STO—and sometimes, the dif-

3 Quoting from FORCED LABOR, we use the ID in the form za000 as indicated in the interview metadata. For full text research and access to more indications of identity, the quoted extracts can, after registration, easily be retrieved at the website indicated below. We use the transcriptions of FORCED LABOR, and the audio files, completing and adapting the transcription according to the standards presented in appendix 5.3.

ference is negotiated: Witness: 'there was only us, the deportees'. Guest: 'you weren't deportees'. Witness: 'we were not political deportees, STO, that's all'. (témoin: *on était les seuls autant dire à être déporté*. Participant: *vous étiez pas déportés* [...] témoin: *on était pas déporté politique / STO c'est tout*, zao80). So, while the participant first spontaneously expresses the idea of being deported, he immediately accepts that he was "only" obliged to participate in Forced Labor.

In another interview, the researcher makes clear that there is a difference between STO and (political) deportees: AMGA (interviewer): 'no, this was in other in other se() in other geographic places where there really were political deportees they came to work but not as in your case': (AMGA (interviewer): *non c'est dans d'autres dans d'autres se() dans d'autres endroits géographiques où il y avait vraiment des déportés politiques qui venaient travailler mais c'était pas votre cas*, zao91).

The use of active vs. passive voice and the related semantic roles seem to be an indicator of the extent of empathy with the young men doing their STO. In LANGAGE, the active voice is compatible with the idea of choice: when a person leaves (A018m76, 4; A024f84), one can suppose a certain responsibility for this act. In contrast, the awareness that the young men were *forced* to participate in STO is expressed in the passive voice; so when the brother of one participant or the participant himself 'was recruited' or a husband 'was called', this is reported in the passive voice (A045m80: 3; A004m83: 3; A013f83, 4). The semantic role of patient, i.e., the direct object of the action, is also attributed in the case where *the STO* forces young men to do it (A031m85, 8: 'the Forced Labor who summoned young French to work in German factories'). This participant, a priest, reports a strong sense of compassion for the young men threatened by recruitment for Forced Labor.

In FORCED LABOR, a similar understanding is realized when the interviewer corrects herself in order to avoid the active voice when asking a question: J. M. (interviewer): 'no, the fact that you uhm the fact that you left that you had to go to Germany, I think ...' (J. M. (interviewer): *on le hum le fait que vous partiez que vous deviez partir en Allemagne* [...] *j'imagine* ..., zao85). This is an adaptation to the content of the witnesses' reports, all of them making clear that it was not by choice that they participated in the Forced Labor.

Interaction

In LANGAGE, the level of interaction between French participants and the German interviewer is explicitly present when participants comment on the term STO, highlighting its historical character (*à l'époque* 'at that time') or *on appelait ça* 'it was called' (A013f83, 3), *ce qu'on appelait* 'what was called' (A31m85; A35f87). This diachronic marker can be combined with an attempt to make sure that the interviewer knew it (A009m80, 5; A013f83, 2). The additional use of the German term *Zwangsarbeiter* (he pronounces the compound as *Zwangarbeiter*, without the epenthetic -s-), together with a question tag, creates a common ground for the German interviewer and the interviewee (A004m83: 3); in this case, the use of the historical term becomes explicitly a resource of interaction. Such comments or "diachronic glossings" on a term that is, in the eye of the speaker, outdated, are quite frequent in the interviews of LangAge. They have several functions (Gerstenberg 2011: 138–147): they are clearly hearer-orientated, implemented to solve potential problems of understanding for the German interviewer. At the same time, the speaker positions him/herself as one who is familiar with the historical term and its signification, maybe forgotten today; he is "being a witness", an activity of membership categorization in the sense of Schegloff (2007).

In Forced Labor, the participants make similar diachronic remarks. With *ce qu'on appelait* 'what was called', one witness introduces words that, in his view, are worth being explicated. In this way, he highlights the historical character of 'small vehicles' (*camionettes*), the 'prohibited zone' established by the German occupiers (*zone interdite*), 'internal networks' (*groupes d'entreaide*), and the 'basic school degree' (*le certificat de premier ordre*, all from za074). The interviewee R. C. uses the expression twice: with 'Pétain parcels', filled with tinned food, cigarettes and books (*colis Pétain*), and with a 'Catholic Club' (*cercle catholique*, za076). Six more occurrences of *ce qu'on appelait* are used in Forced Labor by the interviewee R. S. (za089), each time glossing institutions for young people of the Vichy regime, but also of civilian formation: the 'school of prefecture' (*école de la préfecture*, twice), a higher degree preparing future teachers (*brevet supérieur*), professional schools (*les écoles professionnelles*), an institution where future craftsmen were formed (*artisanat*), additional classes (*cours complémentaires*), the Youth Workcamps (*Chantiers de Jeunesse*, Pécout 2012), and another time when searching for a term he ultimately does not recall.

In Forced Labor, not only the participants but also the interviewer J. M. use the phrase *ce qu'on appelait* to introduce historical terms. Some functions are shared by the interviewer and interviewees; for example in an interviewer's search for the French equivalent of the German *bunker*, the following was recorded: 'these were the bunkers which was ca() the bunkers which was called uhm [pau] the shelters' (*c'était les bunkers ce qu'on les bunkers ce qu'on appelait les euh les abris les bunkers*, za089). Similarly, she looks for 'and what relationships did you have with the the mh the deportees what were the political deportees called?' (*et quels rapports vous aviez avec les les mh les déportés ce qu'on appelait les déportés politiques?*, za090).

The marking of the phrase 'black market' is more specific for her role as interviewer; in this case, there is a double marker: *ce qu'on appelle entre guillemets le marché noir* (za089). The interviewer uses the present tense, and adds 'in quotation marks'. Another case with the double marking of a historical term is 'were you aware of what was called la Relève, that is …' (*est-ce que vous étiez au courant euh de ce qu'on appelait la Relève c'est-à-dire …*, za076). This use is different from what the interviewees do; the interviewer avoids the historical term, reducing the own statement of historical knowledge and thus letting the interviewee take on the role of expert. In this case, the diachronic marker can be considered a politeness strategy (Brown and Levinson 1987: 146).

Concluding Remarks

The linguistic details of spoken language and the features of a term in context indicate on what levels oral history data can be used to show how different facets of meaning emerge and how they are used as a resource in the interaction of interviewee and interviewer. The examples cited also illustrate the crucial role of the details of formulations reflected in a detailed transcription and/or in the aligned audio/video files.

Comparing the 19 participants of FORCED LABOR, invited to specifically talk about Forced Labor, and 11 from LANGAGE, talking spontaneously and in other biographic contexts, about Forced Labor, we found differences suggesting that the use of the term STO differs in many ways depending on individual personal experiences.

The details of linguistic use are, in this regard, significant, as the euphemism *travailler en Allemagne* 'work in Germany' was used by the majority of former STOS as a quotation, while the co-occurrence was automatic and spontaneous in LANGAGE. This euphemistic paraphrase for STO was originally a propaganda slogan. No participant in LANGAGE commented on this fact when using it, while participants in FORCED LABOR made critical remarks on missing the connotation of OBLIGATION expressed in this term.

Both groups have difficulties pronouncing the full compound *Service du Travail Obligatoire*; this can be due to the morphologically odd formation (see 3.1), unconsciously corrected by the speakers. When using verbs for 'go to STO', the semantic roles of patient (passive voice or direct object) were used by the speakers who had experienced STO ('I was recruited') and interviewees sharing their point of view, while the active voice 'leave for STO' was used by contemporaneous speakers without their own direct experiences.

On the level of interaction, the roles of witness and interviewee are activated in many details; we had a closer look at the use of historical terms and the different functions of the marker 'what it's called' introducing them.

Comparing the two corpora gives one the opportunity to compare witnesses and other contemporaries whose speech patterns reflect collective usage. As the number of available speakers is limited, we looked for more evidence in online press archives, including their blogs and discussion forums. It turned out that the observed usage pattern of FORCED LABOR, i.e. STO designating a person and not just the institution, was indeed a highly exclusive pattern of the witnesses of Forced Labor. In conclusion, the semantic trait HUMAN on STO appears when we listen to those who experienced it.

References

Sources

LangAge
http://www.langage-corpora.org
Further details and corpus construction: Gerstenberg 2011.

Forced Labor, French Interviews
http://www.zwangsarbeit-archiv.de/
AAMRDI Grenoble Association des Amis du Musée de la Résistance et de la Déportation de l'Isère (Association Friends of the Resistance and Deportation Museum sère), Grenoble
Responsable and 1st Interviewer: Anne-Marie Granet-Abisset, 2nd Interviewer: Julia Montredon

Cited Works

ACPM = L'Alliance pour les chiffres de la presse et des médias, chiffres / classement presso quotidienne nationale 2015. http://www.acpm.fr/Chiffres/Diffusion/La-Presse-Payante/Presse-Quotidienne-Nationale [09.10.2016]

Baker, Paul, Costas Gabrielatos, Majid Khosravinik, Michal Krzyzanowski, Tony McEnery, and Ruth Wodak 2008. A Useful Methodological Synergy? Combining Critical Discourse Analysis and Corpus Linguistics to Examine Discourses of Refugees and Asylum Seekers in the UK Press. *Discourse and Society* 19(3): 273–306.

Baude, Olivier, and Céline Dugua 2011. (Re)faire le corpus d'Orléans quarante ans après : 'quoi de neuf, linguiste?'. *Corpus* 10: 99–118.

Bergounioux, Gabriel 2004. *Le moyen de parler*. Lagrasse: Verdier.

Blank, Andreas 1997. Prinzipien des lexikalischen Bedeutungswandels am Beispiel der romanischen Sprachen. Tübingen: Niemeyer.

Blog LSP = Blog Langue Sauce Piquante. *Bientôt le STO?* http://correcteurs.blog.lemonde.fr/2016/06/26/bientot-le-sto/ [09.10.2016]

Bödeker, Hans E. 2002. Ausprägungen der historischen Semantik: Begriffsgeschichte, Diskursgeschichte, Metapherngeschichte. In *Begriffsgeschichte, Diskursgeschichte, Metapherngeschichte*, H.E. Bödeker (ed.), 7–27. Göttingen: Wallstein.

Bories-Sawala, Helga 1996. Franzosen im 'Reichseinsatz': Deportation, Zwangsarbeit, Alltag. Erfahrungen und Erinnerungen von Kriegsgefangenen und Zivilarbeitern. 3 vol. Frankfurt am Main: Lang.

Brown, Penelope, and Stephen C. Levinson 1987. *Politeness: Some Universals in Language Usage*, 17th edn. Cambridge: University Press.

Burkhardt, Armin 1991. Vom Nutzen und Nachteil der Pragmatik für die diachrone Semantik. In *Diachrone Semantik und Pragmatik. Untersuchungen zur Erklärung und Beschreibung des Sprachwandels*. D. Busse (ed.), 7–36. Tübingen: Niemeyer.

Deppermann, Arnulf 2013. Interview als Text vs. Interview als Interaktion. *FQS Forum: Qualitative Sozialforschung Social Research* 14(3).

Durand, Yves 2011. La France dans la deuxième guerre mondiale 1939–1945. Paris: Armand Colin.

Fraas, Claudia 1997. Lexikalisch-semantische Eigenschaften von Fachsprachen. In *Fachsprachen. Ein internationales Handbuch zur Fachsprachenforschung und Terminologiewissenschaft*. HSK 14.1 L. Hoffmann, H. Kalverkämper, W. and H. Ernst (eds.), 428–438. Berlin: de Gruyter.

Gerstenberg, Annette 2009. The Multifaceted Category of 'Generation': Elderly French Men and Women Talking about May '68. *International Journal of the Sociology of Language* 200: 153–170.

— 2010. Die Historizität von Bedingungen und Verfahren der Bedeutungsveränderung am Beispiel früher romanischer Entlehnungs- und Verwendungskontexte von lat. AMNESTIA. *Romanische Forschungen* 122: 457–483.

— 2011. Generation und Sprachprofile im höheren Lebensalter: Untersuchungen zum Französischen auf der Basis eines Korpus biographischer Interviews. Frankfurt am Main: Vittorio Klostermann.

Granet-Abisset, Anne-Marie 2010. The French Experience: STO, a Memory to Collect, a History to Write. In *Hitler's Slaves. Life Stories of Forced Labourers in Nazi-occupied Europe*. A. v. Plato, A. Leh, and Ch. Thonfeld (eds.), 113–123. New York: Berghahn Books.

Gumperz, John J., and Jenny Cook-Gumperz 2007. A Postscript: Style and Identity in Interactional Sociolinguistics. In *Style and Social Identities: Alternative Approaches to Linguistic Heterogeneity*. P. Auer (ed.), 477–501. Berlin: De Gruyter.

Harbulot, Jean-Pierre 2003. *Le Service du Travail Obligatoire: La région de Nancy face aux exigences allemandes*. Nancy: Presses Universitaires de Nancy.

Klemperer, Victor 1949. *LTI. Notizbuch eines Philologen*. Berlin: Aufbau.

Koch, Peter, and Wulf Oesterreicher 2011. *Gesprochene Sprache in der Romania: Französisch, Italienisch, Spanisch*, 2nd ed. Berlin: de Gruyter.

Labov, William 1972. The Study of Language in its Social Context. In *Sociolinguistics: Selected readings*. J. B. Pride and J. Holmes (eds.), 180–202. Harmondsworth: Penguin Books.

Löffler, Heinrich 1988. Vergangenheit in mündlicher Überlieferung aus germanistischer Sicht. In *Vergangenheit in mündlicher Überlieferung*. J. v. Ungern-Sternberg and H. Reinau (eds.), 100–110. Berlin: De Gruyter.

Mondada, Lorenza 2001. L'entretien comme événement interactionnel. In *L'espace urbain en méthodes*. M. Grosjean and J.-P. Thibaud (eds.), 197–214. Marseille: Parenthèses.

Morel, Mary-Annick, and Laurent Danon-Boileau 1998. *Grammaire de l'intonation: L'exemple du français oral.* Paris: Ophrys.

Mühlhäusler, Peter 2010. Ecology of Languages. In *The Oxford Handbook of Applied Linguistics*, 2nd ed., R. B. Kaplan (ed.), 1–17. New York (NY): Oxford University Press.

Niethammer, Lutz 1985. Frage – Antworten – Fragen. Methodische Erfahrungen und Erwägungen zur Oral History. In *Lebensgeschichte und Sozialstruktur im Ruhrgebiet 1930–1960*, Band 3: *'Wir kriegen jetzt andere Zeiten'. Auf der Suche nach der Erfahrung des Volkes in nachfaschistischen Ländern.* L. Niethammer and A. v. Plato (eds.), 392–445. Bonn: Dietz.

Ochs, Elinor, and Lisa Capps 1996. Narrating the Self. *Annual Review of Anthropology* 25(1): 19–43.

Pagenstecher, Cord 2017. Testimonies in Digital Environments. (De-)contextualizing Interviews with Holocaust Survivor Anita Lasker-Wallfisch. (in preparation)

Pagenstecher, Cord, and Doris Tausendfreund 2013. Das Online-Archiv 'Zwangsarbeit 1939–1945. In *Erinnern an Zwangsarbeit. Zeitzeugen-Interviews in der digitalen Welt.* N. Apostolopoulos and C. Pagenstecher (eds.), 71–96. Berlin: Metropol.

Paxton, Robert O. 1997. La France de Vichy 1940–1944 [orig. engl. Vichy France, Old Guard and New Order, 1940–1944, 1972]. Paris: Le Seuil.

Pécout, Christophe 2012. Pour une autre histoire des Chantiers de la Jeunesse (1940–1944). *Vingtième Siècle. Revue d'histoire* 116(4): 97.

Plato, Alexander v. 2007. 'Es war moderne Sklaverei'. Erste Ergebnisse des lebensgeschichtlichen Dokumentationsprojekts zur Sklaven- und Zwangsarbeit. *BIOS* 20(2): 251–290.

Portelli, Alessandro 1997. *The Battle of Valle Giulia: The Art of Dialogue in Oral History.* Madison (WI): University of Wisconsin Press.

PRob = Robert, Paul 2016. *Le Petit Robert de la langue française.* Paris: Dictionnaires Le Robert (online).

Roller, Katja 2015. Towards the 'Oral' in Oral History: Using Historical Narratives in Linguistics. *Oral History* 43(1): 73–84.

Sacks, Harvey, Emanuel A. Schegloff, and Gail Jefferson 1974. A Simplest Systematic for the Organization of Turn-taking for Conversation. *Language* 50: 696–735.

Savoie Archives 2005–2009, Conseil général de la Savoie, Archives départementales de la Savoie, Exposition en ligne 'La Savoie des Ombres 1939–1945'
http://www.savoie.fr/archives73/expo_savoie_des_ombres/ [08.09.2016]
Chapitre 10 'Au secours de l'Allemagne'
http://www.savoie.fr/archives73/expo_savoie_des_ombres/pano10/pages/02-01-STOA_1.html› [08.09.2016]

Schegloff, Emanuel A. 2007. A Tutorial on Membership Categorization. *Journal of Pragmatics* 39(3): 462–482.

Schiffrin, Deborah 2003. Linguistics and History. Oral History as Discourse. In *Linguistics, Language, and the Real World: Discourse and Beyond; Georgetown University Round Table on Languages and Linguistics 2001*. D. Tannen and J. E. Alatis (eds.), 84–113. Washington: Georgetown University Press.

Schütze, Fritz 1983. Biographieforschung und narratives Interview. *Neue Praxis* 3: 283–293.

Spina, Raphaël 2012. *La France et les Français devant le service du travail obligatoire (1942–1945)*. Cachan: École normale supérieure de Cachan – ENS Cachan.

Stubbs, Michael 2001. *Words and Phrases. Corpus Studies of Lexical Semantics*. Malden (MA): Blackwell.

Thonfeld, Christoph 2009. Collecting and Interpreting Qualitative Research-Elicted Data for Longitudinal Analysis. The Case of Oral History Data on World War II Forced Labourers. *Historical Social Research* 34(3).

— 2014. *Rehabilitierte Erinnerungen?: Individuelle Erfahrungsverarbeitungen und kollektive Repräsentationen von NS-Zwangsarbeit im internationalen Vergleich*. Essen: Klartext.

Transcripts[4]

The transcription is orthographic and reflects the traits of spoken language, for example interjections, repetitions, uncompleted sentences or words. No punctuation is added, with the exception of '?' for raising intonation in questions without a question word.

If possible, segmentation uses syntactic units. When cited in the text, we mark new lines with a slash. Other conventions include:

(word) reconstructed, incomprehensible
wo() interrupted
[pau] event such as *pau* 'pause'

A018m76

```
1 j'avais comme voisins et amis des des garçons beaucoup
  plus âgés que moi qui étaient euh fils d'un professeur
  du du collège et qui était vraiment euh un grand ami
2 bon ils sont morts tous les trois (enfin) les deux fils
  et le père
```

4 Codes refer to LangAge speaker anonymization as applied in Gerstenberg 2011, see the appendix there for additional metadata. The LangAge transcription guide is used, see LangAge.

3 bon le père c'est normal mais les deux c'est moins normal bon
4 et euh l'un allait être ah ben l'un est parti au au était est parti au STO obligatoire
5 et et il est parti euh dans une usine euh d'aviation près de Vienne
6 et et et il est revenu euh atteint d'une maladie articulaire et a été rapatrié par euh par l'occupant
7 et là bon il a il a vécu au ralenti
8 et le frère pour y échapper euh on l'a euh c'est nous qui nous l'avons fait cacher en d'abord dans le Morvan
1 *I had as neighbours and friends some guys much older than me who were the sons of a college professor and who was really a great friend*
2 *well they all died all three of them the two sons and the father*
3 *well the father, this is natural, but the two* [sons, A.G.] *this is less normal, well*
4 *and one of them went uhm well one of them left was left for Forced Labor* [he uses the acronym, A.G.] *forced*
5 *and he left for an aviation factory near Vienna*
6 *and he came back sick with a joint disease and was repatriated by the occupier*
7 *and then he lived somewhat slower*
8 *and the brother well we took care of hiding him first in the Morvan region*

A015f78

9 [à l'arrivée des Américains, A.G.] un grand soulagement on faisait pas la fête parce que un grand soulagement
10 mais Paris n'était pas encore libéré
11 et puis tous nos prisonniers étaient encore là-bas tous les hommes qui travaillaient le service obligatoire du travail obligatoire
12 donc on pouvait pas rire encore
13 c'était euh un soulagement énorme
14 mais c'était pas euh je peux pas dire que c'était complet hein

9 [When the US soldiers arrived, A.G.] *a big relief not yet a party but a big relief*

10 but Paris was not yet liberated

11 and then all our prisoners were still down there all the men working in the Forced Labor the Service of Forced Labor

12 but we were not able to laugh

13 it was an enormous relief

14 but it was not uhm I cannot say that it was over

A009m80

1 la classe quarante-cinq a été dispensée de service militaire

2 c'était la fin de la enfin la guerre se terminait donc euh

3 par contre il y en a de de de jeunes enfin

4 (vous savez) si j'avais été convoqué au bureau de à l'époque de l'occupation au bureau d'embauche euh allemand pour aller travailler en Allemagne

5 vous avez entendu parler de tra() du Service-Obligatoire euh travail en Allemagne à l' époque

6 et il y a beaucoup de jeunes qui sont partis qui ont été convoqués qui ont été requis en quelque sorte pour aller travailler là-bas

7 c'était le ce qu'on appelait le STO Service-Travail-Obligatoire

8 donc j'ai été convoqué

9 mais on m'a pas pris parce que j'étais boulanger

10 enfin j'ai pas j'y suis pas allé

1 the age-group of 45 was exempted from military service

2 it was the this was the end of, well, the war was over, so

3 but there were these young men

4 (you know), yes, I was called to the office of - at that time - the German recruitment office, to work in Germany

5 you have heard talking about Forced Labor uhm work in Germany at that time

6 and many young men left they had been called or

somewhat recruited to work down there
7 *it was what was called the STO Forced Labor*
8 *so I was called*
9 *but I was not taken, I was a baker*
10 *so I did not I didn't go there*

A045m80

1 dans ma famille il y avait pas de résistants [pau] non
2 ben ma famille était assez réduite puisque je n'avais qu'un mon frère qui avait trois ans plus que moi qui était qui était lui instituteur aussi [tou] [pau] et qui était déjà instituteur lui
3 il était [pau] et il a été réquisitionné pour aller travailler en Allemagne Service du Travail Obligatoire
4 et il se saurait sans doute caché pour ne pas y aller
5 mais il savait que si lui il n'y allait pas c'est moi qui allais être pris à sa place [pau] puisque j'avais vingt ans
6 j'avais dix-neuf ans en quarante-quatre
7 donc euh il a préféré y aller
8 il a passé euh depuis deux ans je crois en Allemagne
9 il a écrit ses mémoires d'ailleurs [tss] de [pau] de Service de Travail Obligatoire
1 *in my family there were no partisans, no*
2 *well, my family was quite small because I had only my brother who was three years older than me and who was who was also a teacher he was already a teacher*
3 *he was and he was recruited to go and work in Germany Forced Labor*
4 *and without any doubt he would have hidden himself in order not to go there*
5 *but he knew that if he didn't go there, I would have been taken in his place, [pau] because I was twenty years*
6 *I was nineteen years old in 44*
7 *so uhm he preferred to go there*
8 *he stayed there two years, I think, in Germany*
9 *by the way, he has written a diary of Forced Labor*

A013f83

1 et on même on a eu chez nous euh un certain temps un un policier qui habitait Paris qui était justement réfractaire euh qui était résistant
2 et re() on appelait ça aussi je sais pas si vous savez le STO
3 réfractaire euh service euh obligatoire S-T-O service comment que c'était [ins] STO service obligatoire en Allemagne ça voulait dire ça hein
4 mon mari d'ailleurs euh a été aussi appelé pour aller travailler en Allemagne
5 mais c'est pareil il n'y est pas allé
6 il s'est sauvé dans la dans la forêt lui
7 il habitait dans la Marne
1 and we had for a while a a policeman who lived in Paris who had actually escaped uhm who was partisan
2 and this was called I don't know if you know that STO
3 rejectionist uhm labor uhm forced STO labor how was it [ins] STO Forced Labour in Germany, that's what it meant, you see
4 and also my husband was called to work in Germany
5 but the same thing, he didn't go there
6 he saved himself in the forest
7 he lived in the Marne region

A014m83

1 j'étais dans une classe euh j() d'un âge où on a eu euh [pau] beaucoup euh de de problèmes de euh de du Service du Travail Obligatoire de comment dirais-je de de réquisition à
2 c'est ce que je disais toujours
3 on avait une définition
4 à mon âge on savait jamais le soir si on couchait dans notre lit hein
5 on pouvait être embarqués
6 on pouvait être réquisitionnés
7 on pouvait être emmenés
8 y a beaucoup qui ont été obligés d'aller travailler sur les côtes de euh de l'Atlantique le mur de l'

Atlantique vous en entendu parler les murs de l'Atlantique hein

1 *I was the age-group that had many problems with Forced Labor, with forced recruitment*
2 *I used to say*
3 *we had a definition*
4 *when I was young, we never knew if, in the evening, we would sleep in our own bed*
5 *we could have been put on a train*
6 *we could have been conscripted*
7 *we could have been taken away*
8 *many of us were forced to work at the Atlantic Coast the Atlantic Wall you have heard about that the Atlantic Wall*

A004m83

1 et puis j'ai commencé d(es) études de droit
2 et puis il y a eu la guerre
3 et étant donné que j'étais (né) en mille-neuf-cent-vingt-deux j'ai donc été euh euh requis pour le service du travail obligatoire Zwangarbeiter [uses the German word, A.G.]
[INT: mhm]
4 voyez bon
1 *and then I started to study law*
2 *and then the war began*
3 *and as I was [born] in 1922, I was recruited for Forced Labor Zwangarbeiter* [sic, German]
4 *you see, ok*

A024f84

1 il y en a [de prisonniers, A.G.] qui se sont évadés
2 il y en a d'autres qui ont fait tout le temps
3 par contre j'ai un ami qui était qui était tué était tué il faut le dire comme ça
4 parce que il était il faisait il était pas prisonnier lui
5 il était parti au titre du STO savez ce que c'est
6 et puis ils avaient des permissions

[INT: mhm mhm]
7 et puis il y en a un de leur groupe qui n'est pas reparti alors bon
8 il a fallu qu'il se paie fallu qu'il y ait quelqu'un qui paie pour lui quoi
9 ça c'était pas très bien de la part de celui qui était pas reparti hein
10 parce que ils étaient détenu X la guerre
11 mais ceux-là en principe ils revenaient
12 parce que ils étaient pour le travail [pau]
13 à part ça les prisonniers ben il y en a qui sont restés il y en a qui [pau]
1 some of them [of the prisoners, A.G.] *escaped*
2 some of them stayed there all the time
3 and then I had a friend who has who was killed must call it like that
4 because he was he made he was not a prisoner
5 he had left with STO you know what it means
6 and then they had permissions/holidays XXX
7 and then one of their group did not return, well
8 and this must be paid someone had to pay for him
9 this was not nice on the part of the person who did not come back
10 because they did not have to go to war
11 but generally these men they came back
12 because it was for work
13 after that from the prisoners, some of them stayed, some of them ...

A025f84

1 non non non non il y a pas eu de de fait de résistance du moins dans ma famille hein
2 si mon beau-père
3 mon mon mari mon mari qui était parti qui a qui a pas voulu faire le STO qui a passé la ligne de démarcation justement pour pouvoir fuir hein fuir le le STO tra() travailler en Allemagne
4 il n'a pas voulu y aller puisqu'il est mon beau-père était militaire
5 il a passé la zone libre et s'est retrouvé dans le

centre de la France

1 *no, no, no, no, there was no fact of resistance at least in my family, you see*

2 *oh yes, my father-in-law*

3 *my my husband who had left who did not want to do the STO who had crossed the demarcation line, indeed in order to have the possibility to escape, you see, to escape the STO, working in Germany*

4 *he didn't want to go there because he is my father-in-law was a military man*

5 *he crossed the free zone and found himself in the centre of France*

A031m85

1 et alors euh évidemment euh j'ai ensuite vécu la guerre un petit peu dans plusieurs endroits de la France

2 car j'étais devenu prêtre

3 et j'étais ce qu'ce qu'on appelait Les Chantiers de Jeunesse

4 et j'étais aumônier [pau] de jeunesse

5 ça a duré un an

6 c'est une période pour moi très riche parce que il y avait là des jeunes un peu désemparés par la guerre hein

7 euh sous la menace de ce qu'on appelait le STO

8 c'était le Service de Travail Obligatoire qui convoquait des jeunes gens français pour travailler dans les usines allemandes

9 donc ces jeunes étaient un peu désemparés

10 et ils avaient bien sûr grande confiance dans le prêtre

11 et là-aussi je je je j'ai eu des des des des des amitiés ah oui

1 *And then obviously I stayed in different places during the war time*

2 *because I had become a priest*

3 *and I was what was called Youth Workcamp*

4 *and I was a priest for the young people*

5 *during one year*

6 *this was for me a time quite rich in experiences because the young men were distressed due to the war*
7 *under the threat of what was called STO*
8 *that is, the Forced Labor who summoned young French to work in German factories*
9 *so, the young men were quite distressed*
10 *and they had a huge confidence in the priest*
11 *and at this point I had many friendships, certainly*

A035f87

1 ah non aucun aucun [résistant en famille, A.G.]
2 euh il y a un de mes frères mon frère prêtre justement qui aurait pu partir au ce au ce qu'on appelait le STO le Service euh Travail Obligatoire
3 et alors lui il a été dans le Sud de la France faire des ce qu'on appelait des Chantiers de Jeunesse
4 et alors c'était pour s'occuper des jeunes
5 et quand il est revenu après la guerre en quarante-cinq il a vu le pont de la Loire
6 et le pont de la Loire qui était effondré par enfin qui était par terre quoi
7 alors ça lui a fait un drôle d'effet
1 *oh no, nobody* [was partisan, A.G.]
2 *one of my brothers could have gone with what was called the STO uhm Service Forced Labor* [the preposition *du "of the"* is missing, A.G.]
3 *and then he was in southern France in order to do what they called the Youth Workcamp*
4 *and this was to take care of the younger ones*
5 *and when he came back after the war in 45, he saw the Loire bridge*
6 *and the Loire bridge was destroyed by well it fell down*
7 *and this had a strange effect on him*

9 HIDDEN DIALOGUES: TOWARDS AN INTERACTIONAL UNDERSTANDING OF ORAL HISTORY INTERVIEWS

Cord Pagenstecher and Stefan Pfänder

Introduction

Bringing together oral history, conversation analysis and interactional linguistics, this chapter studies dialogical patterns in video-taped testimonies of Holocaust survivors. These biographical interviews are understood as results of a recorded interaction: the narration and its layers of meaning are co-constructed in a working alliance between interviewer and narrator, with both participants using specific verbal and non-verbal resources. By analyzing examples of repetitions and of re-tellings within testimonies, the authors explore the potential of an interdisciplinary cooperation between historians and linguists in understanding the dialogical character of oral history interviews.

Usually, the disciplines of history and linguistics work quite separately, although texts are central to both of them, mostly in written form. Gradually, however, researchers in both disciplines are becoming more interested in spoken language corpora (for linguists) or oral history collections (for historians).

Oral history interviews contain important research data not only for historiography, but also for linguistic research, cultural and literary studies, psychology and sociology (cf. Andresen, Apel, Heinsohn 2015, Knopp, Schulze, Eusterschulte 2016). Rarely, however, have they been used in interactional or corpus linguistics, although they constitute a rich and very specific corpus of spoken language. This has several reasons. First, the interview collections are scattered over many, mostly non-academic institutions, poorly catalogued and only partially digitized. Second, in oral history projects, the interviewees are chosen for thematic clusters instead of linguistic or social categories. Third, most transcripts are somewhat polished and are not machine-readable. These obstacles can be overcome, however. With the digital turn in history and the increasing number of digital interview archives, the potential for interdisciplinary cooperation is growing.

On the other hand, oral historians have not worked with existing linguistic corpora for different reasons. Apart from their sometimes limited affinity to digital technology, they often resent quantitative methods applied to such an essentially qualitative source as an individual life-story narration. Deeply rooted in hermeneutical research, oral history is opposed to any kind of de-contextualization and would not analyze short segments of speech without their biographical and historical context, an approach which seems to be widespread in linguistics—and maybe inherent to many digitally supported research approaches. Furthermore, few historians (and other people) are familiar with the specialized terminology applied in many linguistic publications.

Yet, oral history, and also qualitative social research, should cooperate with corpus and interactional linguistics, and vice versa, because both disciplines are not only interested in the same sources (for historians) or data (for linguists). Both also tend to look at the interviews as situated, embodied social interaction. This kind of common ground is essential for all interdisciplinary ventures.

Applying linguistic methods, historians could refine their established historical methods of source criticism, namely applying the *who*, *what*, *where* etc. questions, to oral history interviews. The linguistic analysis of the multimodal interaction shows precisely *how* the sources were created in a dialogical, embodied conversation between interviewer and narrator. In this chapter, the focus on the interviewer's role supports a deeper understanding of *who* created the narration and *to whom* it was addressed, i.e. the target audience intended by the narrator.

In the following sections we will summarize some strands of prior research in linguistics and oral history that might be absolutely familiar to scholars of one, but not necessarily the other discipline.

Interviews in Oral History

Oral history interviews can be defined as audio- or video-recorded biographical narrative interviews. Typically, these two- to three-hour interviews contain few interviewer questions and long autobiographical narrations by the interviewee.

Over the past 50 years, museums, archives, research institutes, and non-governmental initiatives have created large collections of such narratives for individual research or public purposes. Hundreds of interview collections in Europe and beyond contain tens of thousands of interviews, which constitute an extremely useful resource for multidisciplinary research in many fields within the social sciences and humanities.

Thousands of people reflect upon their values and identities, and tell their experiences of war and dictatorship, emancipation and freedom, migration and globalization. For many underprivileged parts of societies, including peasants, migrants, women, opposition groups, or minorities, oral narrations captured in audio-visually recorded interviews were or are the only possible way of expressing their perspectives. These voices constitute a fundamental part of Europe's linguistic heritage, covering a wide range of languages and dialects.

Nonetheless, oral history as a sub-discipline of historiography has remained small and somewhat marginalized in much of continental Europe, contrary to the Anglo-Saxon world and to Latin America. In Germany, it has developed since the 1980s as a qualitative-hermeneutical approach inspired by qualitative social research (Rosenthal 1995) and in opposition to the structural and quantifying paradigm of social history dominant at the time. Case studies using small groups of individual interviews looked for aspects of cultural meaning or personal agency, often focusing on underrepresented groups like women, migrants, or victims of racial and political persecution. Interviews with members of this last group, specifically with Holocaust survivors, are often called testimonies and have received widespread attention in media, culture and politics (Wieviorka 2006; Sabrow and Frei 2012; Andresen, Apel, Heinsohn 2015).

Since the 1990s, life-story interviews have become central in research about the Holocaust and other mass atrocities like Nazi forced labor, communist or Francoist repression. While written documents about deportation, exploitation, and extermination often either reflect the perpetrators' perspective or are missing altogether, the survivors' testimonies convey the victims' manifold *Erfahrungsgeschichte* (Niethammer and Leh 2007) and allow for a deeper understanding of the atrocities' aftermath in individual biographies and post-war societies.

Whereas some historians, usually analyzing contemporary written records, discard survivors' testimonies as unreliable artifacts created long after the historical events, oral historians are eager "to examine the historical agency in these eye-witnesses' narratives […], making historical inquiry the combined study of both what happened and how it is passed down to us" (Young 1997: 56f., cf. Hartman 1996).

In these settings, the individuality of each testimony is highly valued—as is the respect towards a Holocaust survivor's personal life story. Oral historians have always focused on subjective experiences, individual memories, biographical meaning, and cultural context. Any kind of de-contextualization—structural(ist) explanations, generalizing theories, or data-driven statistics—is either not needed or, at worst, distorting.

Given this tradition, this kind of data, and the limited resources in their projects, oral historians usually have analyzed individual interviews, often conducted by themselves (e.g. Felman and Laub 1991; Hartman 1996; Grinchenko 2009; Greenspan 2014). Rarely, however, have they embarked on larger, comparative studies (Browning 2010; Plato et al. 2010; Thonfeld 2014).

Nowadays, the rapid development of digital technologies has inspired the creation and curation of large-scale interview collections (Apostolopoulos and Pagenstecher 2013; Apostolopoulos et al. 2017; Pagenstecher 2017). These digital environments support quantitative and comparative approaches to their corpora and allow one to watch and listen to the interviews in a much more comfortable and efficient way than before.

In the age of the tape recorder, the oral historian usually worked with a textual representation of the recording in the form of a verbatim or lightly edited transcript. This analysis of a written approximation to the spoken word often neglects the non-verbal dimensions of the testimonies. Today, digital technology offers the possibility to study the audio-visual sources themselves, including the multiple modalities of text, speech, silence, gestures and facial expressions captured in the video images and the audio track (de Jong et al. 2008; Lichtblau 2011; Truong et al. 2014). Only few studies, however, have done this, mostly using interviews in Yale's Fortunoff archive (Hartman 1996; Pinchevski 2012; Greenspan 2014; Hamburger 2016) and in Claude Lanzmann's famous *Shoah* film (Chare 2015).

Interviews as Conversation and Interaction

Linguists, especially conversation analysts and interactional linguists, have mostly been interested in everyday conversations such as talk-at-work, dinner conversations, or chats over a drink with friends, but increasingly have also analyzed interviews as real-time interactions. Major obstacles for the study of interviews were the lack of homogeneous data and the lack of data from different languages.

While corpus linguistics has made tremendous progress in the digitally supported analysis of large amounts of written text, the treatment of spoken language has remained a "blind spot" (cf. Mair 2013). Many corpora of spoken language are based on media contexts rather than spontaneous private interaction, and often are accessible only as transcriptions, not as audio or video data.

Oral history collections, however, allow for the investigation of a large and rather homogeneous data set of thousands of interviews in many different languages. The audio- or video-recorded interviews share an overwhelmingly similar setting and similar topics, are of roughly the same duration, and were conducted with interviewees of similar age and elapsed time since their—often traumatic—experiences.

Understanding oral history interviews as recorded conversations can lead to the application of methods of Conversation Analysis (CA) and Interaction Linguistics (IL). CA uses naturalistic observation and detailed microanalysis of participants' conduct in actual instances of naturally occurring interaction as a technique for the empirical description of the practices and methods the participants of an interaction themselves use to produce, interpret, and co-ordinate their actions and activities in social interaction (cf. Heritage 2010). Depending on the sequential context in which it is used, speakers can be shown to use certain practices methodically for implementing various actions (e.g. initiating repair/signaling hearing trouble, foreshadowing disagreement, expressing disbelief). CA does not depart from preexisting analytical categories but intends to reconstruct the participants' categories, employing an emic perspective. In doing so, a given participant's reactions to the other participants' actions are central: In their reactions, participants signal each other how they understood a previous action (next turn proof procedure). This means that interaction is analyzed in terms of sequences of actions and displays of understanding.

Interactional Linguistics (IL) full-heartedly subscribes to the methodological framework and the inventory of communicative actions established by CA, but adds a more linguistic, i.e. structure-oriented perspective, based on the analysis of spoken corpora instead of a single conversation. IL methodology postulates the interdependence between the structure of a language and the structures of interaction (Selting and Couper-Kuhlen 2000: 82). In other words, linguistic structures or patterns are seen to be sedimented solutions for specific tasks. Linguistic structures are "best practiced solutions" so to speak for managing recurrent interactional problems (cf. Selting and Couper-Kuhlen 2001: 261–264).

Thus, IL tries to empirically reconstruct context-specific form-function relationships or patterned regularities between the deployment of certain linguistic forms and specific interactional functions in particular sequential or interactional environments (cf. Barth-Weingarten 2008: 85). In practice, it identifies particular (clusters of) linguistic (e.g., phonetic, prosodic, morpho-syntactic, lexical) resources that are constitutive of specific communicative tasks. In this paper, the repetition of stretches of utterances will be shown to solve the communicative task of negotiating the topic of ongoing speech (see below).

Such linguistic solutions to communicative problems are not seen to be attributable to only one speaker but are inherently dialogic as they serve to manage interactive tasks. Within the methodological framework of corpus-based IL, data is analyzed as an integral part of the context in which it occurs, which may require analytic attention on various levels of granularity (turn-constructional units, turns, a part of or the entire dialogue etc., cf. Linell 2009, 2015).

Interviews as Narrative Dialogue

Through an analysis of these interviews not only as written texts but as multi-modal interactions (from an interdisciplinary perspective cf. Norris et al. 2015) we can investigate the adaptation processes during which the interviewer and the narrator negotiate shared meanings and intersubjective standpoints, anticipate possibilities for misunderstanding (Deppermann 2015), and solve conflicts. The conceptualization of an interview as interactional rather than merely textual requires a comprehensive investigation of at least three types of interaction:

1. Reference and response phenomena between interviewer and interviewee, both verbal after a turn and non-verbal (gestures, looks) as well as verbal during turns, i.e. while one of them is speaking.
2. Adaptation of utterances to the specific interactional partner, where their (expected) background knowledge, interests, identity, and emotions are taken into account (recipient design).
3. Joint construction of meaning through a mutual set-up of contexts. Questions and answers, reactions and interpretations unfold against the backdrop of the context that has been agreed upon and that provides a frame of reference.

For the purpose of this chapter, oral history interviews are thus understood as narrative dialogues, enabled through a working alliance between the narrator and the interviewer.

Obviously, oral history interviews are not only autobiographic sources, but also results of a technically recorded dialogue with an interviewer in a specific setting. This has been underlined by critics who discard survivors' testimonies as unreliable sources for historical events and assign the status of a mere social artifact to these interviews (Bourdieu 1986). Indeed, oral history aims at understanding subjective meanings rather than at retrieving historical facts. Experienced interviewers are well aware of the "dialogical relationship" in oral history, where the "sources are not found, but co-created by the historian [...] in a dialogic exchange" (Portelli 2005).

It is a specific form of dialogue, however: In the biographical-narrative interview, the interviewer tries to elicit long self-structured narrations by restricting himself to short questions and—ideally supportive—interventions. This interviewer, largely silent and mostly invisible in the video recordings, plays a crucial role, however, as a "listener" to and "facilitator" of the testimony (Felman and Laub 1991: xvii; Lichtblau 2011; Pinchevski 2012). Thus, the narrative dialogue is largely a hidden dialogue, mostly not visible on the video, sometimes difficult to hear on the audio, and often not transcribed adequately. The interviewee, on the other hand, takes center-stage in narrating his/her life story, and becomes the narrator—this term will be used throughout this chapter— rather than only the respondent.

This narrative dialogue is a double-layered one: The narrator does not only talk to the interviewer, but also to the camera, and through the camera to an, albeit vaguely defined, audience of future generations (Pinchevski 2012: 149). How this "overhearing audience" of future recipients (cf. Poppe, Buchholz, Alder 2015: 206) is imagined by the speakers is mostly unknown, but definitely depends on the context of the interview project (Michaelis 2013; Shenker 2015; Taubitz 2016).

As Friedman (2014: 291) suggests, "layers of meaning are co-constructed from the embodied interaction of interviewer and narrator". In a successful interview, the narrator and the interviewer build a working alliance, called "complicity" (Jureit 1999: 159) or *Erzählgemeinschaft* (Nägel 2016), which helps the narrator through the difficult and often painful process of remembering, articulating and evaluating personal and sometimes traumatic experiences, and which creates a meaningful narration.

These working alliances—the term we use in a more specific way here than in its original therapeutic meaning—contain negotiations and conflicts. As has been shown for exemplary interview sequences though a scenic narrative microanalysis (Hamburger 2016, cf. also Poppe, Buchholz, Alder 2015), the power-relations between interviewer and narrator have shifting balances. In large collections, researchers like Browning (2010: 6) often come across "impatient and clueless" interviewers who interrupt the narrators. In some—archived, but rarely analyzed—interviews the working alliance is full of tensions or even fails completely. These tussles "are particularly interesting", however, for Cole (in Cole and Greenspan 2016): "Oral history is a co-produced source, but the idea of tussles suggests that co-production is not straightforward."

But how can we identify moments of negotiation or conflict between interviewer and narrator in a testimony in a systematic way? From a linguistic perspective, certain language patterns with a specific dialogical function can signal the ongoing process of creating and maintaining the working alliance. One of these elements is repetition, which will be looked at in the first of two case studies in this chapter.

Although there has been little comparative analysis of interviews from the various, scattered oral history collections, different narrator types with a different degree of agency have been identified in case studies (Michaelis 2013; Laub and Bodenstab 2010). On the other hand, there are also diverging cooperation patterns which can be correlated to the interviewing methods and the institutional settings of a specific interview project (Michaelis 2013: 205ff.), to gender differences of narrators and interviewers (Pagenstecher and Tausendfreund 2015) or to different national cultures of remembrance (Thonfeld 2014; Plato et al. 2010).

Comparisons of different oral history interviews are difficult, however, because of the individual character of each life-story narration. Therefore, repeated interviews with the same narrator, or re-tellings, can facilitate a comparative analysis of the context and dynamics of interaction, and of the hidden dialogue between interviewer and narrator (cf. Kasten 2017: 16–21, *this volume*). Such a re-telling is analyzed in the second case study below.

Sources: Interview Archives at Freie Universität Berlin

The sources (or data) analyzed in this chapter are available at the interview archives at the *Center for Digital Systems* (CeDiS) of *Freie Universität Berlin* (FUB). Since 2006, CeDiS has been creating or hosting four major collections with testimonies focusing on the Second World War and Nazi atrocities. The *Visual History Archive* of the *USC Shoah Foundation* (VHA), the online interview archive *Forced Labor 1939–1945* (Forced Labor), the British-Jewish collection *Refugee Voices* (Refugee Voices), and the new interview archive *Memories of the Occupation in Greece* (MOG) contain thousands of audio-visual life-story interviews, amongst them the interviews with Henry G. and Anita Lasker-Wallfisch analyzed in this chapter. To make the recordings accessible and stimulate their reception in research and education, CeDiS has created transcripts, translations, online archives and learning applications. Additionally, its team is engaged in academic debates through publications and conferences like *Erinnern an Zwangsarbeit* (Apostolopoulos and Pagenstecher 2013) and *Preserving Survivors Memories* (Apostolopoulos et al. 2017).

In 2006, Freie Universität Berlin became the first site outside the United States with full access to the Shoah Foundation's *Visual History Archive* (VHA, VHA-FUB). The collection contains 53 000 interviews with Jewish Holocaust survivors, but also other victim groups like Sinti and Roma, political prisoners, or homosexuals. Liberators and helpers were interviewed, too, as were witnesses of other 20th century genocides.

Whereas the Shoah Foundation had not transcribed the 53 000 interviews in the main archive, CeDiS did transcribe a sub-collection with 908 German-language (plus 50 foreign-language) testimonies following detailed guidelines. These transcripts are time-coded every minute and aligned to the videos, enabling full text search over all 958 interviews (Abenhausen et al. 2012). Among these, there is also the 40-page transcript of Anita Lasker-Wallfisch's interview recorded on 8 December 1998 (VHA, interview 48608) which will be analysed below. The Shoah Foundation offers the German transcripts as a kind of subtitles within their online archive—for universities which have subscribed via the Visual History Archive's new commercial provider ProQuest (USC 2016; currently, FUB's copyright of the transcriptions is not mentioned in the archive). Numerous publications (e.g. Michaelis 2013; Bothe and Brüning 2015; Shenker 2015; Taubitz 2016) shed light on interview settings and methods.

In the interview archive *Forced Labor 1939–1945: Memory and History* (Forced Labor), 590 former forced laborers tell their life stories in 190 video recordings and 393 audio recordings. The testimonies were recorded in 2005 and 2006 by 32 partner institutions in 25 countries (Plato, Leh, Thonfeld 2010; Thonfeld 2014). They have been transcribed, aligned to the media files with sentence-based time-codes, translated into German, indexed and made available in an online archive together with accompanying photos and documents (Apostolopoulos and Pagenstecher 2013). On the project website, some interviewers reflect on their methods and experiences (*Expertengespräche*).

About a third of the interviewees were prisoners of concentration camps—many of them Jews or Roma. The biographical interviews do not only relate to Nazi forced labor, they also touch upon various other historical aspects of the Century of Camps, from Holodomor to Perestroika, from the Spanish Civil War to the Yugoslav Wars. This *Forced Labor 1939–1945* archive contains two video interviews analysed below with Holocaust survivors Henry G. and Anita Lasker-Wallfisch, incidentally both recorded on March 17, 2006, one for two hours in New Haven, the other for 3,5 hours in London (Forced Labor, interviews za577 and za072).

Methods: The MOCA Platform at the Freiburg University of Freiburg

Contrary to other oral history collections where much research still relies on written transcriptions, the new digital environments at CeDiS come with time-aligned transcriptions, media files, and metadata, and allow for thematically focused searches and annotations throughout the video-recordings. From their onset, however, the archives were mainly aimed at historians, educators, and the general public, supporting qualitative and hermeneutic analyses and the respectful engagement of learners with individual testimonies. Therefore, the orthographic transcripts were polished slightly, and no tools for corpus-linguistic analyses were integrated. Given the growing importance of interdisciplinary Digital Humanities approaches, however, using such tools on these collections can provide a future perspective for oral historians and linguists alike.

For the case studies in this chapter, our joint linguistic and historical approach was based on MOCA, an online platform for Multimodal Oral Corpus Analysis. MOCA has been under development since 2001 in the departments of Romance and Germanic Languages at the University of Freiburg, in close collaboration with Universities in Luxemburg and Louvain-la-Neuve. It supports the collaborative analysis of audio and video files with their respective transcriptions and metadata. Based on a MySQL database, it uses PHP as programming language and HTML5 for streaming. As a multi-user environment, MOCA offers safe and personalized access to the data through fine-grained user-rights management. It supports the analysis of audio- and video-taped testimony with a number of different linguistic methods such as the identification of repeated word patterns, as discussed below.

In this chapter, the archives' original orthographic transcriptions are used because they are available for the whole collection of hundreds of interview hours. At later stages of interdisciplinary cooperation, it could be preferable to use a linguistic transcription system (e.g., GAT, the *Gesprächsanalytisches Transkriptionssystem*, Selting et al. 2009) in order to take prosody, pauses, etc., into account, although the digital archives support direct access to the audio-visual data.

Case Study 1: Repetitions in Interviews

Listening closely to an oral history interview, actual dialogues turn out to be much more complex than just a tidy sequence of interviewer questions and narrator answers that we know from journalistic interviews. The analysis of the interviewers' questions and comments, and also of the very moments before and after these interventions, reveals different mechanisms of interaction between both participants: there are pauses and interruptions, cases of simultaneous speaking and of repetition. As the following analysis of a single interview shows, repetitions play an important and changing role in the working alliance between narrator and interviewer.

Working with corpora of authentic interaction, both interactional linguists and conversation analysts have shown time and again that dialogue partners tend to repeat stretches of prior speech almost verbatim (cf. Skrovec 2012 for a comprehensive overview of prior research on this topic). In the dialogue, repetitions create the feeling of being well understood by the interaction partner (Gülich and Mondada 2008). However, repetition also displays synchronization and resonance between the speakers and thus enhances the shared feeling of togetherness (Kim 2015; Pfänder and Schumann 2016), i.e. of sharing similar knowledge and of working together on the same project. In our case studies, both understanding the information and togetherness are not given, but often have to be constructed and negotiated (Ehmer 2011).

In order to both find and analyze strategies of negotiating and of ensuring understanding, we searched for all those moments within a testimony at which either the interviewer or the narrator repeated the other's words exactly. Using the MOCA platform, we searched for repeated bi- and tri-grams, i.e. two or three words that occurred in the exact same order and form at least twice. The two-hour testimony of Holocaust survivor Henry G. (HG), interviewed by Dori Laub (INT) in 2006, is the example we chose for this case study. The interviewer is an experienced interviewer, a well-known psychiatrist specializing in trauma research (Laub and Bodenstab 2010). He is a child survivor himself, just seven years younger than Henry G. Both interviewer and narrator left what today is Ukraine after the Holocaust, first to Israel, then to the USA (Mayer 1998). The fact that the interviewer shares some experiences with the narrator is as important as his approach based on psychoanalysis and trauma research (Hamburger 2016).

This interview contains various instances of repetition, three of which are presented and discussed here—with the repeated word printed boldly. In the first example, repetition is a means for expressing understanding and agreement (or affiliation, as conversation analysts would call it). Talking about pre-1939 religious life and Zionism in his Carpathian home-town, Henry G. describes a local Rabbi's emigration to Israel (Henry G. 2006, tape 1, min. 24:27):

> HG: There was music, trumpets, I don't know, drums, whatever. He had a carriage, he was sitting right in the carriage, and he went to the train station and from the train station he went wherever and he reached Israel.
> INT: **You remember that?**
> HG: **I remember that,** yeah yeah. It was very nice, yeah. I remember, for instance, we went to …

In this sequence, the interviewer voices a slight doubt whether Henry G. really remembers this event personally and asks for clarification "you remember that?". With his repetition "I remember that", the narrator not only confirms this, but starts giving other examples of his detailed childhood memories over the following minutes. Thus, the repetition does not only ensure understanding within the dialogue, but also allows the narrator to shift the topic of the narration slightly and to organize the following stretches of discourse.

In the second example, the interviewer uses repetition in order to pinpoint a topic and ask for more detailed information on that topic (here: the duration of the stay) – thus clearly displaying understanding (Henry G. 2006, tape 1, min. 40:56):

HG: Ultimately they took us to **the brick factory** and they put us in the, in the, in the wagons.
INT: How long were you in **the brick factory?**
HG: Maybe a day, maybe a half of day, you know.

Repetition here slows down the narration and prevents the interviewee from skipping the brick factory episode too quickly and moving on to the topic of the wagons right away. Thus, it allows the interviewer to negotiate what they are talking about. In the minutes before, Dori Laub intervenes several times trying to force Henry G. into a chronological narration of his experiences in the ghetto, the brick factory and the wagons—with limited success.

In the next example, repetition is not so much about negotiating what they talk about, but negotiating the understanding of historical facts (Henry G. 2006, tape 1, min. 31:21):

HG: And the men, the fathers were taken away to the slave battalions, the Munkaszolgálat. It was really rough it was.
INT: Those were battalions sent **with the troops?**
HG: Sent the, yeah, **to the troops,** to serve the soldiers, to serve the soldiers in the battlefield, you know. And uh those didn't fare well.

The narrator mentions the Slave Labor Battalions or *Munkaszolgálat*, which male Hungarian Jews were drafted into after the adoption of anti-Jewish laws in Hungary in 1939. Talking to an expert interviewer, he does not explain this term, but moves on directly to an evaluation. The interviewer interrupts him and asks for an explanation, probably thinking about the future audience of the testimony. At that moment, the narrator echoes part of the interrupting utterance, but substitutes the preposition 'to' instead of 'with', inducing a subtle yet distinct change of meaning, eliminating any notion of togetherness or common experience, let alone collaboration that could arise from the word 'with'.

Sometimes repetition is used as a means for some sort of other-initiated repair. In the following example, the narrator repeats an explanation given by the interviewer to make his own narration understandable (Henry G. 2006, tape 1, min. 30:03):

HG: And the Hungarians came, **they left**, the Hungarians came in, so I pass …
INT: **The Czechs left.**
HG: **The Czechs left,** and the Hungarians came.

Finally, self-repetition may be used to prevent a change of topic. In the next example, the narrator insists on continuing his argument, even though the interviewer wants to change the topic (Henry G. 2006, tape 1, min. 39:37).

> HG: And, uh, I remember some of the people some of the people, uh, they became leaders of the ghetto, you know, and what happens to human nature that they start to act like, uh, I don't know if you've ever heard about Rumkowski. **Rumkowski was a, a fool.**
> DL: Let's talk about your …
> HG: I know, I might. Just to say something: **Rumkowski was a fool,** and he was thinking he was the king of the Jews, and he was serving the Germans.

In this example, the interviewer and the narrator actively negotiate deontic authority, the question of who will talk about which topic at a given time during the interview. The interviewer wants the narrator to focus on his personal experience instead of discussing general historical arguments, but the narrator sticks to his topic, which, as evidenced by the subsequent minutes of the interview, he uses as an example for contextualizing his own experiences by comparing these to an example which would be well-known to his future audience.

Other examples could demonstrate additional functions of repetitions in the narrative dialogue of a testimony, such as expressing empathy, deeply felt understanding or togetherness (Kim 2015), but for reasons of space we cannot go into more detail here. Further studies, using quantitative approaches supported by the MOCA software, will certainly shed more light on the distribution of these different kinds of repetitions throughout a given interview. A higher number of negotiating repetitions could be expected in the first phase of an interview when both speakers have to create their working alliance and its dialogical mode. Turning the argument around, analyzing verbal repetitions could help detecting important or controversial topics and sequences in an interview. Future studies could compare these results with other interviews either by the same or by other interviewers and look for more general tendencies.

Case Study 2: Retellings in Interviews – a Case Study

In different oral history collections, some narrators were interviewed several times over a longer period of time, some wrote written testimonies or testified in court as well. Re-told testimonies with the same interviewers (Laub and Bodenstab 2010, Greenspan 2014) or different interviewers (Kangisser Cohen 2014; Bader 2015) have been analyzed, discussing how institutions, media, and time shape these repeated narrations. Important factors in this are the changing memory discourse in society, the narrator's increased narrative experience, but also different methods and techniques of the interviewer.

Conversation analysis conceptualizes oral re-tellings within the context of actual interaction. These are co-produced by two or more participants and are aligned to the respective contexts and aims of a specific instance of interaction. Linguistic and structural similarities and differences between different instantiations of a retold narration are the result of the adaptation of a particular instantiation to the narrator's communicative goals and the respective interactional situation. A comparative analysis of different instantiations allows one to investigate the impact of individual interactional contexts and individual dynamics in interaction on the composition of individual retellings (Norrick 1997).

This section will discuss a different example, since an earlier interview with Henry G., the narrator quoted above, was not transcribed (Henry G. 1996). Instead, it will compare two testimonies of the well-known Holocaust survivor Anita Lasker-Wallfisch, who had been a cellist in the women's orchestra at Auschwitz and later became co-founder of the English Chamber Orchestra. Apart from publishing her memoirs, she gave many different interviews throughout the decades—from the first BBC interview recorded in liberated Bergen-Belsen in April 1945 to a three-dimensional holographic interview at the University of Southern California in September 2015 (Pagenstecher 2017). The first interview we looked at was conducted in 1998 by Scottish journalist Joanna Buchan, and the second one in 2006 by German historian Christoph Thonfeld. The transcripts quoted below were created in different projects and follow different transcriptions guidelines.

At the age of 18, Lasker-Wallfisch was imprisoned in her home-town Breslau (today Wrocław). In the following excerpts, she talks about an experience in prison before she and her sister were deported to Auschwitz. The prisoners had to work for a toy factory and came into contact with one of the company's forewomen:

Excerpt 1 (Anita Lasker-Wallfisch 1998, min. 22:00 until min. 24:00):

> But the important thing about the soldiers is that the girl who brought these soldiers to the, to the cell, was not a prison guard. She was obviously employed by the, er, toy soldier factory or something. And she used to breeze in and breeze out and soldiers here and colour this and the other. (-) And when my sister had gone she started talking to me and asked me where my sister was. And (--) a really very nice and remarkable relationship (-) developed there. She was obviously a very nice young girl. I would very much like to meet her again. Now she must be over eighty, now, but (-) she was, as far as I am concerned, she was tremendous support. // INT: What was her name? /// <German> Fräulein Neubert. She was very small and we used to call her <German> Püppchen, (-) you know, little doll. <Coughs> And she=er, (-) she used to

open the cell door and say <loud> "What do you need?" <whispers> and then she used to shut it and then we started talking very softly in case another guard hears it. And she was very interested in everything and she used to bring=er_, I found at the bottom of the, the soldiers, (-) some bread or a piece of cake or something, which her mother had sent us. You know, very touchy. To us this was a terribly important thing, you know, nobody was nice to us. (--) She was te-, terrific.

Excerpt 2 (Anita Lasker-Wallfisch 2006, tape 3, min 15:15 until min 16:42).

But even in prison I had a, I don't know whether that interests you, but I had an experience, which was very, I mean, people always ask me, "Was there anything good that ever happened to you in those days?" I said, there is only one good thing that happened, that was the girl that brought us the soldiers to paint, that was our work, to paint the toy soldiers, who was terribly nice. And eventually, we developed a sort of friendship with her, and she used to open the cell, because, you know, prisons are places with a lot of gossip. You mustn't be seen to be nice to the prisoners. She used to open the cell and said, „Brauchen Sie was?" [harshly], and then she used to come in and shut the door, and then we would whisper etc., etc.. And she was obviously, she brought us something, something to eat from her mother, terribly nice, wonderful for us. We used to call her Püppchen, she was a very small lady, and she used to bring these … she showed us what colour and what etc., etc. Anyway, this Püppchen, eventually then my sister wasn't there anymore, and then we started to get more and more talkative, and eventually, when I was sent to Auschwitz, she came to say goodbye and we, sort of, little sayings which her mother sent me to give me courage, and I think, a piece of bread or cake or something. I mean, I shall never forget it, wonderful. OK, end of that story.

A cursory analysis of the two excerpts exhibits striking differences right away. In 1998, Anita Lasker-Wallfisch relates her experience with a female German forewoman as one of several answers to the interviewer's question about how she was treated, and as a single positive exception to the rule. In the moment of stance-taking, she seeks empathy and conformation from the interviewer, using the phrase "you know". The forewoman's nick-name "Püppchen" is introduced before the kernel story, providing an image of the person and setting the tone.

In terms of stance, we find similar stance-taking devices, i.e. ways of positioning herself, in both narrations, but more distance in the second excerpt:

1998	2006
To us this was a terribly important thing, you know, nobody was nice to us. (--) She was te-, terrific.	[...] who was terribly nice [...] terribly nice, wonderful for us.

In 2006, Anita Lasker-Wallfisch proactively narrates her experience without being prompted by the interviewer. She exhibits high agency here, attributing a high level of relevance to her story. Tellability is established right in the beginning with the phrase "people always ask me". The narration starts with "There is only one good thing that happened", and has a clear end marked by "end of that story". It provides much more background information than before. We also find very well-constructed, almost pre-formulated sentences such as "not only do I remember her, she was the highlight of my life in those days", creating an impression of some sort of distance. The forewoman's nick-name "Püppchen" is provided after the core story, just to complete the picture. It is thus part of a story-telling routine. In sum, we can identify the following differences between the two versions:

- The 1998 version is situated in a clearly interactional context, answering an explicit question from the interviewer. The 2006 version, on the other hand, is proactively offered and narrated without any cues from the interviewer. In 1998, the phrase you know is a direct appeal to the interviewer's empathy which is not needed anymore in 2006.
- The 1998 version is shorter, provides fewer details and is less complete as a story as it lacks an ending. It does not provide a lot of background information and includes fewer comments on the narration. The few comments are about how she felt during the events narrated, not about how she feels at the moment of the interview.
- The 1998 version seems more direct and unique, where the 2006 version uses more elaborate structures that are reminiscent of written language, including subordination and formulaic chunks. Its final phrase "end of that story" evokes the notion that "Püppchen" is just one of many stories.

This increased narrative experience becomes very clear when comparing the language in the 1998 and 2006 interviews. Lasker-Wallfisch's performative effort became more elaborate and successful in her later narration in which she directly quotes other people more often. In the 1998 version, she describes her introduction to the orchestra at Birkenau using indirect speech: "So, she asked me to play something." In the 2006 version, however, she uses a direct quotation: "And she gave me a cello and said: 'Play something.'"

This exemplary result is corroborated by several quantitative comparisons: In 1998, there are about 100 instances of direct speech, in 2006 about 320 instances. The transcript of the later interview, which is just over 50% longer, contains more than three times as many quotation marks. This seems to be a general tendency in narrating: When studying re-tellings in other contexts, linguists have found a move towards performativity, marked by an increase in direct speech. More experienced narrators give their testimony with more performative elements and an enhanced narrative authority.

Lasker-Wallfisch's more elaborate narration in 2006 was also enabled by a different interviewing method. A quantitative comparison of the two transcripts demonstrates a different interaction between narrator and interviewer. Both interviewers—Scottish BBC journalist Joanna Buchan in 1998, German Historian Christoph Thonfeld in 2006—intervened roughly once per minute throughout the interview—which seems to be an average value (cf. Michaelis, 2013: 288). But half of Thonfeld's interventions were just supporting incentives to continue (e.g., mumbling "hm"), whereas Buchan asked many factual questions, sometimes interrupting Lasker-Wallfisch's narrative flow. In fact, Lasker-Wallfisch was only able to take up her narration again within no more than five words in merely 13 of Buchan's interventions. Buchan's factual questions (31 what-, 17 how-, 13 where-questions) probably corresponded to the Shoah Foundation's VHA question list (cf. Michaelis 2013: 233).

These results stem from different professional backgrounds of the individual interviewer, but also point to different methodological guidelines in the interviewing projects. Digital interview collections can support such comparative analyses of transcripts on a larger scale, helping us to better understand the working alliance between narrator and interviewer which is influenced by many different factors.

Finally, the language of the quote attributed to the forewoman changes from English in the 1998 version to German in the 2006 version. In the 1998 excerpt, the quote is only a little louder than the rest of the narration and is provided in English, the language the interview is being conducted in.

1998	2006
What you need?	Brauchen sie was?

In the 2006 excerpt, the quote is much louder, very harsh in tone and in German, imitating the narrated event directly. The effect here is one of distance through staging. In addition, it references the cliché of German as a loud and harsh language.

The language used in Anita Lasker-Wallfisch's two testimonies differs remarkably. In 1998, she uses only a handful of German words, apparently taken over from the SS, such as *Zählappell* or *Notenschreiberinnen*. In all survivors' testimonies, the German perpetrators' camp language has entered the victims' memories narrated in another language. In 2006, however, her German mother-tongue surfaces regularly, even for specific topics from the pre-war period (such as *Frontkämpfer* or *Kultur*) and the post-war period (such as *Gedenkstätte* or *Neonazis*). The main reason for this could be the German interviewer. During the second interview, Lasker-Wallfisch certainly knew that Thonfeld would understand every German word, even in its fine-grained nuances. In comparing multiple accounts, it has been noted that bilingual narrators deliberately apply specific wordings in each language. For instance, when Polish Auschwitz survivor—and memorial guide—Jerzy Hronowski called the perpetrators "the Germans" in his Polish, and "the Nazis" in his German-language testimonies, he carefully addressed his different target groups (Bader 2015: 210, fn. 8).

But there may be other reasons as well. In the seven-year period between the two interviews, Lasker-Wallfisch cautiously re-opened herself towards her country of birth and persecution, visiting Bergen-Belsen and other places several times. Thus, it would be interesting to study these deliberate or unwilling German "quotations" in detail, looking for instance at which topics or perspectives are worded in English, and which in German. This could be part of a larger comparative study of multilingual testimonies; this is a very common type of testimony due to many survivors' experiences of deportation and forced or voluntary migration before, during and after the war.

Conclusion

This chapter has studied narrative patterns in video-taped interviews with Holocaust survivors understood as results of a recorded interaction. Three testimonies of two narrators from the oral history archives at Freie Universität Berlin were analyzed with the MOCA software developed at the University of Freiburg. Combining questions and methods from oral history, conversation analysis and interactional linguistics, the chapter has analyzed the working alliance between interviewer and narrator, with both participants using specific verbal and non-verbal resources to co-construct the narration and its layers of meaning.

Two preliminary case studies, one on repetitions and one on re-tellings, analyze the interaction between the interviewer and the narrator that constitutes the oral history interview. The case study on repetitions in Henry G.'s testimony has shown different functions of repetitions in the narrative dialogue. Further studies should analyze the distribution of these different kinds of repetitions throughout other interviews in order to explore the functions of repetitions in different working alliances.

The case study on Anita Lasker-Wallfisch's re-tellings demonstrated a gradually increasing performativity and story-telling experience on part of the narrator, but also the importance of different interviewing methods based on the professional, project and language backgrounds of the individual interviewers. In the future, such re-tellings can be analyzed more systematically in order to identify similar and different dialogical elements.

The resulting array of typical patterns of interaction could then be studied with more quantitative approaches: Similarities and differences can be correlated with biographical or sociolinguistic variables of the narrators and the interviewers such as nationality, age, gender, experience group and professional, institutional or political affiliation. Interactional patterns can probably also be shown to differ with regard to specific topics in the narration.

Going beyond the mere textual analysis, future studies should also address the multimodality of the interaction in video-recorded interviews, and take a closer look at facial expressions, gestures, periods of silence and other elements of non-verbal interaction. Instead of monolingual, monomodal, textual and "tidy" data which existing language technology is most capable of handling, linguistic tools need to address the challenge posed by multimodal, multilingual, spoken, informal and unplanned communication.

The combination of oral history sources, linguistic methods and an interdisciplinary research setting has proved promising. A linguistic approach can help historians to listen more closely to the details of narrating, focusing on specific word patterns rather than on the general historical context. On the other hand, oral history's specific reflectivity on the constructed and medialized character of its sources highlights the interpretative and subjective dimensions in defining types, encoding criteria, and developing algorithms for corpus-linguistic analysis of spoken corpora.

The testimonies studied here are particularly valuable because they constitute a unique record of the narrators' suffering and surviving. This quality is not affected by the mass of a text or sophistication of retrieval and analysis techniques. However, it is through the complementary use of such techniques that we can develop a deeper understanding of the complexity of these narrations.

Sources

Collections:

VHA: Visual History Archive of the Institute for Visual History and Education, USC Shoah Foundation [web page]. Accessed online at <www.sfi.usc.edu>, 05 September 2016.

VHA-FUB: Das Visual History Archive an der Freien Universität Berlin [web page]. Accessed online at <www.vha.fu-berlin.de>, 05 September 2016.

Forced Labor: Interview Archive Forced Labor 1939-1945 [web page]. Accessed online at <http://www.zwangsarbeit-archiv.de/en>, September 05, 2016.

Refugee Voices: Interview Collection Refugee Voices [web page]. Accessed online at <www.refugeevoices.fu-berlin.de>, September 05, 2016.

MOG: Interview Archive Memories of the Occupation in Greece [web page]. Accessed online at <http://www.occupation-memories.org/en>, September 05, 2016.

Interviews:

Anita Lasker-Wallfisch 1998: Interview with Anita Lasker-Wallfisch, interviewed by Joanna Buchan on December 8, 1998, USC Shoah Foundation's Visual History Archive. Accessed online at <www.vha.fu-berlin.de>, interview 48608, February 28, 2016.

Anita Lasker-Wallfisch 2006: Interview with Anita Lasker-Wallfisch, interviewed by Christoph Thonfeld on March 17, 2006, Forced Labor 1939–1945, accessed online at <www.zwangsarbeit-archiv.de>, interview za072, February 28, 2016.

Henry G. 1996: Interview with Henry G., interviewed by Dan Danieli in New Rochelle, NY, USA on April 23, 1996 (length 2:18), Visual History Archive, Interview 14431, http://vhaonline.usc.edu/viewingPage?testimonyID=14625&returnIndex=0

Henry G. 2006: Interview with Henry G., interviewed by Dori Laub on March 17, 2006, Forced Labor 1939–1945, accessed online at <www.zwangsarbeit-archiv.de>, interview za577, February 28, 2016.

Expertengespräche: Website *Forced Labor 1939–1945*, German version, Expertengespräche, accessed online at <http://www.zwangsarbeit-archiv.de/projekt/experteninterviews>, November 18, 2016.

References

Abenhausen, Sigrid, Nicolas Apostolopoulos, Bernd Körte-Braun, and Verena Lucia Nägel (eds.) 2012. *Zeugen der Shoah: Die didaktische und wissenschaftliche Arbeit mit Video-Interviews des USC Shoah Foundation Institute*. Berlin: Freie Universität.

Andresen, Knud, Linde Apel, and Kirsten Heinsohn (eds.) 2015. *Es gilt das gesprochene Wort. Oral History und Zeitgeschichte heute*. Göttingen: Wallstein.

Apostolopoulos, Nicolas, Michele Barricelli, Gertrud Koch, and Ralf Possekel (eds.) 2017. *Preserving Survivors' Memories. Conference Proceedings*. Berlin (forthcoming).

Apostolopoulos, Nicolas and Cord Pagenstecher (eds.) 2013. *Erinnern an Zwangsarbeit: Zeitzeugen-Interviews in der digitalen Welt*. Berlin: Metropol.

Barth-Weingarten, Dagmar 2008. Interactional Linguistics. In *Handbook of Applied Linguistics*. Vol. 2: Interpersonal Communication. G. Antos, E. Ventola, and T. Weber (eds.), 77–105. Berlin: De Gruyter.

Bothe, Alina, and Christina Isabel Brüning (eds.) 2015. *Geschlecht und Erinnerung im digitalen Zeitalter. Neue Perspektiven auf ZeitzeugInnenarchive*. Berlin: LIT Verlag.

Bourdieu, Pierre 1986. L'illusion biographique. In *Actes de la recherché en sciences sociales*, 62–63 (06.1986): 69–72.

Browning, Christopher 2010. *Remembering Survival. Inside a Nazi Slave-Labor Camp*. New York: Norton.

Chare, Nicholas 2015. Gesture in Shoah. *Journal for Cultural Research* 19(1): 30–42.

Cole, Tim, and Henry Greenspan 2016. *Movement and Memory: An Email Exchange with Henry Greenspan and Tim Cole, Part 1*, Oxford University Blog, 22.1.2016, blog.oup.com/2016/01/hank-greenspan-tim-cole-part-1.

De Jong, Franciska, D. W., Heeren W. Oard, and R. Ordelman 2008. Access to recorded interviews: A research agenda. In *ACM J. Comput. Cultur. Heritage 1, 1, Article 3*. (June 2008), http://doi.acm.org/10.1145/1367080.1367083.

Deppermann, Arnulf 2014. Das Forschungsinterview als soziale Interaktionspraxis. In *Qualitative Forschung: Analysen und Diskussionen – 10 Jahre Berliner Methodentreffen*. G. Mey, Günter and K. Mruck (eds.), 133–150. Heidelberg: Springer VS.

Deppermann, Arnulf 2015. Retrospection and Understanding in Interaction. In *Temporality in Interaction*. A. Deppermann and S. Günthner (eds.), 57–94. Amsterdam: Benjamins.

Deppermann, Arnulf 2015. Retrospection and Understanding in Interaction. In *Temporality in Interaction*. A. Deppermann and S. Günthner (eds.), 57–94. Amsterdam: Benjamins.

Ehmer, Oliver 2011. *Imagination und Animation. Die Herstellung mentaler Räume durch animierte Rede*. Berlin: De Gruyter.

Felman, Shoshana, and Dori Laub 1991. *Testimony: Crises of Witnessing in Literature, Psychoanalysis, and History*. New York: Routledge.

Friedman, Jeff 2014. Oral History, Hermeneutics, and Embodiment. *The Oral History Review* 41(2): 290–300.

Greenspan, Henry 2014. The Unsaid, the Incommunicable, the Unbearable, and the Irretrievable. *The Oral History Review* 41(2): 229–243.

Grinchenko, Gelinada 2009. Zwangsarbeit im nationalsozialistischen Deutschland im Kontext des lebensgeschichtlichen Interviews einer ehemaligen ukrainischen Ostarbeiterin. In *Erinnerungen nach der Wende. Oral History und (post)sozialistische Gesellschaften. Remembering after the Fall of Communism. Oral History and (Post-)Socialist Societies*. J. Obertries and A. Stephan (eds.), 133–150. Essen: Klartext.

Hamburger, Andreas 2016. Blick-Winkel. Psychoanalytische Reflexion in der Forschung mit Videozeugnissen. In *Videographierte Zeugenschaft. Ein interdisziplinärer Dialog*. S. Knopp, S. Schulze, and A. Eusterschulte (eds.), 218–256. Weilerswist: Velbrück Wissenschaft.

Hartman, Geoffrey 1996. *The Longest Shadow. In the Aftermath of the Holocaust*. New York: Palgrave Macmillan.

Heritage, John 2010. 'Conversation Analysis: Practices and Methods.' In *Qualitative Sociology. (3rd Edition)*. D. Silverman (ed.), 208–230. London: Sage.

Jureit, Ulrike 1999. *Erinnerungsmuster. Zur Methodik lebensgeschichtlicher Interviews mit Überlebenden der Konzentrations- und Vernichtungslager*. Hamburg: Ergebnisse.

Kasten, Erich 2017. Documenting Oral Histories in the Russian Far East: Text Corpora for Multiple Aims and Uses. In *Oral History Meets Linguistics*. E. Kasten, K. Roller, J. Wilbur (eds.), 13–30. Fürstenberg/Havel: Kulturstiftung Sibirien.

Kim, Young Yun 2015. Achieving Synchrony: A Foundational Dimension of Intercultural Communication Competence. *Intercultural Competence* 48: 27–37.

Laub, Dori, and Johanna Bodenstab 2010. Twenty-five Years Later. Revisiting Testimonies of Holocaust Survivors. In *Hitler's Slaves. Life Stories of Forced Labourers in Nazi-occupied Europe*. A. v. Plato, A. Leh, and C. Thonfeld (eds.), 426–440. New York: Berghahn Books.

Lichtblau, Albert 2011. Opening Up Memory Space. The Challenges of Audiovisual History. In *The Oxford Handbook to Oral History*. D. A. Ritchie (ed.), 277–284. Oxford: Oxford University Press.

Linell, Per 2009. *Rethinking Language, Mind and World: Interactional and Contextual Theories of Human Sense-making*. Charlotte, NC: Information Age Publishing.

— 2015. Dialogism and the Distributed Language Approach: A Rejoinder to Steffensen. *Language Sciences* 50: 120–126.

Mair, Christian 2013. Writing the Corpus-Based History of Spoken English. In *English Corpus Linguistics: Variation in Time, Space and Genre*. G. Andersen and K. Bech (eds.), 11–29. Amsterdam: Rodopi.

Michaelis, Andree 2013. *Erzählräume nach Auschwitz: Literarische und videographierte Zeugnisse von Überlebenden der Shoah*. Berlin: Akademie Verlag.

Nägel, Verena 2016. Zeugnis – Artefakt – Digitalisat. Zur Bedeutung der Entstehungs- und Aufbereitungsprozesse von Oral History-Interviews. In *Videographierte Zeugenschaft. Ein interdisziplinärer Dialog*. A. Eusterschulte, S. Knopp, and S. Schulze, Sebastian (eds.), 347–368. Weilerswist: Velbrück Wissenschaft.

Niethammer, Lutz, und Almut Leh 2007. *Kritische Erfahrungsgeschichte und grenzüberschreitende Zusammenarbeit*. The Networks of Oral History. Sonderband von BIOS für Alexander von Plato. Opladen: Budrich.

Norrick, Neil 1997. Twice-told Tales: Collaborative Narration of Familiar Stories. *Language in Society* 26(2): 199–220.

Norris, Sigrid, and Carmen Daniela Maier (eds.) 2015. *Interactions, Images and Text*. Berlin: De Gruyter.

Pagenstecher, Cord, and Doris Tausendfreund 2015. Interviews als Quellen der Geschlechtergeschichte. Das Online-Archive Zwangsarbeit 1939–1945 und das Visual History Archive der USC Shoah Foundation. In *Geschlecht und Erinnerung im digitalen Zeitalter. Neue Perspektiven auf ZeitzeugInnenarchive*. A. Bothe and C. Brüning (eds.), 41–67. Berlin: LIT.

Pagenstecher, Cord 2017. *Testimonies in Digital Environments. (De-)contextualizing Interviews with Holocaust Survivor Anita Lasker-Wallfisch*. (in preparation)

Pfänder, Stefan, and Elke Schumann 2016. Synchronisation multimodal. Erste empirische Befunde eines interdisziplinären Forschungsprojekts. In *Priscis Libentius et Liberius Novis*. O. Hackstein and Andreas Opfermann (eds.). (in print)

Pinchevski, Amit 2012. The Audiovisual Unconscious: Media and Trauma in the Video Archive for Holocaust Testimonies. *Critical Inquiry* 39(1): 142–166.

Plato, Alexander von, Almut Leh, and Christoph Thonfeld (eds.) 2010. Hitler's Slaves: Life Stories of Forced Labourers in Nazi-Occupied Europe. New York: Berghahn.

Poppe, Christopher, Michael B. Buchholz, and Marie-Luise Alder 2015. Zeugnis ablegen als „DoingTestimony" – Interviewinteraktion in Zeitzeugeninterviews. *Journal für Psychologie* 23(2): 195–232. Accessed online at https://journal-fuer-psychologie.de/index.php/jfp/article/view/383 [05.11, 2016]

Portelli, Alessandro 2005. A Dialogical Relationship. An Approach to Oral History. *Swaraj Expressions Annual*: 1–8.

Rosenthal, Gabriele 1995. *Erlebte und erzählte Lebensgeschichte. Gestalt und Struktur biographischer Selbstbeschreibungen*. Frankfurt a.M.: Campus.

Sabrow, Martin, and Norbert Frei (eds.) 2012: *Die Geburt des Zeitzeugen nach 1945*. Göttingen: Wallstein.

Schumann, Elke, Elisabeth Gülich, Gabriele Lucius-Hoene, and Stefan Pfänder (eds.) 2015. *Wiedererzählen. Formen und Funktionen einer kulturellen Praxis*. Bielefeld: transcript Verlag.

Selting, Margret, Peter Auer, et al. 1998. Gesprächsanalytisches Transkriptionssystem (GAT). *Linguistische Berichte* 173: 91–122.

Selting, Margret, and Elizabeth Couper-Kuhlen 2000. Argumente für die Entwicklung einer interaktionalen Linguistik. *Gesprächsforschung – Online-Zeitschrift zur verbalen Interaktion*1: 76–95.

— 2001. Introducing Interactional Linguistics. In *Studies in Interactional Linguistics*. M. Selting and E. Couper-Kuhlen (eds.), 1–22. Amsterdam: Benjamins.

Shenker, Noah 2015. *Reframing Holocaust Testimony*. Bloomington: Indiana University Press.

Skrovec, Marie 2012. *Répétitions: entre syntaxe en temps réel et rhétorique ordinaire*. Freiburg: Rombach.

Taubitz, Jan 2016. *Holocaust Oral History und das lange Ende der Zeitzeugenschaft*. Göttingen: Wallstein.

Thonfeld, Christoph 2014. *Rehabilitierte Erinnerungen? Individuelle Erfahrungsverarbeitungen und kollektive Repräsentationen von NS-Zwangsarbeit im internationalen Vergleich*. Essen: Klartext.

USC 2016: *USC Shoah Foundation Announces Partnership with ProQuest to Increase Access to Visual History Archive*. Accessed online at http://www.proquest.com/about/news/2016/USC-Shoah-Foundation-Partnership-with-ProQuest.html [05. 09. 2016]

Wieviorka, Annette 2006. *The Era of the Witness.* New York: Cornell University Press.
Young, James E. 1997. Between History and Memory: The Uncanny Voices of Historian and Survivor. *History and Memory* 9(1/2): 47–58.

NOTES ON THE CONTRIBUTORS

Lyudmila S. Bogoslovskaya, (1937–2015), was a specialist in marine mammal and bird behavior and brain morphology before she eventually switched to indigenous subsistence, cultural and heritage studies in the course of her many years of fieldwork in the Russian Arctic, primarily in the northern Bering Sea-Bering Strait region. During the 1970s and 1980s, she surveyed Russian coastal areas around the Bering Strait using animal hide boats with local Yupik and Chukchi hunting crews. From 1993 until 2010, she was the Head of the Center for Studies of Traditional Subsistence Practices at the Russian Institute for Cultural and Natural Heritage in Moscow, Russia. She made major contributions in support of indigenous maritime hunting and traditional ecological knowledge of the Native people of Chukotka.

Michael Dürr, Ph.D., is an anthropological linguist specializing in Mesoamerica and in the North Pacific Rim. He works as a librarian in Berlin and also teaches anthropology and Mayan languages at the Freie Universität Berlin. His publications include studies on Franz Boas's text collections for the languages Sm'algyax̲ and Kwakw'ala of the Northwest coast, and he has also co-authored an introduction to descriptive linguistics in German. For many years, he has participated in the language preservation and publishing activities of the Foundation for Siberian Cultures. Currently he is focussing on editing 16th to 18th century dictionaries and grammars in K'iche' and Mixtec.
http://www.lai.fu-berlin.de/homepages/duerr/index.html

Ophira Gamliel completed her Ph.D. in the Indian Studies Department at the Hebrew University of Jerusalem in 2010. She published three anthologies of translations: two from Sanskrit to Hebrew (1999, 2000) and a third from Malayalam in a bilingual Malayalam-Hebrew book (co-author Scaria Zacharia, 2005) with Jewish Malayalam women's songs. She is currently employed in a research project on Eastern Jewish-Christian relations funded by the European Research Council at the Ruhr University Bochum (jewseast.org).

Annette Gerstenberg has been a professor of Romance linguistics (French and Italian) at Freie Universität Berlin since 2013. She holds a Ph.D. from University of Saarland (2003) and worked as postdoctoral researcher at Ruhr-Universität Bochum. Starting in 2005 she conducted biographical interviews with French senior citizens in the city and urban agglomeration of Orléans (France), which continued as a longitudinal study until 2016. The interviews are contained in the LangAge database and are currently being prepared for anonymized publication as part of the network Corpora for Language and Aging Research (http://www.langage-corpora.org).

Erich Kasten, Ph.D., studied social and cultural anthropology and taught at Freie Universität Berlin. He has conducted extensive field research in the Canadian Pacific Northwest and in Kamchatka and has curated international museum exhibitions. As the first coordinator of the Siberian research group at the Max Planck Institute for Social Anthropology in Halle, he studied transformations in Post-Soviet Siberia. In ensuing projects for the UNESCO and the National Science Foundation, he documented and analysed indigenous knowledge. Since 2010 he has been the director of the Foundation for Siberian Cultures in Fürstenberg/Havel (Germany).
http://www.kulturstiftung-sibirien.de/kasten_E.html

Sonya Kinsey taught English in South Korea for three years and then attended the University of Regensburg, where she completed her Master's Degree. She then began her Ph.D. in English Linguistics at the University of Freiburg. She conducted her fieldwork in Moricetown, B.C., working with the Witsuwit'en people of North Central B.C. She is interested in language contact, second language acquisition, World English varieties, First Nations English varieties and variationist sociolinguistics.

Igor Krupnik received his Ph.D. in anthropology/cultural ecology at what was then the Institute of Ethnography in Moscow, Russia (1977) and has been active in Arctic socio-cultural and heritage research since the 1970s. He currently works as Curator of Arctic and Northern ethnology at the National Museum of Natural History of the Smithsonian Institution in Washington DC. He was the leading force behind including socio-cultural and indigenous themes in the program of the recent International Polar Year 2007–2008. He has conducted fieldwork in local communities in the Russian Arctic and in Alaska, especially in the northern Bering Sea-Bering Strait region.

Cord Pagenstecher, Ph.D., studied history and has published on forced labor in Nazi Germany, on oral and visual history, tourism research, history of migration as well as historical education and remembrance. He works at the Center for Digital Systems of Freie Universität Berlin where he conceptualizes and curates oral history archives like Zwangsarbeit 1939–1945 (www.zwangsarbeit-archiv.de) and related educational applications (www.lernen-mit-interviews.de, www.berliner-geschichtswerkstatt.de/forced-labor-app.html). In the past, he worked with the Berlin History Workshop and the Ravensbrück Memorial Museum.

Stefan Pfänder, Ph.D., is an interactional linguist and professor at Freiburg University. One of his research areas is collaborative storytelling / retelling, which developed out of an interdisciplinary research project on social psychology, funded by the Fritz Thyssen Foundation (10.11.2.066 *Wiedererzählen*). Narrative research within the Thyssen project was followed up during a Freiburg Institute for Advanced Studies (FRIAS) senior fellowship and thanks to the successful co-acquisition of a Research

Training Group funded by the German Research Foundation (DFG-GRK 1767 *Faktuales & Fiktionales Erzählen*) and a project collaborating with cultural anthropology and psychosomatics / body psychotherapy. The latter project investigates and models the synchronization of interactants in everyday, aesthetic and therapeutic interaction and is co-funded by FRIAS and the European Union.
http://www.romanistik.uni-freiburg.de/pfaender/

Michael Rießler holds an M.A. in Scandinavian studies from Humboldt University Berlin, a Ph.D. in general linguistics from the University of Leipzig and is an adjunct professor in Finno-Ugric studies at the University of Helsinki. He is the head of the Freiburg Research Group in Saami Studies, a junior research group at he University of Freiburg focusing on linguistic documentation and description of indigenous languages in the Barents Sea region. He is also the co-applicant for a large-scale interdisciplinary research project funded by the Academies' Program at the University of Hamburg with the aim of creating systematic linguistic documentation for several Uralic and other languages of Siberia. He is currently a fellow at the Freiburg Institute for Advanced Studies. In addition to documentary linguistics, he has written on language contact, language typology and language sociology. He is also working with applied research on language revitalisation in Russia, Norway and Finland.
https://www.frias.uni-freiburg.de/de/personen/fellows/aktuelle-fellows/riessler

Katja Roller obtained a Ph.D. in English Linguistics from the University of Freiburg. She worked as a research assistant and lecturer in English Linguistics at the University of Freiburg as part of the FREDDIE team (FReiburg English Dialect Database for Instruction and E-learning). In 2015, she co-hosted the interdisciplinary workshop "Oral History Meets Linguistics" with Stefan Pfänder and Bernd Kortmann. Her research interests include Welsh English, perceptual dialectology, usage-based linguistics and the interface between linguistics and oral history. Currently, she is completing her practical teacher qualification (*Referendariat*) in Rottweil, Germany.
http://frequenz.uni-freiburg.de/roller-curriculum

Joshua Wilbur, Ph.D., is a general linguist who has been working on documenting and describing Pite Saami, a highly endangered Uralic language of northern Sweden, since 2008. In addition to publishing a grammar of Pite Saami in 2014, he developed an orthographic standard for the language and edited the first Pite Saami – Swedish– English dictionary, both of which were released in 2016. He is currently a post-doctoral researcher at the Freiburg Research Group for Saami Studies, and the principle investigator in a project aimed at describing Pite Saami syntactic structures.

Kasten, Erich and Tjeerd de Graaf (eds.)

Sustaining Indigenous Knowledge: Learning Tools and Community Initiatives for Preserving Endangered Languages and Local Cultural Heritage.

2013, Fürstenberg/Havel: Kulturstiftung Sibirien
284 pp., 22 color photos,15,5 x 22 cm
Euro 26; paperback
ISBN: 978-3-942883-12-2

Exhibitions and Symposia
http://www.siberian-studies.org/publications/exsym_E.html

Erich Kasten and Michael Dürr (eds.)

Sustaining Indigenous Knowledge: Comparative Views on Indigenous Learning Situations from Russia, Peru and Papua New Guinea

2015, Fürstenberg/Havel: Kulturstiftung Sibirien
DVD (77 min.) English / Russian / Spanish subtitles
Euro 18
ISBN: 978-3-942883-21-4

Films on DVD
http://www.siberian-studies.org/publications/films_E.html

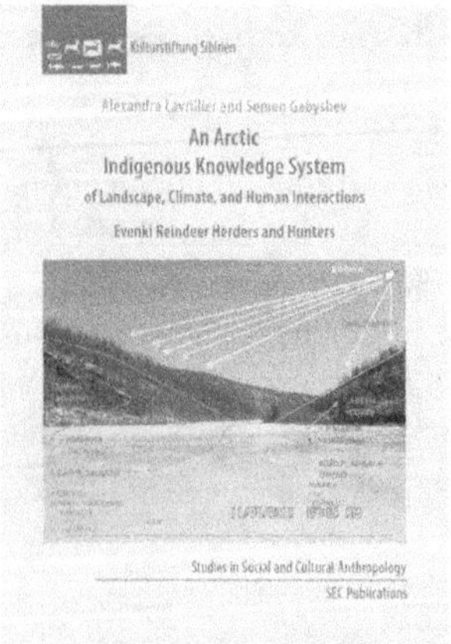

Alexandra Lavrillier and Semen Gabyshev

An Arctic Indigenous Knowledge System of Landscape, Climate, and Human Interactions: Evenki Reindeer Herders and Hunters

2017, Fürstenberg/Havel: Kulturstiftung Sibirien
ca. 470 pp., ca. 300 color photos, 15,5 x 22 cm
Euro 68; paperback
ISBN: 978-3-942883-31-3

Studies in Social and Cultural Anthropology
http://www.siberian-studies.org/publications/studies_E.html

Erich Kasten and Michael Dürr (eds.)

Ительменские тексты
Itelmen texts

2015, Fürstenberg/Havel: Kulturstiftung Sibirien
120 pp.,15,5 x 22 cm
Euro 18; paperback
ISBN: 978-3-942883-22-1

Languages and Cultures of the Russian Far East
http://www.siberian-studies.org/publications/lc_E.html

Erich Kasten (ed.)

Родовые мелодии и танцы коряков-нымыланов, с. Лесная, Камчатка
Songs and Dances, Coastal Koryaks (Nymylans), Lesnaya, Kamchatka

2016, Fürstenberg/Havel: Kulturstiftung Sibirien
160 pp., 15,5 x 22 cm
Euro 18; paperback
ISBN: 978-3-942883-29-0

Languages and Cultures of the Russian Far East
http://www.siberian-studies.org/publications/lc_E.html

Erich Kasten (ed.)

Духовная культура коряков-нымыланов, с. Лесная, Камчатка
Worldviews and Ritual practice, Coastal Koryaks (Nymylans), Lesnaya, Kamchatka

2017, Fürstenberg/Havel: Kulturstiftung Sibirien
ca. 150 pp.,15,5 x 22 cm
Euro 18; paperback
ISBN: 978-3-942883-32-0

Languages and Cultures of the Russian Far East
http://www.siberian-studies.org/publications/lc_E.html

Erich Kasten and Raisa Avak (eds.)

Духовная культура эвенов Быстринского района
Even Tales, Songs and Worldviews, Bystrinski district

2014, Fürstenberg/Havel: Kulturstiftung Sibirien
200 pp., 15,5 x 22 cm
Euro 18; paperback
ISBN: 978-3-942883-20-7

Languages and Cultures of the Russian Far East
http://www.siberian-studies.org/publications/lc_E.html

Alexandra Lavrillier and Dejan Matic (eds.)

Эвенские нимканы Дарьи Михайловны Осениной
[Even tales of Dar'iia Mikhailovna Osenina]

2013, Fürstenberg/Havel: Kulturstiftung Sibirien
160 pp.,15,5 x 22 cm
Euro 18; paperback
ISBN: 978-3-942883-15-3

Languages and Cultures of the Russian Far East
http://www.siberian-studies.org/publications/lc_E.html

Raisa Bel'dy, Tat'iana Bulgakova, Erich Kasten (eds.)

Нанайские сказки
[Nanai tales]

2012, Fürstenberg/Havel: Kulturstiftung Sibirien
268 pp., 24 color photos,15,5 x 22 cm
Euro 26; paperback
ISBN: 978-3-942883-06-1

Languages and Cultures of the Russian Far East
http://www.siberian-studies.org/publications/lc_E.html

Tat'iana Bulgakova

Камлания нанайских шаманов
[Nanai shamanic healing texts]

2016, Fürstenberg/Havel: Kulturstiftung Sibirien
56 pp., 13 Farbabbildungen,15,5 x 22 cm
Euro 18; paperback
ISBN: 978-3-942883-28-3

Languages and Cultures of the Russian Far East
http://www.siberian-studies.org/publications/lc_E.html

Cecilia Odé (ed.)

Илья Курилов: Моя жизнь, песны
Il'ia Kurilov: My Life, Songs (Yukaghir)

2016, Fürstenberg/Havel: Kulturstiftung Sibirien
56 pp., 13 color photos,15,5 x 22 cm
Euro 18; paperback
ISBN: 978-3-942883-28-3

Languages and Cultures of the Russian Far East
http://www.siberian-studies.org/publications/lc_E.html

Cecilia Odé (ed.)

Акулина Иннокентьевна Стручкова:
Разные рассказы, юкагирским детям
Akulina Innokent'evna Struchkova:
Various Tales, for the Yukaghir Children

2016, Fürstenberg/Havel: Kulturstiftung Sibirien
92 pp., 12 color photos,15,5 x 22 cm
Euro 18; paperback
ISBN: 978-3-942883-27-6

Languages and Cultures of the Russian Far East
http://www.siberian-studies.org/publications/lc_E.html

---

www.ingramcontent.com/pod-product-compliance
Lightning Source LLC
Chambersburg PA
CBHW052050220426
43663CB00012B/2513